The Story of the City of New York

CHARLES BURR TODD

The Story of the city of New York, C. Burr Todd
Jazzybee Verlag Jürgen Beck
86450 Altenmünster, Loschberg 9
Deutschland

ISBN: 9783849671730

www.jazzybee-verlag.de
admin@jazzybee-verlag.de

Printed by Createspace, North Charleston, SC, USA

CONTENTS:

PREFACE.

In writing the story of New York, it has been the author's purpose to present a brief but comprehensive survey of the causes which led to the founding of the city, and of the various agencies which contributed to its marvelous growth, and to combine with this a narrative of such domestic details and romantic or picturesque incidents as would serve to render the picture clear and complete. The author hopes that his volume, while planned more particularly for the requirements of younger readers, may be found of service to citizens of all ages who may wish to inform themselves concerning the chief events in the history of the great city of the New World, and who may not find time for larger and more elaborate histories. It is startling to think that in twenty-five years, if the present rate of increase is continued, New York, with her history of two hundred and fifty years, will surpass London, with a life-time of twenty centuries, and will become the capital of the world — that is, in wealth and population. The onward rush of material forces will give her this vantage; but whether she becomes the capital in a larger sense— in art, letters, science, and moral influence, in great museums and universities of art, in free libraries for the people, and storehouses of learning for the scholar, in that literary and artistic atmosphere which attracts the author, poet, and painter, and develops the best that is in them, — this possibility rests largely with the young people of to-day, who, for the next fifty years, will shape her destinies. Manifestly they will work with greater interest toward this end, if they know that their city has a noble and dignified history, that, notwithstanding grave drawbacks and difficulties, her progress has been such as to challenge the wonder of students of social science the world over, and that her future is so full of possibilities that no man can hope to forecast it. This result the author has also had in view.

Some details have been unavoidably omitted — an omission supplied in part by the chronological record in the Appendix. In treating of the modern period, the writer has adopted the view of most scholars, that history ceases fifty years back of the present time — contemporary record taking its place, — and has treated of the modern period only so far as seemed necessary to the completeness of the narrative.

It would be impossible to name here the numerous authorities consulted. The author has, however, derived special benefit from the labors of such original investigators as Messrs. Brodhead, O'Callahan, and Valentine. From the "Corporation Manual," compiled by the last-named gentleman, many of the illustrations, as well as many curious facts, have been taken. He is also indebted to the various histories of the city— by Miss Mary C. Booth, David T. Valentine, Mrs. Martha J. Lamb, Colonel William L. Stone, and Benson J. Lossing, — and to the scrapbooks and files of old papers in the Astor and Society libraries. Acknowledgment is also due Mr. George H. Putnam for his encouragement and co-operation.

New York, January 1, 1888.

INTRODUCTORY.

The year 1524 was a very good year to have been born in. Men in one corner of the world, at least, were waking up. Kings were learning that merchants and navigators had their value as well as men-at-arms. Thirty-two years before, Columbus had discovered America. Twenty-seven years before, De Gama had opened up the passage to India around the Cape of Good Hope and had given the merchants of Spain and Portugal the treasures of India; and five years before, Magellan had rounded Cape Horn, and triumphantly circumnavigated the globe. Just now the strife among navigators was for the discovery of a shorter passage to India, either around the frozen pole or through newly found America. One of the great captains who aspired to make this discovery was Jean Verrazano, a native of Florence, but who easily found in Francis I., King of France, a patron willing to commission and dispatch him on such an errand. Verrazano left France late in the year 1524 with two ships — the Norman and the Dolphin, — but was forced by a terrible storm "to land in Bitaine " and repair his ships. His account of the voyage that followed, given in his quaint " Relation," brings back the soft-toned atmosphere of the age.

" Afterwards," he says, with the Dolphin alone we determined to make discoverie of new countries, to prosecute the navigation we had already begun. . . . The 17th of January, the yeere 1524, by the grace of God, we departed from the dishabited rock by the isle of Madeira, apperteining to the king of Portugal, with 50 men, with victuals, weapons, and other ship munition very well provided, and furnished for eight months. And sailing westward with a faire easterly wind in 25 dayes we ran 500 leagues, and the 20 of Februarie we were overtaken with as sharp and terrible a tempest as ever any sailors suffered, whereof with the divine helpe and mercifull assistance of Almighty God, and the goodnesse of our shippe, accompanied with the good happe of her fortunate name, we were delivered, and with a prosperous winde followed our course west and by north, and in other 25 days we made about 450 leagues more, when we discovered a new land never before seen of any man either ancient or modern."

This new land was probably the Jersey shore. Verrazano first sailed southward in quest of a harbor; but finding none, he returned and coasted north until he found " a very pleasant place situated among certaine little, steepe hills; from amidst the which hills there ranne downe to the sea an exceeding great streme of water which within the mouth was very deepe, and from the sea to the mouth of the same with the tide, which we found to rise 8 foote, any greate ship laden may passe up. But because we rode at anker in a place well fenced from the wind we would not venture ourselves without knowledge of the place, and we passed up with one boate onely into the sayd river and saw the country very well peopled." This bay in which the Dolphin rode "fenced in from the wind," most geographers agree was the bay of New York, and the "exceeding great streme of water" between the hills must have been the Hudson itself. Verrazano was, therefore, the first European to discover and sail into the bay of New York. Without doubt his first act on going ashore was to take possession of the country in the name of his royal master in the beautiful and dramatic fashion peculiar to explorers of the Latin race. Landing with the pomp and display of arms, he planted first a large wooden cross in the ground, and near it a cedar post bearing a metal plate on which was engraven the royal arms of France. Then standing beside the cross, with head bared and his men-at-arms grouped about him, he repeated these words:

" In the name of the most high, mighty, and redoutable monarch, Francis, first of that name, most Christian king of France and Navarre, I take possession of this island, as also of the bay, river, and all countries, rivers, lakes, and streams contiguous and adjacent thereunto, both those which have been discovered, and those which may be discovered hereafter, in all their length and breadth, bounded on one side by the seas of the north and west, and on the other by the south sea; declaring to the nations thereof that from this time forever, they are vassals of His Majesty, bound to obey his laws and to follow his customs, promising them on his part all succor and protection against the invasion and incursion of their enemies; declaring to all other potentates, princes, sovereigns, states, and republics, to them and their subjects, that they cannot and are not to seize or settle upon any parts of the aforesaid country, save only under the good pleasure of His Most Christian Majesty, and of him who shall govern in his stead, and that on pain of incurring his displeasure and the effort of his arms."

Having thus imparted to our island this pleasant touch of mediaeval romance and chivalry, Verrazano sailed away to France, where, at Dieppe, he wrote a " Relation " of his discoveries, as has been remarked. The French king, however, made no attempt to settle his new territories, his attention that year being fully absorbed by his campaign against the Spanish Emperor Charles V.; a campaign which ended in the defeat of Francis at Pavia, and in his being carried off to Spain a prisoner.

For nearly one hundred years the island retained its primeval wildness and beauty; vessels passed by in the distance, — discoverers, fishermen, traders, pirates — but none came into the bay, or if they did they left no traces of their presence. At length, however, on a September day in 1609, a ship sailed in — a craft of moment. She was, indeed, an odd-looking vessel, with carved prow, a stern much higher than her bows, and carrying square sails on the two masts of a schooner. She flew a banner new among nations — the Dutch flag: orange, white, and blue, in three horizontal stripes, — and she was in fact a Dutch craft, " the Texalina vessel," called the Half Moon. I cannot clearly explain her presence here without speaking somewhat at length of the people to whom she belonged. These people were called the Dutch, their country lay along the southern shore of the North Sea, and was called indiscriminately the Netherlands, the United Provinces, and the Low Countries. It was so very flat and low that the quaint writers of the day described it as " a bridge of swimming earth," and the people as " living lower than the fishes, in the very lap of the floods." The Dutch were of an ancient civilization. Originally formed of various rude tribes, the Frisians, Batavi, and Belgae, of whom Caesar speaks, and later mingled with the conquering Franks and Saxons, they grew to wealth and power under the successive rule of the great Charlemagne, of the lords and bishops of the feudal age, and of the dukes and kings of the house of Burgundy. In 1550, we read, under Charles V. they had 208 walled cities, 150 chartered towns, 6,300 villages, and 60 fortresses. The Netherlands were Protestant in religious faith — disciples of Calvin of Geneva. This did not please Catholic Spain, to which country they were subject, and she so bitterly persecuted them that seven provinces revolted and formed themselves into a republic. Another terrible war followed this act, which had been closed six months before the Half Moon sailed into New York Bay, by both parties agreeing to a truce

3

for twelve years. You will find the whole story graphically told in Mr. Motley's " Rise of the Dutch Republic." I will speak briefly of the political divisions of the state into which the seven provinces had been welded.

Its government was republican in form, though much more complex and unwieldy than is our own beautiful system. Four great bureaus or departments managed its affairs — the States-General, the Council of State, the College of the Admiralty, and the Chamber of Accounts. The States-General was the principal bureau and will be most frequently referred to in our pages. This chamber was usually composed of twelve deputies from the various provinces, and its powers more nearly approached those of the president of modern republics. It was the executive body of the system. The genius of the Netherlands was almost purely commercial. It was a nation of great merchants, not of shop-keepers, as Napoleon later styled the English. It had at the time of which we write three thousand ships, one hundred thousand sailors, and a trade of sixteen millions per annum, against England's six millions. Old Peter Heylin tells us that at Amsterdam in 1623, at one tide, one thousand ships were seen to go out and in, and that though scarce a stick of ship timber grew on their soil, yet they supplied the world with ships. Its great mercantile corporation — the privileged East India Company, chartered after the rupture with Spain to secure the rich trade of India and the East which Spain and Portugal had so long enjoyed, was now the wealthiest and most powerful association of merchants on the globe. The Dutch Company had, however, a rival in the English East India Company, chartered in 1600, and which, though not then so strong, eventually outstripped it.

Both companies were eager rivals in the discovery of a shorter passage to India than that by the Cape of Good Hope around Africa. The Dutch company believed that such a passage existed through the " Frozen Ocean behind Norway," that is, around the northern shores of Europe and Asia, and in 1608 had fitted out the Half Moon, and given her in charge of the famous English navigator, Henry Hudson, with orders to sail by the way of Nova Zembla and the Straits of Arian in search of this passage. Hudson sailed into those frozen seas until his path was blocked by ice, and then returned, and began coasting southward along the shore of America, searching for a passage through the continent. He reached Virginia without discovering this passage, and then turned and sailed back by the way he had come, examining the shores more closely than he had previously done. In this way, on the 3rd of September 1609, he discovered, and the next day entered, the beautiful bay of New York. Hudson no doubt believed that the long-sought passage to India was found, and after resting for several days, and exploring the neighboring shores, he made sail and continued on up the river where keel of white man had never before ventured. The freshening water and shoaling channel must soon have convinced him that he was in no strait, but a river, a sad disappointment no doubt to the enterprising, ambitious sailor; nevertheless, with a resolution that increases our respect for him, he decided to press on and explore the mighty stream. He was nine days ascending to the present site of the city of Albany, sailing only by day. Some nights the Half Moon cast anchor under the frowning mountains. At other times she was so enshrouded in spectral mists that the mariners could see nothing except what fancy pictured for them.

Often they stopped to trade with the Indians, sometimes going on shore for the purpose. One of these occasions is thus quaintly described by Captain Hudson in his narrative of the voyage. " I went ashore in one of their canoes with an old man who was chief of forty men and women, whom I found in a house made of the bark of trees, and was exceeding smooth and well finished within, and all round about. I found there a great quantity of Indian corn and beans, and indeed there lay to dry, near the house, of those articles, as much as would load three ships, beside what was still growing in the fields. When we went to the house two mats were spread to sit on, and immediately eatables were brought to us in wooden bowls well made, and two men were sent off with their bows and arrows to kill wild fowl, who soon returned with two pigeons. They also killed immediately a fat dog, and in a little time skinned it with shells they got out of the water."

The natives also brought to barter for trinkets; skins and furs, pumpkins, squashes, grapes, and apples. When the Half Moon had reached nearly to the present site of Albany, the channel became so shallow that she could go no farther, and the ship's boat was sent some twenty miles farther on until it reached the head of navigation. When it reported this fact Hudson made preparations to return, and on the third of October, after a voyage of ten days, anchored in the bay of New York, having beaten off a party of hostile Indians, on the ninth day of the return, and killed several warriors. On this voyage Hudson first acquainted the Indians with the taste of rum, which they at once named, from its most prominent quality, fire water." At the same time far north on the banks of Lake Iroquois, Champlain was giving the same race its first lesson in the use of gunpowder.

On the fourth of October, 1609, the Half Moon " went out of the mouth of the great river," and set sail for Europe. Instead of continuing on to Holland, however, Hudson put into the port of Dartmouth, England, where he proposed to spend the winter, and in the spring proceed again to the north with a different crew. A proposition to this effect, together with a full account of his discoveries, he forwarded to his employers in Holland, who responded with a peremptory order for him to return at once with the Half Moon. But ere he could do this the English authorities seized him on the ground that, being an English subject, he had no right to engage in the service of a rival power; the Half Moon, therefore, proceeded without her captain. The subsequent fate of this eminent navigator was a sad but heroic one. The next year, 1610, he was sent by the Muscovy Company — an English corporation chartered in 1555, to prosecute the trade with Russia — into the northern seas to search for the baffling passage to India, and in pursuit of it discovered the great bay and strait still known by his name. Almost in the moment of his success, however, the crew mutinied and set him adrift on the waste in an open boat with his son and other adherents. No traces of the party were ever after discovered, though an expedition was sent out from England to search for them.

Two years later, in 1611, the intrepid Dutch navigator Adrian Block visited Manhattan Island, coasted the shores of Long Island Sound, discovering the Connecticut River and the island still bearing his name, and then, returning to Holland, published a very graphic and detailed account of his voyages. But the haughty East India Company saw nothing to attract them in the western wilderness, and still continued their search for a shorter passage to the East. There were certain shrewd merchants in Amsterdam, however, who had not been admitted to a share in the profits of the East India Company, and who saw what a rich trade in furs and other commodities might be established with the new country. They proceeded to form a trading company, which was formally chartered by the States General and given the exclusive privilege of trading to " New Netherlands," for the term of three years, counting from January 1, 1615. In this charter the country was first called New Netherland. The merchants began by building a trading house and fort on an island, near the present site of Albany, and another on Manhattan Island, and enjoyed a profitable trade, but the company was endowed with no civil powers and effected no settlement. Meanwhile, at home, a company was growing up which was to exert a great influence on the destinies of Manhattan. This company, after thirty years of dissensions, was at length chartered by the States-General. It was known as the West India Company, and was one of the most unique and privileged corporations in history. It was a private company yet exercised many of the functions of a sovereign state. It could make war or peace, contract alliances, administer justice, appoint or dismiss governors, judges, and men-at-arms, build forts, ships, cities — in fact, do anything that a sovereign state might do to promote trade and secure its stability. It had also a monopoly of the trade for the Atlantic coasts of Africa and America. Its charter granted by the States General is dated June 3, 1621, — the very year in which the truce with Spain terminated. Its projectors were certain merchants of the popular or anti-Spanish party, who had, in forming it, a twofold object: the crippling of Spain by attacks on her American possessions and on the vessels trading thither; and the control of the rich trade in furs, herbs, native woods, and precious stones and metals in which the hills and woods of the New World were believed to abound. It was because this company was intended to act against the public enemy that such enormous powers were conferred upon it. As this company was the real founder of our city, some details of its organization may not be out of place. This was much like that of its great compeer, the East India Company.

It was governed by five " Chambers " or " Boards," called, respectively, the Chamber of Amsterdam (which had control of four ninths of the company's interest), the Chamber of Zealand having two ninths, of Maeze with one ninth, of North Holland with one ninth, and of Friesland with one ninth. There were twenty managers for the Chamber of Amsterdam, twelve for that of Zealand, and fourteen for each of the other three. Each chamber had its separate directors and vessels and fitted out its own voyages. The combined capital of the various chambers amounted to twelve millions of florins equal to nearly five million dollars of our money. This great company having received from the States General a grant of the whole magnificent territory discovered by Hudson, erected it into a province and committed its affairs to the care of the Amsterdam Chamber, while the other boards began actively to prosecute operations against the Spanish. For some time the Amsterdam Chamber paid little attention to the savage province in the west. Its attention, too, was absorbed by the fierce war with Spain. Immense fleets, many of them numbering seventy armed vessels each, were sent against the Spanish possessions in America, and captured prizes of such value that dividends ranging from twenty-five to seventy-five per cent, were declared. Bahia, in Brazil, was taken in 1624, "the great silver fleet" of armed vessels carrying treasure from the South American mines to Spain in 1628, and in 1630 the rich city of Pernambuco in Brazil. All Netherlands rang with the exploits of the privileged West India Company. But a clause in the charter of this company provided that it should " advance the peopling of the fruitful and unsettled parts," which had been granted it, and its enemies soon

6

began to complain that it was doing nothing to carry out the conditions of this clause. Spurred on by these attacks, the company in 1624 sent thirty families of Protestant Walloons to New Netherlands, with orders to make a settlement at Fort Nassau, while eight men were to remain and establish a post on Manhattan Island. These first settlers, the Walloons, were a worthy people, inhabitants of the frontier between France and Flanders, who had distinguished themselves in the wars with Spain by their valor and military spirit.

In 1625 the company, encouraged by its South American successes, advertised for "adventurers" to the New World, offering free transportation, employment, and other inducements. Many hastened to enroll themselves, and toward the close of the year three large ships and a yacht were fitted out and dispatched to Manhattan, bearing forty-five persons, men, women, and children, with their household furniture, farming utensils, and one hundred and three head of cattle. This event marks the founding of the colony of New Netherlands, later known as New York. Four years before, the Pilgrims had landed on Plymouth Rock, while Boston was founded three years later. Sir Walter Raleigh's colony had already been seventeen years established at Jamestown, Va. At St. Augustine, Fla., the Spaniard had been domiciled for nearly sixty years — since 1565. Everywhere else along the vast stretch of coast the forest still waved and the savage held possession. But the company hesitated to organize a government and send out a governor. It feared the English, who laid claim to the whole coast of North America, by virtue of the discoveries of the Cabots — John and Sebastian — in 1497 and denounced the Dutch as interlopers. In 1625, however, this fear was removed by the forming of an alliance between England and the Netherlands, for the better prosecution of the war against Spain. The West India Company at once proceeded to form a government for the new country and to appoint a director, or, in English, a governor. This director was Peter Minuit, of Wesel, in Westphalia, a man who had had experience of new countries while in the employ of the East India Company. He was, too, of a kind, conciliating disposition, and possessed of a faculty for governing — in fact, much the best ruler that New Netherlands ever had. Minuit left Amsterdam for Manhattan in December, 1625, in a ship picturesquely named the Sea Mew, and bearing with him quite a reinforcement of colonists.

PART I. THE DUTCH DYNASTY
I. PETER MINUIT.

Sometimes I allow fancy to picture the appearance of the island on that 4th of May, 1626, when the Sea Mew cast anchor off the point of the Battery. Nature's temples, not man's, then adorned it. Somber forests overhung the Jersey shore and fringed the water-line of the island. A chain of low, craggy hills covered with noble forests of oak, chestnut, hickory, and other trees, with pretty grassy valleys between, extended from the Battery to near the present line of Canal Street; on either side along the river banks were wide marshes stretching away to the north; at Canal Street they bore directly across the island, and were so low that on high tides the water flowed across from river to river. In the sheltered valleys were the maize fields and queer villages of the Indians, and the rude log-cabins of the settlers who had come over the year before. Cow-paths crossed the marshes to the upper part of the island, which was much wilder and more savage, with precipitous ledges, and in many places dense thickets of grape-vines, creepers, blackberry and other bushes which no one could penetrate. The settlers did not allow their sheep and calves to cross this marsh, lest they should be throttled by the wolves, bears, and panthers that lurked in the thickets, and in their letters home they complained of the deer and wild turkeys that broke in and destroyed their crops. Minuit's first step — probably before landing his people — was to purchase the island of its Indian owners. He had been directed to do this by the company for two reasons: first, to satisfy the Indians and gain their friendship; second, to strengthen the company's title to the country, as against the English. This recognition of the property right of the Indian was the uniform custom of the Dutch in settling New Netherlands. The bargain was made on the 6th of May, 1626, on the present site of the Battery, perhaps on the very spot where Verrazano had planted his cross one hundred and two years before. Old Knickerbocker's delightful account of the affair, in his version of the story of New York, will at once recur to the reader; but Knickerbocker's exuberant fancy often played sad pranks with his historical faculty. The scene as it actually occurred must have been exceedingly picturesque.

On the one side were the savages, clad in deerskins or in waist-belts of woven grass; on the other, stern, bearded men whose brave costumes and dignified bearing were well calculated to overawe the rude natives. The Hollanders wore long-skirted coats, some loose, some girt about the waist with a military sash, velvet breeches ending at the knee in black Holland stockings, and for foot-gear military boots with high flaring tops, or low shoes adorned with silver buckles. Their hats were made of felt and were low in the crown with very wide brims, which were looped up or not, at the fancy of the wearer. In a sash, slung over the right shoulder and passing under the left arm, a short sword was suspended, but no other warlike weapons were visible. A strong sea-chest of the solid though clumsy workmanship peculiar to Dutch artificers stood open between the two parties, filled with beads, buttons, ribbons, gayly embroidered coats, and similar articles, which were spread out before the delighted savages and were offered in exchange for their island. The red men were only too glad to accept, and thus, for baubles worth scarcely twenty-four dollars, the island, now covered with miles of splendid buildings, passed into the hands of Europeans.

The Dutch, as we have seen, found the Indians in possession of Manhattan Island. It is quite time that the reader was introduced to these Indians. This particular tribe was called the Manhattos or Manhattans, whence the name of the island. They were a branch of the great Algonkin-Lenape family of aborigines. Their neighbors, with whom they were often at war, were the Hackensacks and Raritans, who lived on the opposite shore of the Hudson; the Weekqueskucks, Tankitikes, and Packamies, whose territories lay north of the Raritans; and the Canarsees, Rockaways, Menikokes, Massapeagues, Mattinecocks, Missaqueges, Corchaugs, Secatauges, and Shinnecocks, Long Island Indians. On the western bank of the upper Hudson, extending inland some seventy miles, were the fierce Mohawks, a part of the great clan of the Five Nations. Opposite, inhabiting the country between the Hudson and the Connecticut, were the Mohegans, another powerful tribe. With these tribes the colonists were often in contact. Their first peculiarity, as noted by the curious settlers, was their color, which was of a dull copper, or obscure orange hue, like the bark of the cinnamon tree. Their clothing was, in summer, a piece of deer-skin tied around the waist, in winter the skins of animals sewed together, and hanging loosely from the shoulders. After the Dutch came they used in place of buckskin a piece of duffels, or coarse cloth, thrown over the right shoulder and falling to the knees, which served as a cloak by day and a blanket by night. The men went bareheaded. Their hair was coarse, black, and very strong. Some had hair only on one side of the head, some on both, but all wore the scalp-lock; it was a point of honor with them. This lock was formed as follows: a strip of hair three fingers broad was first allowed to grow on the top of the head from the forehead to the neck. This was cut short, except a tuft on the top of the head three fingers long, which was made to stand erect like a cock's-comb by smearing it with bear's-grease. The women or squaws allowed their hair to grow and bound it behind in a coil shaped like a beaver's tail, over which they drew a square cap ornamented with wampum. The Indians were extremely fond of ornament; even the implements the Dutch gave them were devoted to this use. Heckewelder, for instance, relates that they hung the axes and hoes given them about their necks, and used the stockings for tobacco-pouches; and Creuxis tells of a Huron girl reared by some Ursuline nuns, who on her marriage was given a complete suit of clothes in Parisian style; but what was the surprise of the nuns a few days later to see the young husband arrayed in the finery and strutting up and down before their convent with an air of exultation which was greatly increased on seeing the nuns at the windows smiling at his queer appearance! Wampum played an important part in their economy. It was their money, their measure of value. " It was an ornament, a tribute; it ratified treaties, confirmed alliances, sealed friendships, cemented peace, and was accepted as a blood atonement." In making it the Indian artificer took the inside of the stem of the great conks cast up on the shore, and fashioned from it a small, smooth, white bead, through which he drilled a small hole. For another kind he took the inside purple face of the mussel shell, and made beads shaped like a straw, one third of an inch long, which were then bored lengthwise, and strung on hempen threads or the dried sinews of wild animals. These were then woven into strips of a hand's width and two feet long, called " belts" of wampum. The white beads were served in the same way, but their value was only half that of the purple beads. " They value these little bones," said Dr. Megapolensis, " as highly as many Christians do gold, silver, or pearls, valuing our money no better than they do iron.'

9

In political economy these people were communists, socialists. The land was held in common; the hunt, the fisheries, were free to all, and their condition is an excellent illustration of the utility of socialism when its principles are put into practice. They were anarchists, too, in that they had no law. Each did as he pleased, restrained only by his savage instincts of right and wrong. Minor crimes were unpunished. Murder was avenged by the next of kin, provided he met the murderer within twenty-four hours after the deed was committed. If he did not, the crime could be atoned for by the payment of wampum. Each tribe had its own chief, and separate practices and government. The houses of the Indians were mere huts made by binding the tops of saplings together, and covering the frame thus formed with strips of birch bark; some of the dwellings were communal — inhabited by many families. One shown in the engraving, found on Manhattan Island by the Dutch, was one hundred and eighty yards long by twenty feet wide. There were within it pots and kettles for cooking food, sharpened stones for axes, sharpened shells for knives, wooden bowls from which the food was eaten, beds formed of bulrushes or the skins of wild animals. The Indians used for food the flesh of animals and fish cooked whole, corn, pumpkins, roots, nuts, and berries. They had boats made of birch bark or hollowed out of the trunks of trees, the largest being capable of holding fourteen men, or one hundred and fifty bushels of grain. Calmly considered, these savages were not a people calculated to inspire respect. They were uncleanly in their food, their dwellings, and their persons. They had neither arts, science, nor commerce, as we understand those terms and there was much in their character and condition to justify the opinion freely expressed by the Dutch, that they " were children of the Devil," " mere cumberers of the ground."

In the midst of this wild, untamed people Minuet set up his orderly government — the product of a thousand years of judicial wisdom and patriotism. Let us consider it briefly. The Director was absolute monarch of his little world, except that he could not execute the death penalty; his subjects also had the right of appeal to the home company, and even from that body's decision to the States-General. Minuit was also instructed to appoint an advisory council of five of the wisest and most prudent men of the colony, to whose opinions he was expected to give due weight. There were but two other officers in the colony — the secretary of the Council Board and the Schout-fiscal — the latter an official who makes as great a figure in the early records of Manhattan as the Director himself. He was sheriff and constable, State's attorney to convict, and prisoner's council to defend, collector of the customs too, and beadle and tithing-man on Sunday. If we fancy him, with his wand of office in his hand, preceding the Burgomasters and Schepens to church on the Lord's Day, and during service patrolling the streets, seeing that no slave or Indian profaned the hour by gaming, or tapster by selling beer, we shall view him in the guise most familiar to the people. The men whom Minuit governed were little more than fiefs or servants of the company. They could not at this time hold land, not even the ground on which their dwellings stood; nor lawfully engage in trade with the Indians, nor among themselves, nor manufacture the necessaries of life. The privileged West India Company held the right to do all these things. Minuit had brought with him a competent engineer — one Kryn Fredericke, — and his first step after forming his government was to build a fort to defend it. It was a triangular earthwork with bastions and red cedar palisades and stood on a slight elevation near the point where

Broadway enters the Battery. Minuit named it Fort Amsterdam. Next the busy workers opened quarries in the island crags, and of the " Manhattan stone " found there, built a rude, strong warehouse for housing the company's stores and other property. This warehouse was a creditable work — considering the means at hand for building it — with its stone walls, roof thatched with reeds, and those quaint crow-step gables dear to the heart of every Dutchman, of which one may still see a good specimen in the pretty cottage of Washington Irving at Sunnyside. The next public work was a " horse mill," for the grinding of grain by horse-power — for they seem to have lacked the tools and gear to build a windmill, after the fashion of Hollanders. Some thirty small cabins were also built along the East River shore, and a store was opened in a corner of one of the great warehouses and placed in charge of a salaried servant of the company. Only a church and a minister were lacking to complete the equipment of the village, but church and minister as yet there was not. That the people might not be wholly without spiritual counsel, however, the company had sent out two " Zukenstroosters," or Consolers of the Sick " (lay readers, we should call them), and they called the people together on the Sabbath and expounded the Scriptures to them. Their church — the first church in the city of five hundred temples — was the loft of the horse-mill, rudely fitted up with benches and chairs.

Two years later, a regularly ordained pastor, the Rev. Jonas Michaelis, arrived and organized a church, whose lineal descendant we shall find in Rev. Dr. Terry's church, on the corner of Fifth Avenue and Twenty-first Street. Minuit was also busy in extending and cementing trade with the Indians. His voyageurs, in sloop, ship's boat, and canoe, explored every bay and creek of the North River where an Indian lodge was planted, exchanging their beads, axes, knives, and gayly colored cloths for furs, and inviting the Indians to come down and trade with their white brothers at the fort. Many accepted the invitation, and soon parties of savages in blankets or skins, some laden with bales of fur, others with venison, turkeys, wild fowl, and other game, were familiar objects in the streets of Manhattan. The company's warehouse became a busy place.

The ship Arms of Amsterdam which sailed for Amsterdam September 23, 1626, carried home " 7,246 beaver skins, 178 otter skins, 675 otter skins, 48 minck skins, 36 wild-cat skins, 33 minck skins, 34 rat skins, and much oak and hickory timber," the whole valued at 45,000 guilders, or nearly $19,000. This ship also took samples of the " summer grain " the colonists had gathered at their recent harvest, viz., wheat, rye, barley, oats, buckwheat, canary seed, beans, and flax. And she bore, too, news of the birth of the "firstborn Christian, daughter" in New Netherland — Sarah Rapaelje, daughter of Jan Joris Rapaelje, born June 9, 1625.

An incident occurred this autumn which involved the colony a few years later in a terrible Indian war, and did much to destroy that confidence between the Dutch and Indians which the Director was anxious to cultivate. A Wukquaesguk Indian coming to town to trade, accompanied by his nephew, a mere lad, was set upon by three of the Director's negro slaves, and not only despoiled of his goods but barbarously murdered. The lad escaped, and as soon as he became a man wreaked bloody vengeance, not, as we shall see, on the guilty negroes, but on the innocent whites.

From the Indians who came to trade with him, Minuit heard scattered bits of news about his neighbors, the English on Plymouth Bay, and felt a desire to communicate with them. So he wrote two letters to Governor Bradford, of Plymouth, " in a very fair hand, the one in French and the other in Dutch," and signed by Isaac de Rasieres as provincial secretary, inquiring after his Excellency's health, and offering to accommodate him with any European goods the English might want in exchange for beaver skins and other wares. Governor Bradford replied very courteously, saying that he had not forgotten the kindness shown the Pilgrims in Holland, but that for the current year they were well supplied with necessaries; "thereafter" he would be glad to trade " if the rates were reasonable." At the same time -he expressed a doubt as to the propriety of the Dutch traffic with the Indians on English territory. Director Minuit replied promptly, and, as evidence of good-will, sent a " rundlet of sugar and two Holland cheeses "; but he firmly maintained the right of the Dutch to trade in the disputed territory. Governor Bradford, in his reply, modestly disclaimed the titles bestowed by his worthy and loving " brother of New Netherlands as being " over high " and beyond his deserts, but asked that an ambassador be sent to confer on the matter. Isaac de Rasieres, the secretary, was chosen for this delicate and important mission. Now Rasieres was by nature a very presentable man, and we may be sure that on this occasion he was made to appear at his best. He donned his long coat with its silver buttons, his velvet breeches, and black silk stockings, slipped on his military boots, thrust his sword into its sash, and with a noble retinue of trumpeters and men-at-arms, marched down to the company's dock, where the barque Nassau, neatly painted and furnished, and loaded with wampum, a chest of sugar, and " cloth of three sorts and colors," was waiting to receive him. Of the voyage we have, happily, a minute account by de Rasieres himself, given his patron, Samuel Bloemmaert, in Holland.

The Nassau sailed through Long Island Sound, we learn, bravely flying the orange, white, and blue flag at her peak, threaded the island passages of Narragansett Bay, and then ran " east by north fourteen miles to Frenchman's Point, where in a little harbor where a stream came in the English had an outpost." This was the present Manomet, in the town of Sandwich, at the head of Buzzard's Bay, on the south side of the isthmus connecting Cape Cod with the mainland, and which will be shortly the southern terminus of the Cape Cod ship canal. Plymouth was twenty miles north, across the isthmus " four or five miles " then by boat up the coast. At Manomet the Nassau anchored, while the ambassador dispatched a trumpeter to Governor Bradford with a message saying he had come in a ship to visit him and to report to him " the good will and favor which the Honorable Lords of the American West India Company had toward him." He mentioned the cloth of three sorts and colors, the chest of white sugar, and the seawan (wampum), that they might trade, and begged the Governor to send a conveyance for him, as he had not walked so far " in three or four years." Governor Bradford accordingly sent a boat for him, and he came " honorably attended by a noise of trumpets," as the Governor himself records. De Rasieres spent several days in the village courteously entertained by Governor Bradford and laid the foundation of a very lucrative trade between the two lone colonies. He gives in his letter a graphic description of Plymouth, and of the customs of its people. Among other pleasant details he tells us how the Pilgrims attended church.

" They assemble by beat of drum, each with his musket or firelock, in front of the captain's (Miles Standish's) door; they have their cloaks on, and place themselves in order, three abreast, and are led by a sergeant without beat of drum. Behind comes the Governor in a long robe; beside him on the right hand the preacher with his cloak on, and on the left hand the captain (Miles Standish) with his side arms and cloak on, and with a small cane in his hand, and so they march in good order, and each sets his arms down near him."

The secretary's mission seems to have been successful in every particular. The Pilgrims were much pleased with his genteel appearance and courteous behavior, and when he returned in triumph to New Amsterdam he bore a letter from Governor Bradford to his " very loving and worthy friends and Christian neighbors," the Dutch, assuring them of his disposition to trade, and of his great regard and friendship.

The little colony prospered, however, without English trade. Six farms or " boweries " were opened by the company in the natural meadows along the shores of the East River, which were stocked with cattle, goats, hogs, and sheep, and tilled by its servants. Ships were continually arriving from the father-land, bringing colonists, cattle, and household goods. By 1628 the number of inhabitants had risen to two hundred and seventy. In 1629 the imports amounted to 113,000 guilders (about $45,200), and the exports to 130,000. The company, however, was not satisfied with this progress, nor with the rich future it promised. The expense of colonizing the new country, under the liberal terms granted emigrants, was very great, and the directors now perfected a plan by which this outlay might be met, in part at least, while their privileges should be retained.

There were many wealthy merchants among their stockholders, who, it was thought, would value a title and an estate. To these men they said, in effect:

" We have a vast territory in America lying along the Mauritius River (the Dutch name of the Hudson) and on the shores of the sea. To each of you who will, at his own expense, establish a colony there we will freely grant these privileges: an estate extending sixteen miles along the one bank of a navigable river, or eight miles on both banks, and stretching inland as far as you can explore; a title, the title of patroon or feudal chief; exempt you and your people for ten years from taxation: grant you freedom in trade, except in furs, which we reserve to ourselves, and full property rights; protect you from enemies, and supply you with negro servants. You may take up this land anywhere but on Manhattan Island, which we reserve to ourselves. You shall forever possess and enjoy these lands, with the fruits, rights, minerals, rivers, and fountains, the supreme authority and jurisdiction, the fishing, fowling, and grinding; and if you shall so prosper as to found cities, you shall have authority to establish for them officers and magistrates. In return you must agree to satisfy the Indians for the land taken; to plant a colony of fifty souls above fifteen years age within four years; to provide a minister and schoolmaster for the colony as soon as possible, and until that is done ' a comforter of the sick.' "

Several directors of the company were willing to accept these terms, and a charter styled the " Charter of Freedoms and Exemptions" was granted by the Assembly of the XIX., as the governing body of the West India Company was called. It was dated June 7, 1629, and was a lengthy document containing thirty-one articles, from which we can learn something more of these curious feudal establishments in free America.

The patroons were to govern their people conformably to the rules of government made or to be made by the directors of the company. They were to have liberty to sail or traffic all along the coast from " Florida to Terra Neuf," provided they "entered " the goods received in this trade at the company's custom house at Manhattan, and paid a duty of five per cent, upon them; they were to have two thirds of all prizes taken from the Spaniards, the company reserving the other third; they might trade in furs in places where the company had no " factories " or stations, provided they paid the company one guilder on each merchantable beaver and other skin. It was further provided that in cases tried before the patroons, where more than fifty guilders were involved, an appeal might be taken to the commander and council in the New Netherland. If anyone should discover " minerals, precious stones, crystals, marbles, or any pearl fishery" on the estate, it should remain the property of the patroon, he paying the discoverer a certain price to be agreed on be forehand. The people were not to make any woolen, linen, or cotton cloth, or weave any other stuffs, on pain of banishment. Finally, the colonies lying in the same neighborhood were to appoint a deputy, who should give information to the governor and council of all things transpiring in his district, and who was obliged to report at least once in every twelve months. This charter was the outcome of the social system then prevailing in Europe and among nearly all civilized nations. At this very moment the French were founding " lordships " and " seigneuries " of similar character in Canada, while forty years later the English proprietors of Carolina attempted to introduce the same system into that province in the guise of landgraves and caciques. Its merits were that it satisfied the Indian for his soil, it provided schools and churches, and settled men in strong, well-ordered communities; its evils were that it introduced monopoly, servitude, and aristocratic privilege. Colonies were quickly established under this instrument.

On June 1, 1629, Samuel Bloemmaert and Samuel Godyn, through agents, purchased of the Indians a tract of country on the southwestern shores of Delaware Bay two miles in width, and extending inland from Cape Henlopen thirty-two miles. The next spring, April, 1630, Kilian Van Rensselaer, a pearl merchant of Amsterdam, and also a director, purchased of the Indians, through agents, a large tract of land on the upper Hudson, which was increased by subsequent purchases until he was master of a territory twenty-four miles long by forty-eight broad, and of an estimated area of seven hundred thousand acres; a tract now comprising the counties of Albany, Rensselaer, and a part of Columbia. Next month. May, 1630, directors Godyn and Bloemmaert increased their estate by buying a tract on the shore of Delaware Bay, opposite their former purchase, sixteen miles long by sixteen square. Michael Pauw another director, finding the best lands on the Hudson and the Delaware taken, purchased, in June, the territory called Hoboken-Hacking, situated opposite New Amsterdam, on the west side of the Hudson, to which he added, in the course of the following month, Staten Island and the territory north of his first purchase, now known as Jersey City. These lands were in all cases bought of the Indians, through agents, and were duly ratified before the director and council at Fort Amsterdam, who " sealed them with the seal of New Netherland in red wax." The tract on the Delaware was called Zwanendael or the Valley of Swans. Pauw gave his purchase the pleasant-sounding name Pavonia; the estate on the upper Hudson was called Rensselaerwyck. Zwanendael was the cradle of the present State of Delaware, and

Pavonia that of New Jersey. These purchases of the more desirable lands in the company's territory excited the jealousy of the remaining directors, and to appease them, and also to secure their aid in settling the lands acquired, several others were allowed to share in the enterprise; Godyn, De Laet the famous Dutch historian, Bloemmaert, Adam Bissels, and Toussaint Moussart, being admitted to a share in Rensselaerwyck, and six directors together with Captain Petersen De Vries sharing Zwanendael among them. The latter was soon colonized, and farmers, cattle, and farming implements were sent to Rensselaerwyck, which soon became a flourishing settlement. Kilian Van Rensselaer, the patroon, did not himself remove to the colony, but entrusted the management of its affairs to an agent called a Seneschal. His sons, however, emigrated and became successive lords of the great estate, founding a family that has held an honorable place in the annals of the city and State. Michael Pauw also founded on his patroonship, a village which he called " the Commune," and which occupied the present site of Communipaw, and no doubt gave its name to that ancient village. Very soon the directors had cause to regret giving the patroons such privileges, for they found the latter much more eager to secure the rich trade in furs, than to clear and cultivate their lands. The patroons based their right to the fur trade on the fifteenth article of their charter, which gave them the privilege of trading on the coast from Newfoundland to Florida, and in the interior anywhere " where the company had no commissaries at the time the charter of 1629 was granted," and their ships and their agents were soon out trading at almost every point.

The directors held that this was too liberal a rendering of the fifteenth article; that the whole tenor of the charter was to give the company a monopoly of the fur trade, on which it chiefly depended for its revenues, and a bitter quarrel arose which greatly retarded the progress of the colony. The charter to the patroons was revised, new articles were propose— some of the directors even advocated doing away with the charter altogether. The quarrel was carried before their High Mightinesses the States-General, and complaints were made against Director Minuit, who had officially ratified the purchase of the patroons, and who, it was charged, had favored them as against the company. Another circumstance aided in bringing Minuit into disrepute at this time. A short time before, two Belgian ship-carpenters had appeared in New Amsterdam and, seeking out the Director, had asked his aid in building a famous ship, the largest that had ever floated. The Director, seeing in the project a means of exhibiting to Holland merchants the resources of his colony in ship timber, consented, and in due time the New Netherlands, a ship of eight hundred tons and thirty guns — one of the finest pieces of naval architecture that had ever been built — was launched. It cost much more than had been expected, however, and the bills were severely criticized at home both by the stockholders and by the press. Incited by all these complaints, the States-General decided to investigate the Director, the patroons, and the affairs of the West India Company in general, the result being that Minuit was recalled and the privileges of the patroons restricted. Minuit embarked for Holland in the spring of 1632, in the ship Eendracht (Union), — which also carried five thousand beaver skins belonging to the company — leaving the affairs of the colony m the hands of his council. But his troubles were not yet over. His ship was driven by stress of weather into Plymouth, England, and was seized by the authorities there on the charge that she had traded to and obtained her cargo in countries subject to the English king. Minuit promptly advised the directors, and himself hurried up to London and laid the case before the Dutch ambassadors, by whom it was brought to the attention of King Charles. The ambassadors also wrote to the States-General, asking them to send over all the documents proving the right of the Dutch to trade to New Netherland, " as that right will undoubtedly be sharply disputed in England." A long and spirited correspondence followed, in which the right of the two nations to the disputed territory was freely canvassed without accomplishing any result, the English government at last consenting to release the Eendracht, " saving and without any prejudice to His Majesty's rights." The seizure, however, had served to assert the claim of the English to New Netherlands, which uninterrupted possession by the Dutch might have impaired. Director Minuit will again appear in our history. He had ruled the infant colony for six years, in general, it must be said, with wisdom and moderation. Under his sway it had increased in wealth, trade, and population, and had escaped serious difficulties with the Indians on the one hand, and with the English on the other. Of the four governors of New York under the Dutch dynasty none are worthier of more kindly remembrance than Peter Minuit.

II. WOUTER VAN TWILLER.

The directors, after much laying of their heads together, and canvassing of numerous candidates in their great oak-paneled chamber in Amsterdam, fixed on Wouter Van Twiller as Minuit's successor. " Wouter Van Twiller," — the name provokes a smile as one recalls the famous description by Knickerbocker:

" He was exactly five feet six inches in height, and six feet five inches in circumference. His head was a perfect sphere, and of such stupendous dimensions that Dame Nature, with all her sex's ingenuity, would have been puzzled to construct a neck capable of supporting it; wherefore she wisely declined the attempt, and settled it firmly on the top of his backbone just between the shoulders. His body was oblong and particularly capacious at bottom. His legs were short but sturdy in proportion to the weight they had to sustain; so that when erect he had not a little the appearance of a beer-barrel on skids."

A grotesque figure truly, and not all caricature, for Van Twiller was stout of body and slow of thought; in habit something of a roysterer, with a burgomaster's fondness for good dinners and good wine, and withal of a petty spirit and narrow mind — a man totally unfitted for the place.

He had been a clerk in the employ of the West India Company, we are told, and had been appointed at the instance of the powerful patroon and director, Kilian Van Rensselaer, whose niece he had married, and whose interests he might be trusted to look after, which seems all the more queer when we consider that the chief grievance against Minuit was that he had favored the patroons at the expense of the company. Van Twiller arrived early in April, 1633. As he came ashore, he saw between two and three hundred men and women with stolid Dutch faces, the men clad in wide, deep-seated breeches tattered and earth-stained, the women in shabby kerchiefs and short gowns; behind them Indians looking curiously on; and, forming the background, noisome marshes and fens, a few clearings and cornfields, and a great deal of forest.

He took up his quarters in the fort, and the people went on with their daily tasks as though nothing unusual had occurred. It was but a few days later that a quaint, tub-like craft furled her sails in the harbor, and dispatched a boat shoreward, bearing a stranger differing much in appearance from the average voyageur of that day. He was slight and compact in frame, with fair, Saxon features, curly hair, and kindly blue eyes — one of the most polite, humane, and interesting of the knights-errant of his time — the co-patroon, Petersen De Vries. At home he was known as the rich merchant, but having early become interested in America, as we have seen, had been among the first to plant a colony in the new countries. A sad story he told the Director over their wine that night. He had left Holland, he said, the November before, in his yacht, with provisions and stores for his colony of Zwanendael, but on arriving there found only blackened ruins and the bones of his massacred people. An Indian was enticed on board and induced to tell the pitiful story.

The Dutch, they learned, had reared a pillar on a prominent point in their territory, to which they had affixed a piece of tin bearing the arms of Holland, as an emblem of sovereignty. An Indian chief spying it, had innocently taken it to make himself a tobacco-box. Hoossett, whom De Vries had left in charge of the colony, on discovering the theft, had expressed great indignation, whereupon certain Indian allies greatly attached to him had killed the offender. The murderers were sternly rebuked by the commander and sent away in disgrace. But in the Indian code blood

17

must atone for blood, and one day, as the colonists were nearly all in the tobacco fields, a band of savages had rushed upon them and massacred them all — thirty-two in the tobacco-fields, Hoossett and a sick man in the company's house. They had further glutted their vengeance by setting fire to the company's buildings. All the money and labor spent on the plantation had been made useless in a moment; worse than all, his confidence in being able to keep peace with the Indians had been rudely assailed. Being now without occupation, De Vries lingered a long time in the settlement, and one day witnessed an incident which showed the Director's mettle. They were chatting and smoking on the fort parapet after dinner one day, when they saw a vessel pass the Narrows and head directly for the fort. She flew the Red Cross of England, but her straight lines and " ship-shape " appearance sufficiently proclaimed her nationality. She came to under the guns of the fort, and presently dispatched a boat to the shore. A man in resplendent uniform stood in its bow. " What ship is that? " growled Van Twiller, as the boat grounded. The William, of London," replied the officer, with a deep obeisance, and last from Boston." "Who commands?" pursued the Director. " Jacob Eelkens," was the reply. " I know the varlet," said De Vries, quietly; " he was post trader at Fort Orange (Albany) for the first Dutch trading company and was dismissed for thievery." " What doth he here? " continued the Director. " Prithee, to trade with the savage," replied the envoy. The Director bit his lip. Here was the old vexed question of English supremacy again presenting itself. In fact, like Banquo's ghost, it was continually popping up in those days on the most inopportune and unexpected occasions. " He hath sent me to present compliments," continued the envoy, " and to invite your Excellency and the Honorable Councilors to dine with him to-morrow. He bade me say there shall be no lack of good wine and ale."

The pleasures of the table were the Director's chief failing, and though De Vries tried to dissuade him, he decided to accept Eelkens' invitation. Next day, two boats conveyed the Director, his mighty councilors, and De Vries to the William, where, as the patroon afterward told the home company, the songs and mad antics of Van Twiller in his cup did grievously tend to bring the Dutch government into disrepute and caused the English to laugh at the Director's authority. The William lay five days before the town, and then Eelkens coolly announced his intention of sailing to Fort Orange to trade with his old friends, the Indians, there. The Director was almost beside himself at the audacity of this proposal, and the measures he took to prevent it were characteristic of the man. He gathered the whole crew of the William into the fort and, to overawe them, mustered his men-at-arms, ran up the tri-colored flag, and ordered his gunner to fire three pieces of ordnance in honor of the Prince of Orange. But Eelkens, no whit dismayed, sent his gunner on board ship with orders to throw the Union Jack to the breeze and fire a whole broadside in honor of King Charles, — or in defiance of Van Twiller. While this was being done he hurried on board with his crew, weighed anchor, and stood up the river, his sailors twirling their thumbs at the Dutch garrison, which stood petrified at the audacity of it. Van Twiller was first to recover speech. He ordered a barrel of wine to be brought and broached, and then invited the entire village, which had been attracted to the spot by the guns, to join him in drinking it. Then made valiant by the potion he swung his hat and shouted: " All ye who love the Prince of Orange and me, emulate me in this and aid me in repelling the violence of that Englishman."

As quickly as was consistent with Dutch stolidity three armed vessels — a pinnace, a caravel, and a hoy — were got ready, and, manned with one hundred and four soldiers, stood up the river in pursuit. Meantime, Eelkens had proceeded to a point about a mile below Fort Orange, landed his cargo, raised a marquee and began a brisk trade with the Mohawks who were delighted to meet again their old friend and ally. It was in vain that Houten, the Dutch factor at Fort Orange, came in his shallop, wreathed in green boughs, with a trumpeter making stirring music, sat up a Dutch booth beside the English, and did his utmost to disparage their goods and hinder their trade. Eelkens was familiar with the Indian language and tastes, and was fast disposing of his cargo, when, fourteen days after his arrival, the three-armed vessels we have seen leaving New Amsterdam hove in sight. Getting ashore as quickly as possible, the Dutch officer in command gave Eelkens two letters protesting against his action and ordering him to depart forthwith. There were soldiers from " both the Dutch forts, armed with muskets, half-pikes, swords, and other weapons," to enforce these demands. Eelkens not complying as promptly as they desired, they attacked the Indians who were trading with him and " beat them well," and then, disregarding the trader's pleadings that he was on British soil and had a right to trade there, they pulled his tent about his ears and hurried his goods on board the William; as they did so, they added insult to injury by sounding a trumpet in their boat " in disgrace of the English." Eelkens and his goods being on board the William, the Dutch took possession of her and escorted her to the mouth of the river; or, as Eelkens described it: " The Dutch came along with us in their shallop, and they sticked green bowes all about her, and drank strong waters, and sounded their trumpet in a triumphing manner over us."

Thus ended the third attempt of the English to assert their right to the Hudson as against the Dutch.

Van Twiller was soon embroiled in a deeper quarrel with the English colonies on the east. Both parties cast covetous eyes on the Fresh River (the Connecticut), which had been discovered by Adrian Block, in 1614, and which had since been visited at stated periods by Dutch traders who derived a yearly revenue from it of ten thousand beaver skins, beside other peltries. The Dutch claimed the river by virtue of Block's discovery; the colonies of Plymouth and Massachusetts Bay by grant of the English king. To strengthen his claim. Van Twiller, in 1632, bought a large tract of the Indians at Saybrook Point at the mouth of the river; and in the summer of 1633, he sent his commissary, Jacob Van Curler, with a piece of duffels twenty-seven ells long, six axes, six kettles, eighteen knives, one sword-blade, one shears, and some toys, to buy a large tract called " Connittecock," embracing the present site of the city of Hartford. Van Curler built on his new purchase a trading post fortified with two cannons, which he called the House of Good Hope. This act of the Dutch caused great uneasiness when it was reported at Boston and Plymouth. Governor Winthrop contented himself with an emphatic protest, but Governor Winslow, of Plymouth, proved himself a man of action. The frame of a house was quickly made ready and placed on board a vessel. A company of emigrants also embarked, and the little craft then proceeded coastwise to the mouth of the Connecticut and up that beautiful stream. Sped by favoring winds, it soon came to the House of Good Hope, where Van Curler stood by his guns to forbid her passage. " Halt," he cried, " or I shall fire! " But the English kept right on. "They were obeying the orders of the Governor of

Plymouth," they said, " and they should go on, though they died for it." They passed unmolested, and founded a settlement at Windsor, a few miles above Hartford, which became the nucleus of the State of Connecticut. Van Twiller protested, but his protests were treated with contempt by the English; he then dispatched an armed force of seventy men to clear the river. The doughty warriors finding the English resolute, and the woods (in their imagination) full of hostile savages, returned valiantly to New Amsterdam, without striking a blow. The Director seems to have made no further attempt to dislodge the intruders, but to have contented himself with sending protests, and dispatching lengthy accounts to his superiors at home. In a short time the English had established settlements at Springfield above Good Hope, at Wethersfield, just below, and at Saybrook, and were in virtual possession of the river.

On the Delaware, however, Van Twiller was more fortunate. A fort (Nassau) had been early established on this river to command its trade, and then temporarily abandoned. A party of Virginia cavaliers seized this fort early in the summer of 1635, pretending that it came within the confines of their territory. A deserter bore the news to Fort Amsterdam, and the Director at once dispatched a body of troops to capture the invaders. They returned in due time with the crest-fallen cavaliers as captives. There was great rejoicing in New Amsterdam — fanfare of trumpets, and toasts in honor of the victors, — but the Director was sorely puzzled to know what to do with his prisoners. At last he hit upon a plan, and calling them before him, he first soundly lectured them for their thievery and trespassing, and then shipped them " pack and sack " to Virginia — which was certainly a very wise thing to do.

In the management of his internal affairs, Governor Van Twiller was much more fortunate. He had some trouble with the powerful patroons who abated no whit of their pretensions, but otherwise affairs ran smoothly. An honorable peace was concluded with the Raritan Indians. New farms and villages were continually being opened in the vicinity. De Vries purchased Staten Island and founded a colony there. East of the Walloon settlement, on the present site of Brooklyn, Jacob Van Corlear bought a large tract of the Indians and founded a plantation. Andries Hudde, of the Governor's Council, in company with Wolfert Gerritsen, bought a large tract next to Van Corlear's, and the Governor himself purchased another adjoining them on the east, the whole forming the present town of Flatlands. Van Twiller also bought for himself Nutten, now Governor's Island, Blackwell and Great Barn islands. Under him, too, was given another grant to which we shall later refer; that to Roelof Jans of sixty-two acres, which was later incorporated into the King's Farm, and now forms a part of the estate known as the Trinity Church property. In the erection of public buildings, and the giving in general a substantial and civilized air to the crude little town Van Twiller had an honorable record. Fort Amsterdam was completed, and a substantial guard-house of brick was erected within it for the Director, with barracks for the soldiers on the East River shore above the fort, and nearby a parsonage and stable, to which Domine Bogardus soon added a fine garden. A country house of brick was also built, " on the plantation," for the Governor. A barn, dwelling, brewery, and boat-house " to be covered with tiles " on Farm No. 1, a goat's stable " behind the five houses," several mills, and dwellings for the smith, cooper, corporal, and other officials. All this was done at the expense of the West India Company, which had now become a wealthy and powerful corporation, owning one hundred and twenty vessels fully armed and equipped, and employing an army of nearly nine thousand men. The furs annually exported from Manhattan had reached a value of one hundred thousand guilders, and Van Twiller reasoned correctly that a part of this revenue should be expended in making his capital more presentable. The company, however, did not agree with him, and partly for his action in this respect, but chiefly because of charges by such responsible persons as De Vries and Van Dinclage, the Schoutfiscal, that he was diverting the company's moneys to his own enrichment, they decided to remove him. Van Twiller left the colony under a cloud. Wilhelm Kieft, his successor, took the oath of office at Amsterdam, September 2, 1637.

III. WILHELM KIEFT.

The good barque Blessings bearing Kieft and his party, arrived on the 28th of March, 1638, but the new Director did not receive a very hearty welcome from the motley throng gathered on the quay to receive him. Tales not at all to his credit had preceded him. He had failed as a merchant in Holland, it was whispered, and his portrait had been affixed to the gallows — a lasting disgrace; and, when later, through the influence of friends he had been appointed Minister to Turkey, and funds for the redemption of Christians held by the heathen had been placed in his hands, he had turned the money to his own use, and the poor captives had continued to languish in bonds. Such were the popular tales. His personal appearance as he stepped ashore was not well calculated to win love or confidence. He was a little man with sharp, pinched features, a cold gray eye, a suspicious look, and the air of an autocrat. A man of good natural abilities, but of little education; a shrewd trader, austere in morals — in happy contrast to Van Twiller, — of a fiery, peppery temper, conceited, opinionated, and tyrannical; the very man to embroil himself with his people, and his people with their neighbors. The citizens soon found that the new Director was bent on establishing a despotism — one that chafed all the more because of the lax rule of Van Twiller. The company had given him authority to fix the number of his council. He chose but one, and further curtailed the power of that one, by adopting a rule that in conducting the government his council should have but one vote, while he had two. His powers in other respects were so extraordinary as to create him a despot. His will was absolute. He erected courts, appointed all public officers, except such as were commissioned by the company; made laws and ordinances and executed them, imposed taxes, levied fines, incorporated towns, and had every man's property at his mercy by his power of raising or lowering the price of wampum, then the chief circulating medium of the country. He extinguished Indian titles to land at his pleasure; no purchases from the natives were valid without his sanction. No contracts, sales, transfers, or engagements were of effect unless they passed before him. He not only made and executed the laws, but construed them, as judge. He decided all civil and criminal cases without the aid of a jury. He was the highest court of appeal in the colony.

The council had heretofore been the only check on the governor's action, and this abolished, he became at once an absolute monarch. Having arranged matters to his liking, Kieft, in his shrewd, business like way, began investigating the affairs of the colony, and found n:iatters in very bad condition, as he reported to the company: the fort open on every side except " the stone point," the houses and public buildings all out of repair, the magazine for merchandise destroyed, every vessel in the harbor falling to pieces, only one windmill in operation, the farms of the company without tenants and thrown into commons, the cattle all sold or on the plantations of Van Twiller. Vice, too, was prevalent, but the greatest evil was the illicit trade with the Indians. Everybody, from the patroon to the negro slave, he said, was engaged in it. Even Hans, instead of quietly toiling on his little farm, would secrete his demijohn of rum or canister of gunpowder, and barter it slyly with the Indian for his coveted beaver or otter skin.

Another evil was the great lack of farmers. The Dutch colonists had a great repugnance to agriculture. Even if placed on farms, they would follow their hereditary instincts and become traders; very different from their neighbors, the

English pioneers, who immediately cleared their lands for farms, and soon became self-supporting freeholders. The Director thought he could change all this by a few strokes of the pen. One morning, on their way to business, the people were surprised to see the trees, walls, rocks, and corners of the houses covered in part with proclamations written in a bold, free hand, and signed with the Director's name. They read on them certain new laws for the government of the colony. Whoever sold powder or fire-arms to the Indians should suffer death; if a servant of the company was found trafficking with the latter, he should lose his office and his wages; if an outsider, his goods should be confiscated, and he himself corrected. No articles could be exported without the governor's permission; no one could trade in any? part of the company's territories without a license. Sailors could not remain on shore after sunset without special leave; the company's servants of every grade must proceed to and leave off work at stated hours, and " not waste their time." Fighting, rebellion, theft, false swearing, calumny, " and all other immoralities " were sternly forbidden. Lastly, the instrument appointed Thursday of each week for the regular sitting of the council for the trial of criminal cases and hearing of complaints. A second proclamation forbade all " except those who sold wine at a decent price and in moderate quantities " to sell any liquor under a penalty of twenty-five guilders. An inspector of tobacco was also appointed. The regulation that the colonists deemed the most oppressive, however, was one declaring that no contracts, bargains, sales, or public acts should be deemed valid unless they were written by the secretary of the province, a law similar in character to the famous " stamp act " of a century later. Another unwise regulation that Kieft soon made was one affecting the Indians. On the plea that the company was put to heavy expense for forts and soldiers on their account, he levied a tribute of maize, seawan, or furs, and when they refused to pay it, threatened to compel them by force. The effect of such stringent laws on a community so mixed and impatient of restraint was what a wiser man would have foreseen and guarded against. The ordinances were treated with contempt and openly violated. Prosecution and punishment followed; there were some executions for murder and mutiny, and the little Governor, lacking the respect of his subjects, was soon involved in constant broils in the effort to maintain his authority.

We have spoken of the deplorable lack of farms in New Netherlands. To remove this state of things and promote trade, the West India Company this year, 1638, published a very important instrument, which abolished its monopoly of trade and of lands. By the provisions of this paper, any merchant in the Netherlands, "its allies or friends," might send cargoes to America in the company's ships, paying as freight ten per cent, of their value; while " to people the lands there more and more, and to bring them into a proper state of cultivation," every immigrant to the new country was promised as much land as he " by himself and his family can properly cultivate," provided he paid after four years of cultivation one tenth of the produce to the company.

Religious freedom had always been enjoyed in New Netherlands, and these generous terms attracted a large immigration not only from Europe, but from New England, where the Puritans were beginning to prosecute the Quakers and Anabaptists and drive them from the country.

Scarcely was this matter settled when another foreign invasion threatened New Netherlands and put the fiery Director in a glow of martial rage and patriotism. The

Swedes this time were intent on carving a slice from Dutch territory. The attempt is interesting, as showing how nearly every great nation of Europe was concerned in the settlement of our country. Sweden had long turned a covetous eye upon America, and her Parliament, in the time of the great Gustavus Adolphus (1626), had created a corporation similar in character to the Dutch West India Company for its settlement, but the German war and death of Gustavus on the field of Lutzen (1632) prevented the company from being organized. Minuit had doubtless heard of this fact, and on being dismissed from his government had hurried to the good Swedish Queen Christina, and had offered his services, the result being that as Director Kieft sat in his great chair of state one day, a breathless messenger hurried in with news that a Swedish frigate and her tender had sailed into Delaware Bay, and up the river, until brought to by the guns of the Dutch Fort Nassau. He further said that the frigate was commanded by Peter Minuit, who, though ordered by Peter Mey, the Dutch commander, to halt and show his commission, had refused, saying: " My queen hath as much right here as thou; I shall pass, therefore, and erect a fort to be called by her name." Director Kieft is said to have been thrown into paroxysms of rage by this news, but as soon as he could control himself, he sat down and dictated, by his secretary. Van Tienhoven, a truculent message to Minuit, which is so good an example of the style and thought of the men of that day that we print it, without further apology. " I, Wilhelm Kieft, Director General of New Netherland, residing in the island of Manhattan, in the Fort Amsterdam, under the government of the High and Mighty States-General of the United Netherlands and the West India Company privileged by the Senate Chamber in Amsterdam, make known to thee, Peter Minuit, who stylest thyself commander in the service of Her Majesty, the Queen of Sweden, that the whole South River of New Netherland, both upper and lower, has been our property for many years, occupied with our forts, and sealed by our blood, which also was done when thou wast in the service of New Netherland, and is therefore well known to thee. But as thou art come between our forts to erect a fort to our damage and injury, which we will never permit, as we also believe Her Swedish Majesty hath not empowered thee to erect fortifications on our coasts and rivers, or to settle people on the lands adjoining, or to undertake any other thing to our prejudice; now therefore we protest against all such encroachments and all the evil consequences from the same, as bloodshed, sedition, and whatever injury our trading company may suffer, and declare that we shall protect our rights in every manner that may be advisable."

This document he dispatched to Minuit by his commissary Jan Jansen Van Ilpendam. Minuit however treated the protest with contempt, and continued building his fort, which stood nearly on the present site of the city of Wilmington. Kieft did not dare attack him, his timidity arising from the fact that though a tyrant he was also amenable to the chamber in Amsterdam.

It is not necessary to give an extended account of Kieft's subsequent acts. His reign was marked by cruelty to the Indians — which in return brought savage vengeance on the colony — and by oppression of the people. One day in 1640, word came that some swine turned loose in the forests of Staten Island to feed on mast were missing. The Director at once asserted that the Raritan Indians had stolen them and sent out a company of men-at-arms with orders to kill, burn, and destroy. The soldiers surrounded the unfortunate tribe in their village, slaughtered them without

24

mercy, burned their wigwams and cornfields, and returned — to learn that a party of the company's servants on their way to Virginia had taken the swine. The Raritans in return descended on the bouwerie of De Vries at Staten Island, killed four of his planters, and burned his house and tobacco-barn. Kieft, frenzied with rage, now swore to exterminate the Raritans, although he had been enjoined by the company to keep peace with the Indians. He offered his allies, the River Indians, ten fathoms of wampum for every head of a Raritan, and twenty fathoms each for the heads of those who had committed the Staten Island massacre. This reward set five hundred human hounds on the trail of the wretched Raritans, and in a few days Pacham, the chief of the Tankitikes, who resided about Sing Sing, brought in, dangling on the end of a stick, the head of the chief who had slain De Vries' men. At the same time, so fierce was the hunt that the Raritans came in and begged for peace. Another day there arose a great outcry in the village, and the gossips learned that an inoffensive old man, Claes Smit, the village wheelwright and a general favorite, had been murdered in his cottage in the suburbs, where he lived alone, and it was soon known that the murderer was the Weckquaesgek Indian, whose uncle had been murdered twenty years before in the time of Peter Minuit. Kieft promptly demanded the murderer from the Weckquaesgek chief, but the chief refused the demand. " He was sorry," he said, " that twenty Christians had not been killed." The Indian had but performed a pious duty in avenging an uncle whom the Dutch had slain twenty years before." The Director would have declared war at once, but feared the people, who were beginning to murmur at the results of his Indian policy, which threatened them all with the torch and tomahawk of the savage. A little cowed by these complaints Kieft made a concession to popular rights — he called a meeting at the fort, of the patroons and heads of families to advise with him in the emergency, and this meeting, quick to improve the occasion, appointed a council of twelve wise men to advise with the Director in the affair, much to the latter's disgust. The council, with Captain De Vries at its head, advised delay in declaring war for three reasons: the crops were still unharvested; the cattle in the woods; and the people scattered about on their farms. In the winter, they argued, these conditions would not exist, while the Indians could be taken at great disadvantage. The impatient governor was therefore forced to wait until the winter had set in.

In January the twelve gave their consent, and at the same time ventured to call the Director's attention to certain evils in his government, and to ask for their removal, as well as for certain concessions to popular rights — a council being one of them. Kieft promised fairly at the time, but soon after issued a proclamation dismissing the council, which had been called to advise on the murder of Claes Smit, and, " which now being done," he thanked them for the trouble they had taken, and promised to make use of their written advice with " God's help and fitting time," " but," concluded the paper: "we propose no more meetings, as such tend to dangerous consequences and to the great injury both of the country and of our authority." The calling of any assemblies or meetings in future was therefore prohibited, on pain of punishment. Being now unfettered in action, Kieft ordered his ensign, Hendrick Van Dyck, to proceed with eighty soldiers from the fort against the Weckquaesgeks and punish them with fire and sword. The party set out on its errand but became bewildered in the forests and returned without having even seen the foe. The

Weckquaesgeks, however, soon discovered the trail pointing toward their village, and, alarmed at the dangers they had but barely escaped, came in and sued for peace.

In 1643, the governor's policy provoked a general Indian war — the gravest misfortune that could have befallen the colony. In this war the River Indians, the Connecticut Indians, and the Long Island tribes formed a confederation to exterminate the Dutch. Fifteen hundred savage warriors were arrayed against two hundred and fifty whites. Soon the outlying farms and settlements were attacked and given to the flames, their people being killed or driven in terror to the fort; and as the Indians continued to increase in numbers, the people were in mortal terror lest the fort itself should be taken. We at this distance can have little conception of the terror and dismay which beset the people in those troublous times. The Director acted like one bereft of his senses. He would not listen to counsel; his troops in their expeditions were ordered to spare no one. Terrible massacres, at which humanity shudders, were committed by his stern orders.

In February, 1643, for instance, the Weckquaesgek and Tappaen tribes came fleeing breathless and trembling to the fort for protection. The Mohawks, they said, had made a descent on them and had slain seventy of their people, besides carrying many into captivity. Every instinct of humanity would seem to have pleaded for these helpless refugees, but Kieft, deaf to the entreaties of the humane De Vries and others, sent a force which surprised them at night and butchered everyone, man, woman, and child, in cold blood. An expedition against the Canarsees, in 1644, destroyed one hundred and twenty warriors with the loss of but one man killed and three wounded. Again, in February, 1645, the Stamford tribe of Indians was surprised in their village as they were celebrating a festival, their wigwams were burned, and between five and six hundred men, women, and children perished by fire and sword. These massacres, we may be sure, were avenged by the allied tribes to the full extent of their powers. Meantime De Vries had retired to Holland in disgust, and the people had sent petition after petition to the home authorities, reciting the crimes and arbitrary acts of the Director, and demanding his recall. But the influence of the Patroon Van Rensselaer and other of Kieft's friends was so powerful in Amsterdam that for a long time these complaints were unheeded. At length, in the spring of 1645, on the colonists threatening to desert the island in a body unless the Director was removed, he was recalled, and Petrus Stuyvesant was appointed in his stead. Kieft will not again appear in our history in any official capacity. In taking leave of him it is but just to set over against the evil that he wrought, the good that he did. For he certainly did much to make Manhattan Island more beautiful and habitable. He straightened the streets and enacted laws for keeping them in better sanitary condition. He repaired the fort and other public buildings, and set out orchards and gardens, and encouraged others to do so. He built, in 1642, a great stone tavern, which later became the Stadt Huys or City Hall, and he began within the fort and nearly finished a large stone church, to be paid for in part by the company's funds, and in part by popular subscriptions; and the dwellings that he built for the company's servants and on the company's farms were of such character as to add much to the beauty and solidity of the future city.

IV. PETRUS STUYVESANT.

We may be sure that the news of a new governor was received with the wildest delight by the oppressed people, and that long before his appearance in New Netherland, his personal history, character, and appearance were known and had been freely canvassed. He was a native of Friesland, the gossips said, son of a clergyman there. Educated to the profession of arms, most of his life had been spent in the service of the West India Company, in those brilliant battles, sieges, naval combats, and descents against the Spanish in the West Indies and South America, which, if they had ever found a competent historian, would form one of the most brilliant episodes in American colonial history. As governor of Curacao, Stuyvesant had undertaken to reduce the Portuguese island of St. Martin, and, losing a leg in the action, had returned to Holland for medical advice. There the West India Company had seized on him as the proper person to bring order and prosperity to their mismanaged colony. His portrait shows him to have been a marked character, — strong, intellectual, energetic, austere, an autocrat by nature and training. The colonists therefore derived little comfort from his appointment. It was regarded as meaning that the company would still continue its despotic form of government. But anything was preferable to that under which they had suffered for ten years; and when, on the nth of May, 1647, Stuyvesant's fleet was reported below, the whole populace, ex-Director and all, hastened to the landing to welcome him. It was quite a gallant fleet of four large vessels, and it bore a noble company — the Director, his wife, a beautiful and accomplished lady; Mrs. Bayard, the governor's widowed sister, and her three boys; the Vice-Director, and Council, which had been appointed in Holland as a check to the Director; soldiers and colonists. They had been on their way since the Christmas before, having steered south to Curacao and the West Indies on some business of the Director's. As the party came to land, the people waved their hats and handkerchiefs, and the guns of the fort thundered a salute. Kieft then made an address of welcome, to which the new magistrate responded in a way that did not at all please his hearers. His air and bearing, they observed, was that of a prince come to reign over conquered subjects. " I shall be in my government as a father over his children, for the advantage of the privileged West India Company, the burghers, and the country," he told them. The new Director was inaugurated on the 27th of May, and his speech on the occasion confirmed the ill impression produced by his former remarks. Said an eye-witness: " He kept the people standing, with their heads uncovered, for more than an hour, while he wore his chapeau as if he were the Czar of Muscovy." The same day Stuyvesant announced his council, which had been appointed, as we have seen, in Holland. Lubbertus Van Dinclage to be Vice-Director, and La Montague, Adraen Keyser, and Captain Bryant Newton, an Englishman, who had been twenty years in the company's employ, to be counsellors. The former secretary. Van Tienhoven, was retained. Hendrick Van Dyck was made Schout-fiscal. Two new offices had been created — an English secretary and interpreter, and a master of equipage. A court of justice was also established, with Van Dinclage as presiding judge, and the Director acting as a court of appeals — a concession to the people,

Stuyvesant's name has become classic through the pages of Knickerbocker, and the portrait of him there given comes much nearer the truth of history than those of his predecessors in office. His long reign of seventeen years was marked by some events of great importance, though all were overshadowed by his last act, the surrender of the city to the English. We will consider these events in their order, with special reference to their influence on the fortunes of the city.

The Director's first act taught the people that no concessions might be expected from him. Cornelis Melyn, the president, and Jochim Pietersen Kuyter, a member of the council appointed by the people in Kieft's day, having lost heavily in the Indian war, petitioned that an inquiry as to its causes might be made, and that the testimony of citizens under oath might be taken for use in an investigation of the case before the company in Holland, Stuyvesant appointed a commission to decide on the merits of the petition; but considering it a dangerous precedent for the people to call any acts of their rulers in question, he went before the commission and told them that in his opinion " the two malignant fellows were disturbers of the peace, and that it was treason to complain of one's magistrates, whether there was cause or not." The petition was therefore refused. But the matter was not allowed to rest here. Kieft, secure of the favor of the governor, had the two burghers arrested on a charge of " rebellion and sedition." Their trial followed quickly, Stuyvesant himself occupying the bench with the newly-appointed judge. Van Dinclage, by his side. It was a remarkable trial in its way — one in which justice was outraged and humanity had little place. There were no lawyers to be had, and the prisoners pleaded their own case — and made an able defense. They proved the truth of the charges against Kieft, and that in preferring them they were not moved by vindictive feelings. They admitted having complained to the company, as they believed they had a right to. All had been done openly. Yet in the face of the law and evidence the prisoners were declared guilty. Hanging them was for a time seriously considered. The right of appeal was denied. " If I was persuaded that you would bring this matter before their High Mightinesses, I would have you hanged on the highest tree in New Netherland," said Stuyvesant, as he pronounced their sentence, which for Melyn was banishment for seven years and a fine of three hundred guilders, and for Kuyter banishment for three years and a fine of one hundred and fifty guilders. This act of Stuyvesant, regarded from any standpoint, must be pronounced most impolitic and unfortunate. He meddled in a quarrel which did not concern him, and which might well have been referred to the company at home. He angered the people, and he did not save his prerogative; for his action violated both the law and traditions of the fatherland, and brought on him a stinging rebuke, when, in 1649, Melyn returned restored to his full rights, and bearing a summons to the governor from the States General and Prince of Orange to appear before them and answer for his conduct, either in person or by his attorney. But we anticipate. At the time of the trial the ship Princess was about to sail for Holland, and the banished men took passage on her. With them sailed Domine Bogardus, Kieft and his ill-gotten fortune, and a large company — in all over one hundred souls. The Princess, however, never reached her destination, for a fierce storm overtook her and drove her violently on the rocky Welsh coast. Kuyter and Melyn, with some eighteen others, escaped. Kieft, Domine Bogardus, and the rest of the ship's company perished. Kieft's fate excited little sorrow either at home or in his former government; it was generally accepted as a fitting retribution. Said De Vries in Holland, on hearing of his death: " I told William Kieft in 1643 that I doubted not that vengeance for the innocent blood he had shed in his murderings would sooner or later come on his head." Soon after his coming,

Stuyvesant called a public meeting, which named nine men to advise and assist him in the government. His next step of importance was a journey to Hartford (not Boston, as Diedrich Knickerbocker records) to confer with the authorities there on boundaries, runaway slaves, the attitude of the Indians, and other vexed questions. The Director went by vessel in military state, with a retinue of servants, trumpeters, and men-at-arms, and four days after setting out reached the Connecticut capital, where he was received with equal state by Governor Winthrop and the dignitaries of New England there assembled. After a week spent in discussion, it was agreed to submit the questions at issue to arbitrators; and after remaining several days longer, feted and feasted by his very good friends, the Director-General returned as he had gone to his seat of empire. But he soon found that he had acted unwisely: his somewhat refractory subjects were jealous of his friendship with the English; and the fact that he had entrusted the interests of New Netherlands to the two English arbitrators was made the cause of fresh charges against him at home. It was charged that the Director looked for support to his English rather than to his Dutch subjects, which was perhaps true, for the monarchical English were no doubt much more to the Director's taste than the republican Dutch.

In the fifth year of Stuyvesant's reign, April, 1652, a great event occurred. New Amsterdam was made a city — endowed with municipal rights. Two hundred and thirty-five years have passed since then, and for that reason the reader will wish to know all that can be known of this first city charter. It was modelled after the ancient charter of Amsterdam, which provided for the election by the people of a schout, four burgomasters, nine schepens, and an advisory council of thirty-six men. The first fourteen comprised the board of city fathers, and made the laws and ordinances governing the city. They were the " Fathers of the Burghery," guardians of the city poor, of widows and orphans, principal church-wardens, and farmers of the excise, and they held in trust and managed the city's funds and franchises. No burgher could be seized for debt unless it was done in their presence; no sentence of death could be pronounced without their consent or executed without they were present. They were custodians of the city seal; all official documents were drawn in their name, and they had authority to preserve the peace of the city even to the calling out of the burgher guard. They also constituted a city court for the trial of civil and criminal cases. Both boards were of great antiquity, the board of schepens dating back to the year 1270, and that of burgomasters to the fourteenth century.

In granting to New Amsterdam this great dignity the company limited the number of burgomasters to two, and of schepens to five, and stipulated that they should be elected by the citizens as in the city of Amsterdam. Governor Stuyvesant proclaimed the new city on the 2nd of February, 1653, at the feast of Candlemas, but instead of allowing the people to choose their own officers as the company had directed, he proceeded to appoint them, and he gave the city fathers to understand that their existence would not lessen his authority, but that he should preside at their meetings when he deemed it necessary, and advise them in matters of importance. It was a privilege very distasteful to the autocratic governor, and he did all he could to restrict the people in their enjoyment of it. The two burgomasters named were Arent Van Hattan and Martin Cregier, the latter a man of importance in the city, captain of the burgher guard and landlord of a popular tavern situated opposite the Bowling Green. The five schepens were Paulus Van der Grist, commander of the Gellert,

Stuyvesant's flag-ship, Maximilian Van Gheel, Allard Anthony, a wholesale merchant, Petro Van Couwenhoven, and William Beekman, the ancestor of the Beekman family in New York, who had come over in the same ship with Stuyvesant, and who later rose to distinction in the government. The old stone tavern built by Kieft was remodeled, cleaned, and furbished up and set apart as a Stadt Huys or City Hall, and here the city fathers held their sessions. So on that far-off February day the city came into being. It contained about fifteen hundred inhabitants, some three hundred houses, a few of stone, but most of them rude wooden structures, no trade of its own, and scarcely farms enough to supply it with the necessaries of life. Two years now passed without incident. In the December of 1654 Stuyvesant decided to make a voyage to the West Indies. His jurisdiction also included the islands of Curacao, Buenaire, and Aruba, and he wished to see how affairs were progressing there; he thought, too, that he might be able to arrange for a trade with the Spanish possessions in that quarter. News of this voyage created quite an excitement in the little city. The Common Council called a special meeting, and resolved that, " Whereas, The Right Honorable Peter Stuyvesant, intending to depart, the burgomasters and schepens shall compliment him before he takes his gallant voyage, and shall for this purpose provide a gay repast on Wednesday next in the Council Chamber of the City Hall." The dinner came off and was a grand affair, with a long list of edibles, Jamaica rum, potent Hollands, and rare old Madeira in abundance. Under its influence the austere governor mellowed, and, in a happy speech, presented the city with its long-delayed seal. The city fathers, crowded round to examine it. It bore the arms of old Amsterdam — three crosses saltier, with a beaver for a crest, and above on the mantle the initial letters C. W. I. C, meaning the " Chartered West India Company." A wreath of laurel encircled the legend, " Sigilluni Amstello Famensis in Novo Belgio " (Seal of Amsterdam in New Belgium).

The governor returned in July of the same year to find awaiting him a message from Holland that inflamed all his military ardor. It was an order to drive the Swedes from the South River, where, as we have seen, they had been planted by Director Minuit in Kieft's time. Never had he set about executing an order from Holland with greater alacrity. His trumpeters were sent out to beat up town and country for volunteers. Three armed vessels had been provided by the directors. The city fathers furnished one. Three more were chartered, and on Sunday, September 5th, " after the sermon," seven vessels, with a force of seven hundred men on board, including the Domine Megapolensis, sailed out into the ocean. There were two Swedish forts and settlements on the Delaware — Trinity and Christina; the latter near the present site of Wilmington, the other a few miles below. On Friday the fleet appeared before Fort Trinity, and the trumpeters were sent to demand its surrender. Captain Schute, the commander, asked time to consult with Governor Risingh at Christina, but this was denied; then he asked for an armistice till next morning, which was granted. When morning came he demanded as conditions of surrender that he should be allowed to march out with his body-guard of twelve men, fully accoutered and colors flying, the other soldiers to retain their side-arms, and the commander and other officers their private property. Stuyvesant willingly granted these terms, and on Saturday the Dutch troops took possession. Next day Domine Megapolensis preached a " sermon of thanksgiving," in return for the bloodless victory. Stuyvesant, like a good general, pushed on at once to invest Fort Christina, where Governor

Risingh with the balance of the Swedish force, comprising some thirty men, was entrenched. Again the trumpeters sounded their demand, but Governor Risingh showed a disposition to parley and to argue the matter. He recited the whole history of the Swedish occupation and proved that the present attack was a gross outrage on a people with whom the Netherlands were at peace, and only to be justified on the plea that " might makes right." The parley lasted for several days; at length Stuyvesant, finding himself worsted in the argument, became angry, and threatened to assault the fort and " to give no quarter," unless the Swedes promptly surrendered. On the 25th, therefore, their colors were lowered, and the Swedish empire in the New World ceased to exist. Governor Risingh, however, succeeded in making generous terms for himself and people. They were to " march out with their arms, colors flying, matches lighted, drums beating, and fifes playing." The cannon were to be sent to Sweden, if desired. Such Swedes as wished to remain were to be protected in their rights of person and property.

Thus without bloodshed New Sweden fell, but in the first flush of victory a courier arrived with such terrible news that the governor forgot his triumph and hastened back with all possible speed to his capital. The Indian was again on the war-path, and a general massacre of the Dutch was threatened. This was the story the courier told. A few days after the fleet had left, ex-Sheriff Van Dyck surprised an Indian woman in his orchard stealing peaches one morning and shot her dead on the spot. The murder provoked her tribe to vengeance. Knowing that the governor and militia were away, they rapidly gathered the warriors of all the river tribes, the Connecticut and Long Island Indians, into an army, and suddenly appeared before the city, nineteen hundred strong, in sixty-four canoes. It was just at daybreak, September 15, 1655, that the savages spread through the city, breaking into a few houses on the pretense of looking for enemy Indians, but, probably to satisfy themselves that the murderer. Van Dyck, was in the city. The burgomasters and schepens went around among them in a kindly way, and asked to see their sachems, and when they had gathered them in the fort, prevailed on them to call their forces out of the city. The Indians retired to Nutten (now Governor's) Island, but soon after dusk returned, hastened to the house of Van Dyck, and killed him. Schepen Van der Grist, who lived next door, hurried out and was stricken down by an Indian with an axe. At once the hue and cry of murder was raised. The few remaining soldiers, with the burgher guard, sprang to arms, and, after a brisk action, drove the savages off, killing three and wounding others. The Indians, enraged at this punishment, hastened to Hoboken and Pavonia, where they killed every person they could find, and ravaged the plantations; thence they hurried to Staten Island and other parts of New Jersey, where the same scenes were enacted.

In three days one hundred men, women, and children were murdered, and as many more made captives. Twenty-eight fruitful plantations were wholly laid waste, and property to the value of eighty thousand dollars destroyed. Quite as bad in its results was the general feeling of terror and insecurity that prevailed, driving farmers from their boweries, and retarding settlement of the country. Stuyvesant, on his return, acted much more wisely than Kieft had done on a similar occasion. Instead of retaliating, he called the Indian chiefs together, and by kind words and presents succeeded in placating them and restoring confidence.

The last years of Stuyvesant's reign were marred by cruel religious persecutions, which seem the more cruel because they were in open violation of the company's instructions as well as the traditions of father-land. " Allow all the free exercise of their religion in their own houses," said the company, but the Director would recognize only the Dutch Reformed Church. He sent back to Holland the Rev. Ernestus Goetwater, a Lutheran minister, who was sent over in 1656 by his co-religionists to found a Lutheran Church in his city; and he fined and imprisoned Lutheran parents who refused to have their children baptized in the Dutch Church. By and by he did much harsher things than these. One day, hearing that a Baptist clergyman in Flushing who had not been licensed by him had administered the Sacrament and baptized some converts, he ordered him brought before him, and fined him one thousand pounds and banished him from the province. The Quakers, however, met with the harshest treatment. Many of these peculiar people had been banished from New England about this time, and had taken refuge in New Netherlands, where they met the hearty reprobation of the clergy and the Director. Domine Megapolensis complained that the scum of New England was drifting into New Netherlands. Domine Dresius boldly asked the Director why he harbored persons who were driven from the other colonies as worse than a pestilence. By and by Robert Hodshone, an Englishman, a leading Quaker, began preaching in Hempstead. One day, soon after, while walking in his garden, he was seized and brought before a magistrate of Hempstead, one Richard Gildersleeve, who bound him over for trial, and hastened to acquaint Stuyvesant with the facts. The latter, all zeal, ordered his schout-fiscal to proceed that evening with a guard of musketeers and secure the prisoner and his effects. This was done. The soldiers seized Hodshone, bound and tied him securely, face down, to the rear end of a cart. Two women, one with a babe at the breast, who had been arrested for sheltering the preacher in their houses, were then placed in the vehicle, and the cavalcade took its slow way to the city. We can imagine the laughter and rude jests it elicited, as it wound though the streets to the common gaol, where the prisoners were thrust into separate dungeons. In a few days the Director and council met in the City Hall to dispose of Hodshone's case and pronounced sentence — a fine of two hundred and forty dollars, and in default of payment, two years' hard labor with a negro at the wheelbarrow. Having neither money nor friends to discharge his fine, the prisoner was chained to the barrow with the negro malefactor; he was quite as obstinate as his persecutors, however, and refused to work, saying that he knew not how to do manual labor, and could not endure it if he did. The poor man was imprisoned, cruelly beaten, hung up by the thumbs, and otherwise illtreated, but would not yield. At last, on the appeal of Mrs. Bayard, the Director's sister, he was set at liberty. This severity excited the general horror of the people, and although many more arrests were made, the governor did not again proceed to such extremities.

Thus for years, slave to a despotic governor, vassal to a private corporation, controlled by a people with no genius for colonization, the city struggled for existence, and was outstripped in the race by everyone of the several English colonies on the north and on the south. But in the year 1664 there came a turn of fortune's wheel, and New York also became an English colony. England, as we have tried to make prominent in the preceding pages, had never relinquished her claim to the territory covered by New Netherlands. In the year 1664, believing that the fruit was ripe, she stretched forth her hand and plucked it. Events all through the reign of Stuyvesant had been leading up to this consummation. Charles I. of England had been deposed and beheaded. Oliver Cromwell had governed as Protector, and after his death, by a natural reaction, the monarchy was restored and Charles II. ascended the throne of his father. Charles was a weak, pleasure-loving king, and the management of foreign affairs fell into the hands of his ministers and of his abler brother, the Duke of York. From this moment aggressions began upon the little strip of Dutch territory in America, which were intended to sweep it out of existence. In 1662, because a man whom he very much liked — John Winthrop the younger — desired it, Charles granted to Connecticut a charter which gave her jurisdiction over the territory bounded east by Narragansett Bay, north by the Massachusetts line, south by the sea, and west by the Pacific Ocean, with all the islands " thereunto belonging." Lord Baltimore, proprietor of the colony of Maryland, claimed the Dutch possessions on the South River under his charter, its northern boundary being the fortieth parallel. In 1664, however, ignoring these prior grants, Charles gave to James, Duke of York, the entire territory claimed by the Dutch, and that energetic nobleman at once set about taking forcible possession of his property. He had no love for the Dutch, by whom he had once been libeled without being able to obtain satisfaction. Besides, personal interest was involved. He was Governor of the Royal African Company, an association of merchants which traded to the Gold Coast, and which had been nearly driven from the field by the superior business talent of their Dutch competitors. He was also quite ready to provoke a war with Holland, in which he might distinguish himself, and thus fix the attention of the nation upon himself, for he already had his eye on the throne. Nor were the ministers of King Charles at all backward in aiding the prince in these ambitious designs. Four men-of-war, the Guinea of thirty-six guns, the Elias of thirty, the Martin of sixteen, and the William and Nicholas of ten, were borrowed of the king, and four hundred and fifty soldiers — men of the line, under command of Colonel Richard Nicolls, a veteran officer — were placed on board of them. Colonel Nicolls was appointed Deputy Governor of the province when it should be taken. Under him were three commissioners, Sir Robert Carr, Sir George Cartwright, and Samuel Maverick, who were given power to erect the conquered territory into an English colony. These men also bore orders to the governors of the New England colonies to furnish men and means to aid in conquering the Dutch. The fleet left Portsmouth about the middle of May, 1664 and arrived at Boston late in July. Here the commissioners made their demand on the Massachusetts authorities for aid, and also on Connecticut by an express sent to Governor Winthrop at Hartford. Massachusetts, whose Puritan sympathies were not heartily enlisted in King Charles' cause, responded tardily, but Connecticut, which had been in almost constant collision with the Dutch on her western border, gladly aided the enterprise. Meantime peace and tranquility brooded over New Amsterdam. Not the slightest preparation had been made to receive an enemy. Of the thirteen hundred pounds of powder in the fort seven hundred were unserviceable. There were one hundred and fifty regular soldiers to garrison it, and two hundred and fifty militia, but these so heartily detested the Director that they could not be depended on in an emergency. No provision had been made for a siege.

A certain merchant, one Richard Lord, of Lyme in Connecticut, sent his vessels both to Boston and New Amsterdam. He reached Manhattan from Boston, about the time the English fleet was expected there, and informed Stuyvesant that it was common rumor in Boston that the fleet was intended for the Dutch. The Director and council, alarmed, began active preparations for defense, but on the heels of the merchant came a letter from the Amsterdam Chamber, saying that the English fleet need not be feared, that Charles had only sent a few ships to introduce Episcopacy in New England. All efforts were therefore relaxed, and a few days later the Director set out for Albany, on official business, but before he could finish it, a messenger, spurring in hot haste, reached him with news that Nicolls had left Boston for New Amsterdam, and that the city was in hourly expectation of an attack. It would be interesting could we analyze the emotions of the Director in the mad gallop back to his capital, which followed. Probably rage that both he and the Amsterdam Chamber had been so cleverly duped by the caitiff Englishman was the ruling passion. Twenty-four hours after reaching home, as he walked the fort parapet, he saw the red-cross flag of St. George gleam in the lower bay and caught the dim outlines of the Guinea moving up through the mist. Evidently the threatened English invasion was near.

Stuyvesant's faults were those of a soldier. He had also the virtues of a soldier: bravery, energy, and decision of character were among the latter. He at once determined to hold the town against all odds. And yet it seemed almost an act of madness. The fort at the Battery would protect only that point, and there was the town behind exposed to the enemy's frigates on both sides. He could muster but four hundred men all told, and of these a number were Englishmen and not to be depended on. He had an uneasy feeling, too, that his own countrymen would willingly exchange his iron rule for that of the duke, if they could be assured of protection. Nevertheless, he began active preparations to withstand a siege. Every third man was ordered to repair to the defenses with spade, shovel, or wheelbarrow, which many refused to do. A guard was placed at the city gates; the brewers were forbidden to make grain into malt; the Director's slaves were set to thrashing grain at his farm and conveying it to the fort. "The frigates anchored in a cluster in the bay, and a messenger was dispatched to Stuyvesant with a summons to surrender.

On this unexpected letter," say the burgomasters and schepens of New Amsterdam in their account of the capture to the West India Company dated September 16, 1664 — "On this unexpected letter the Heer General sent for us to determine what was to be done in the matter. Whereupon it was resolved to send some commissioners thither to argue the matter with the General and his three commissioners, who were so sent for this purpose twice, but received no answer except that they were not come here to dispute about it, but to execute their order and commission without fail . . . Three days' delay was demanded for consultation. That was duly allowed, but meanwhile they were not idle. They approached with their four frigates, two of which passed in front of the fort. The others anchored about Nooten (Governor's) Island, and sent five companies of soldiers who encamped themselves at the ferry opposite this place (Fulton ferry, Brooklyn), together with a newly raised company of horse and a party of new soldiers both from the north (Connecticut) and Long Island, mostly all our deadly enemies, who expected nothing else than pillage, plunder, and bloodshed, as men could perceive by their cursing and talking."

Nicolls on his part performed his delicate mission with the tact of the accomplished soldier and courtier. On his arrival he issued a proclamation couched in the kindliest, most conciliatory terms, offering to everyone who would submit, life, liberty, estate, and the fullest enjoyment of every right whether of person or property. These he scattered as firebrands in the enemy's camp, and waited, hoping to secure the prize without incurring the odium of firing on a town filled with women and children. Meantime, while the commissioners were going to and fro, the city was in a ferment. There lay the frigates with the black muzzles of their guns looking on the town, — silent monitors. An inkling of Nicolls' proclamation had reached the people, and they clamored for submission. Stuyvesant sternly refused. The city fathers counselled delay, and an urging on of the preparations for defense, that better terms might be obtained. Nicolls' formal summons to surrender had been made on Saturday, August 30th. He had omitted to sign it, and it was returned that the informality might be remedied, thus giving the besieged precious time. All day Sunday men wrought on the defenses. On Tuesday morning a row-boat left the fleet and approached the city. It contained six dignified gentlemen, men of mark, the commanding figure of Governor Winthrop of Connecticut, whom Stuyvesant had met in council and at fete during his memorable visit to Hartford, being conspicuous. They were met at the wharf with stately courtesy, a salute was fired in their honor, and they were conducted to the City Hall, where Stuyvesant and his council were waiting to receive them. Winthrop broached his mission, which was to deliver a letter from Colonel Nicolls, and to urge the Director to give over a hopeless struggle and submit to the English. Many weighty arguments were advanced with the persuasive eloquence for which the elder Winthrop was famous, but all in vain. The lionhearted Director would defend the city to the last. On taking leave Winthrop left the letter from Colonel Nicolls. Unsealing it Stuyvesant read:

" Mr. Winthrop: — As to those particulars you spoke to me, I do assure you that if the Manhadoes be delivered up to his Majesty, I shall not hinder but that any people from the Netherlands may freely come and plant there, or thereabouts; and such vessels of their own country may freely come thither, and any of them may as freely return home in vessels of their own country, and this and much more is contained in the privilege of his Majesty's English subjects; and thus much you may, by what means you please, assure the Governor, from, Sir, Your very affectionate servant,

Richard Nicolls."

It was a very timely and politic document. The burgomasters at once asked that it be read to the citizens, who had gathered en masse outside to hear the result of the conference, but Stuyvesant feared its effect on them, and refused; a wordy quarrel ensued; at last the Director, in a burst of passion, tore the offending letter to pieces, whereupon Cornelis Steenwyck condemned this violence in no measured terms, and with his fellow-officials quitted the place. The people received the news with suppressed rage, and covert threats, and presently deputed three prominent citizens to call on the Director and demand the paper. The fragments were shown them, but they demanded the letter. Stuyvesant himself appeared before the people, and tried to reason with them, but his voice was drowned in clamorous shouts for the letter. " That," said Stuyvesant, " was addressed to the officers of the government, and does not concern the commonalty "; but the people could not be pacified, and, amid bitter curses against the company and himself, the Director withdrew and shut himself up in the fort, while Nicholas Bayard, like the accomplished courtier that he was, joined the torn fragments of the letter, and thereupon made a copy which he read to the people, and thus partially appeased them. Still the murmuring was deep and loud.

" Why should we fight for the governor and company? " we can fancy them saying. " He has always treated us as children and slaves, and the company has regarded us as a mere trading post for the filling of its coffers. The English colonies have had much better treatment. Look at Connecticut on the east. What a liberal charter 1 There the people elect their own governors and councils; make their own laws. And Maryland on the south. No man there was ever persecuted for conscience' sake; every man has equal rights as respects property, religion, and the suffrage. Why should we fight to sustain a despotism, and expose our property to ruin and our families to violence? "

So they reasoned. Meantime Stuyvesant was busily penning a letter in reply to Nicolls, in which he gave an exhaustive account of the Dutch discovery and right to Manhattan and emphasized their claims to it. This he sent by four of his wisest councilors. But Nicolls declined argument. " He stood on no question of right," he said. "If his terms were not accepted he must carry out his orders and attack." The delegates still wished to argue the matter, but Nicolls refused. " On Thursday I shall speak with you at the Manhattans," he said significantly. He was told that he would be welcome if he came in a friendly manner. " I shall come with my ships and soldiers," was the reply, " and he will be a bold messenger who will dare to come on board and solicit terms." " What then is to be done?" asked one. " Hoist the white flag of peace at the fort, and I may take something into consideration." They entreated that the ships should not fire upon the city without warning, but he denied their request that the troops should not be brought up nearer the city. " To-day I shall arrive at the Ferry," he added; " to-morrow we can agree with one another." On the 25th of August (old style) he landed three companies of regulars at Gravesend, and marched at their head to the Brooklyn Ferry, where the Connecticut and Long Island volunteers were already massed. At the same time two frigates sailed up and cast anchor off Governor's Island. A little later the other two came up under full sail, with their ports open, and guns shotted, ready to pour in a broadside if opposition was made, and so ran past the fort, and came to anchor in the river above. Stuyvesant stood on the ramparts as they came on, feeling that the crisis had come. No doubt he remembered Governor Risingh and Fort Christina. Then he was the piper, and the poor Swedes danced; now the terms were reversed. As the ships came on, the old soldier's ardor was aroused, and he would have ordered his gunners to fire, but at the critical moment good Domine Megapolensis laid his hand upon his shoulder. " It is madness," said he; "what can our twenty guns do in the face of the sixty-two pointed toward us on yonder frigates? Will you be the first to shed blood? " So the ships sailed by without testing the caliber of the Dutch guns. Once past, however, the governor's resolution returned, and taking one hundred men he hurried up into the city to resist any attempt of the foe to land. But there he was met with a remonstrance signed by ninety-three of the leading citizens, including the city magistrates and the clergy, urging him to accept the terms of the English and save the city from sack. Women and children came to him and begged him with tears to save them from violence. At last the grim veteran, hero of a hundred battles, gave way. " I had rather be carried to my grave," he said, but finally he ordered the white flag raised above the fort. And thus peaceably fell New Amsterdam in the year of our Lord 1664.

The articles of capitulation were agreed on next morning. There were twenty-four of them, and they embodied in substance the terms made known by Nicolls in his proclamations and conversations with the Dutch delegates. Never were more favorable terms offered a conquered people. Citizens of every nationality were to be secured in person, property, customs, and religion. Free intercourse with Holland was to continue. The public buildings and records were to remain intact, and public officers were to hold over until the time came for a new election. For himself and his soldiers Stuyvesant asked much the same terms as he had granted to Governor Risingh under exactly similar conditions. They were to march out carrying their arms, with drums beating, colors flying, and matches lighted, and embark on the vessel which was to convey them to Holland. This programme was fully carried out on Monday, September 8th. As Stuyvesant and his troops marched out, the forces of Nicolls and Carr entered the town and raised their " meteor flag " over the fort and public buildings. In the council-chamber the grave burgomasters and schepens proclaimed Nicolls Governor of the province. The fort was rechristened James, in honor of the duke, and the province was named New York for the same reason. Rensselaerwyck and the forts on the South River soon yielded, and thus, without bloodshed, England secured the whole wide territory of New Netherlands — a territory, it is but just to add, which she had always claimed, and to which she was clearly entitled by the law of nations. The United Provinces exclaimed loudly against the injustice of the seizure and waged a long and bloody war with England on account of it, quite ignoring the fact that they had committed a precisely similar act in driving the friendly Swedes from Fort Christina, on the sole plea that they had settled on territory claimed by the Dutch. The grim old Director, too, was harshly blamed for yielding up the fort — as if he had not for the last five years, by every ship that sailed, importuned the half-moribund company to send him men and munitions of war to put it in a proper trim for a siege. Stuyvesant went to Amsterdam and made an able defense of his course. Afterwards, as all his family and property interests were in New York, he returned, and, taking up his residence at his bouwery or country-seat, he lived there, for several years, an active and useful life, though studiously refraining from politics. His estate was a large one and cost him sixty-four hundred guilders. Its fields, sloping down to the East River, were kept in the highest state of cultivation and stocked with the finest breeds of horses, cattle, and sheep. He had there a large, roomy house of Dutch architecture, with square stone chimneys and diamond-paned windows, which was burned in 1777, to the city's permanent loss. It was surrounded by flower-gardens and orchards of peach-, pear-, and apple-trees, in which the owner took great delight. One of his pear-trees was for many years a landmark of the city. Stuyvesant brought it from Holland on his return and set it out in his garden. The tree lived and flourished for two hundred years; and when the city streets were laid out through its ancient home, found itself exactly on the corner of Thirteenth Street and Third Avenue. There it burgeoned and fruited for many a year, never asking a penny for the golden fruit it strewed to the people so generously. At last it fell, and its clean, firm wood was cut up into mementos, and is treasured in scores of city homes to-day. Governor Stuyvesant died in 1672 and was buried in the family vault in the chapel built by himself on his farm, and which stood exactly where

St. Mark's Church now stands, the original tablet of the vault being built into the east wall of the church. He whom it commemorates was a strong, heroic figure, and one may not pass it by without a thrill at the contrast between the city of to-day and that which struggled upward under his iron reign.

V. SOCIAL AND DOMESTIC LIFE.

If in preceding chapters we have touched but lightly on the social and domestic life of the colonists, it was not because we deemed it unimportant, but from a desire to give the reader a clear and graphic sketch of the founding of New York and of the events which, like the stairway of some noble temple, led up to its settlement. But few social amenities were possible to the early settlers. The Rev. Jonas Michaelis, the first pastor, in a letter to " his beloved brother in Christ and kind friend," Rev. Adrianus Smoutius, of Holland, gives a graphic account of the trials and hardships which beset the first pioneers. His letter is dated " Island of Manhata in New Netherlands, the 16th of August, 1628." At the first celebration of the Lord's Supper, he says, they had full fifty communicants — Walloons and Dutch. The Sacrament was administered once in four months " until a larger number of people should otherwise require." The natives he found entirely savage and wild.

" Strangers to all decency, yea, uncivil and stupid as posts, proficient in all wickedness and godlessness, devilish men who serve nobody but the devil — that is, the spirit which in their language they call Manetto. . . . They have so much witchcraft, divination, sorcery, and wicked tricks, that they cannot be held in by any bands or locks. They are as thievish and treacherous as they are tall, and in cruelty they are more inhuman than the people of Barbary, and far exceed the Africans."

Servants were scarce, except Angola slaves, which were " thievish, lazy, and useless trash," and there were no horses, cows, or laborers to be had for money. The rations given out at the company's store, and " charged for high enough," were hard, stale food, such as was used on shipboard, and frequently " this was not good." The Indians brought in fish and flesh of various kinds, but unless one had wares, such as knives, beads, and the like, or wampum, one could not buy. From this letter we learn that in 1628 the colonists felled much wood for father-land, that they had a grist-mill, and were building a windmill, and a " fort of good quarry stone "; that they baked brick, burned lime from oyster-shells, made salt by evaporating sea-water, and had tried to make potash from wood-ashes without success. " The country is good and pleasant," the letter concluded, " the climate healthy notwithstanding the sudden changes of cold and heat."

At the time of which we now write, however — the close of the Dutch dynasty, — New Amsterdam had become a city with many of the comforts and refinements of civilization. Perhaps we can best depict the people's daily life by inviting the reader to join us in a stroll through the city — the time a clear, cool September day in 1663. Shall we enter by this arched gate-way at Broadway and Wall Street, or by the "Water Gate," at the point where Wall Street now meets the East River front? The latter. Then we will take the river road leading through fine old forests from what is now Fulton Ferry into the city. At what is now Maiden Lane we come upon a footpath leading west toward Broadway, and skirting the shores of several clear-water ponds whose outlet is a little brook purling down to the East River; and here we come upon a pretty scene — a bevy of maidens with bare, dimpled arms, some washing linen in the ponds, others spreading it to dry on the green sward of the hill on the west. The path has been made by these maidens and their mothers, from which circumstance it is called Maagde Paatje — maidens' path, which when the English came to name the street was changed to Maiden Lane.

Chatting over the pastoral scene we ride on, and a few moments later, at the present line of Wall Street, come upon a blank wall of palisades, stretching quite across the island to the Hudson. As intelligent strangers we stop and survey the scene with interest. On the left, where the wall abuts on the water front, is a square block-house pierced for musketry, and beyond, built out into the water, a little half-moon battery of two guns, with a sentinel in gray blouse and baggy breeches patrolling it. Before us is an arched gate-way, the key of the arch grotesquely carved and surmounted with a carved cupola and gilded weathercock. The wall is of palisades — beams of wood twelve feet high, imbedded three feet deep in the earth, sharpened at the upper end, and strengthened by planks nailed transversely. There are block-houses at intervals, and *chevaux de frise* of stumps with the roots upturned, and we find on entering that it is defended within by a sod rampart and by a fosse or ditch. A good-natured burgher whom we accost tells us that the wall is 2,340 feet long and cost 3,166 guilders, and that it was built in 1653, when the people feared an attack from the Indians and English.

A broad lane 100 feet wide flanks the wall as far as Broadway and is lined on the south side with rude wooden cabins — the quarter of the chimney-sweeps and low tapsters. Numbers of the former — ragged, soot-begrimed urchins — swarm upon us with their cry of " Sweep ho! " and fight and scramble for the handful of farthings we dispense, until at length the burgher falls upon them with his cane and drives them screaming to their dwellings. Meantime we have been riding slowly down the water-front, examining each object with the curious eye of one new to the place and people. The odd, half-moon docks, with placid, very fat burghers seated on them, fishing and smoking; the quaint buildings with peaked, many-storied roofs, dwellings above and stores beneath; the great stone Stadt Huys, or City Hall, with its gallows in front, the Indian canoes and the shipping in the river, all amuse and interest us. The city dock, shown on the left of the picture, with a vessel inside its piers, is at this moment a busy place.

This dock was the first built on Manhattan, the pioneer of our thirty miles or more of wharves. The merchants call it the " Hooft," and the river in front the " Roadstead." It is a busy place, as we have said. A fleet of scows is plying back and forth between the dock, and the great, clumsy, high-pooped ships anchored in the roadstead. These boats are laden with various articles, according to the cargoes of the ships they are discharging. For instance, one from a " Holland ship " carries dry goods, hardware, and groceries of all sorts, with some of those " cow calves " and " ewe milk sheep " that formed so large a part of early Dutch imports. Another from a Virginia " ketch " is laden with hogsheads of tobacco. A third brings dried fish and English goods from the Snow just arrived from Boston. A fourth is laden with savage, repulsive-looking African negroes from the slave ship White Horse, last from the coast of Angola, on their way to the slave market to be sold at public auction. A pinke from Barbadoes is loading a fifth scow with barrels of sugar and hogsheads of molasses, while the patroon of Rensselaerwyck's sloop — yacht the burghers call it — is sending ashore bales of costly furs — beaver, otter, mink, and others, — and a galley from Curacao costly dyestuffs, fruits, and other tropical products. Gangs of negro slaves are on the dock receiving the goods. One of these gangs, the strangers learn, is owned by Cornelis Steenwyck, a second by Pieter Cornelissen Vanderveen, a third by Isaac Allerton, and a fourth by Govert Loockerman, the four greatest merchants of New Amsterdam at this time, and the four are there in their baggy breeches and blue-cloth coats with silver buttons, to see that no thievery or unthrift is practiced. Indeed, so careful is Cornelis Steenwyck, that he has a negro woman with needle and thread following him about to sew up any rents in bags or bales that have been consigned to him. A part of the bales, barrels, and hogsheads are rolled across the street into the merchants' warehouses, but the bulk of them are carted off to the five great stone warehouses of the company between the present Bridge and Stone Streets. Vessels were not then allowed to come to the dock for two reasons: first, to prevent smuggling; and, second, to keep the sailors on board their ships, as commanded by a city ordinance.

A guide-board off Coenties Slip warns vessels of fifty tons or under not to anchor between that board and the Battery under a heavy penalty. Another near the present Fulton Ferry forbids any vessel to anchor above that point. Quite a fleet of vessels are swinging at anchor between the two points, and we find ourselves studying with interest the names painted in quaint letters on their sterns. There is the Little Fox and the Little Crane, pioneer ships in the Manhattan trade, the Herring, man-of-war, armed with two metal guns, sixteen iron, and two stone guns, the Flower of Guilder, the Sea Mew, Orange Tree, Three Kings, Blue Cock, New Netherland' s Fortune, Black Eagle, Great Christopher, Pear Tree, King Solomon, New Netherland Indian, Morning Star, and others. As we stand viewing the scene, old Gilles de Voocht, the haven-master, making his round of the wharves, draws near, and we address him. " Aye," he replies, " a rare fleet, driven in mostly by the last noreaster. D 'ye mind the Hope, there? a fine craft, a regular Amsterdam liner. Her skipper, Julian Blanck, was the first sea-captain to build a house in New Netherlands; the New Amsterdam, yonder is another regular packet. Captain Adrian Bloemmaert. Her consort, the Prince Maurice, was lost on Fire Island beach in 1659; not the last ship, I warrant thee, to lay her bones on those devilish sands. A pretty craft, is she not? The patroon's yacht yonder plies between New Amsterdam, Sopus, and Fort Orange (Albany). She will take thee quite to Orange for ten florins. She hath a gun on the deck forward hung on a pivot, and her skipper may by law suffer fine and imprisonment if he keep not a strict watch on the way both against the Tankitikes and Wequaegeseeks, the Mohawks, and Mohegans."

We are about leaving the dock when a commotion arises and looking up we see that the flag on the fort flagstaff has been hoisted to the mast-head, which means that a Holland ship is in the offing. To modern Manhattanese such an event seems a trifle, but to the ship and to the burghers of that day it was a great event. To the former it meant the end of an eight weeks' voyage, a tedious course by the Canaries and Guiana, the Caribbean and Curacao, Bahamas and Bermudas. To the people it meant news from home — of fathers and mothers, husbands, wives, children; it meant the news of the day — whatever had been done abroad for the last two months in war, politics, science, art, or religion; it meant to the merchants news of ventures, fate of argosies. Even while we look scores of boats filled with men, eager for news, put off and urge their way toward the ship, while the populace throng the Battery and welcome the new-comer with cheers and waving of hats and handkerchiefs. By and by a single gun thunders from the fort. The vessel rounds to off the Battery, the naval master boards her, inspects manifests and papers, and she

41

is then allowed to proceed to. her anchorage and to transfer her passengers in boats to the shore.

In our leisurely progress we next halt on the arched stone bridge spanning the canal at Broad Street and look up that thoroughfare. It is well built up with solid stone and brick houses having checker-work fronts and quaint crow-step gables, as seen in the engraving, and right through the center of the street runs a canal, with houses and the travelled way on either side. The homesick burghers must have something to remind them of father-land, so they have widened and deepened the bed of a brook that originally flowed through the street, planked its sides, and formed a canal navigable for boats, skiffs, and canoes, and very useful to the farmers and Indians who are wont to land there with loads of produce and game for the markets in the vicinity.

Let us now turn into Whitehall Street and ride slowly up to our tavern, which stands near the point where that street debouches on the Bowling Green. Whitehall was then the patrician quarter of the city. Stuyvesant's town mansion stood at its foot, being known far and wide as " the White Hall," and giving the street its name. On its northern side were rows of quaint Dutch houses such as have been described, and that looked down on the Battery and beyond over the sparkling bay. Behind each house was a garden aglow with flowers, and still behind that an orchard well stocked with apple, peach, plum, pear, quince, and apricot trees; for the old chroniclers all agree that at this period the fruit and flower gardens of the New Amsterdam far outrivaled the old. Tall oaks and chestnuts, spared from the native forests, pelt us with glossy brown nuts as we pass, while squirrels, red and gray, chatter in their tops.

By and by we come to the inn. It is a tall, two-story structure of Holland brick, with checker-work cornices, and at each gable an immense chimney of Manhattan blue stone, which bears, in clumsy iron figures, the date of its erection. There are the usual crow-step gables, and in addition, three long, narrow windows in the roof, the upper surface of each flush with the ridge-pole, the whole much resembling those curious structures built by the wasp on the interiors of barns and out-buildings in summer days. Projecting over the street is a wide, brick-floored, vine-covered stoop, or porch, furnished with wooden benches, while a long wooden arm extending over the street suspends a creaking sign-board, on which, in the guise of a very fat bow-legged Dutchman, is painted Saint Nicholas, the patron saint of Old and New Amsterdam.

As soon as we draw rein, the host, worthy Martin Cregier, president of the burgomasters and captain of the burgher guard, appears at the door to welcome us, while a hostler holds our stirrups, for the inn prides itself on being able properly to entertain distinguished guests. Governors of the neighboring colonies, commissioners seeking the Dutch city to settle vexed questions of boundaries or runaway slaves, titled visitors from abroad, military and naval officers, great merchants, Virginia cavaliers, bookmaking travelers, — in fact, every visitor of quality seeking the city, is at once referred to the inn of Burgomaster Cregier. We will pass through the two-leaved oaken door into the wide hall. On one side is the parlor or drawing-room, with oiled floor and cumbersome Dutch furniture; on the other, the great public room of the inn. We look curiously about. The floor is sprinkled with fine white sand brought in the " Vlie boats " from Coney Island, and done into many quirls and curlicues by Gretchen's broom. On the walls are hung deers' antlers, serving as racks, on which rests the long goose gun of the landlord and the fire-arms of his guests. There is also a great cupboard in the corner, well filled with decanters, glasses, and black bottles of ancient Hollands and rare old Madeira, and near it a rack stuck full of long pipes, each inscribed with the name of the owner. The tap-room opens of¥ from the apartment in the rear. This public room is a sort of meeting-place or exchange for the merchants and gentry of the town — a club-house where they meet to hear and retail the news and discuss new ventures and projects. Two stout merchants are already there seated at a little table, drinking Sopus beer and smoking contemplatively. Placards quite cover the walls, and we have noticed many on the doors and sides of the buildings and on street corners as we passed. One, as we read, gives us a vivid idea of the iron rule of the Director.

" Item. Tavern-keepers and tapsters, from now henceforward, shall not sell, barter, nor give as a present either by the first, second, or third hand, nor provide the natives with any beer, wine, brandy, or spirituous liquors, on pain of forfeiting their business, and an arbitrary correction at the discretion of the Judge.

"Item. To prevent all fightings and mischiefs, they shall be obliged to notify the officer immediately in case anyone be wounded or hurt at their house, on pain of forfeiting their business, and one-pound Flemish for every hour after the wound or hurt has been inflicted and is concealed by the tapster or tavern-keeper.

" Item. The ordinances heretofore published against unreasonable night reveling and immoderate drinking on the Sabbath, shall be observed with more strict attention and care by the tavern-keepers and tapsters, to wit: that they shall not admit nor entertain any company in the evening after the ringing of the farmer's bell, nor sell, nor furnish beer or liquor to any person — travelers and boarders alone excepted — on the Sunday before three o'clock in the afternoon when divine service is finished, under the penalty thereto affixed by law."

And on another placard, this bounty:

" Whereas, we are informed of the great ravages the wolf commits on the small cattle; therefore, to animate and encourage the proprietors who will go out and shoot the same, we have resolved to authorize the assistant Schout and Schepens to give public notice that whoever shall exhibit a wolf to them which hath been shot on this island, on this side Haarlem, shall be promptly paid therefor by them, for a wolf fl. 20, and for a she-wolf fl. 30 in wampum or the value thereof."

As the sun sinks behind the noble forest trees that line Broadway, we sit with other guests on the stoep, where pipes and spiced sangaree are brought us by neat-handed Phillis. Looking down the line of Whitehall Street, we see on every stoep beautiful women and staid, bearded men, the former laughing and chatting among themselves or with acquaintances who, strolling by, stop for an exchange of friendly gossip; the latter stolidly smoking their pipes. We view the moving panorama before us with undisguised interest. Down on the fort the sentry paces his beat. Lovers, two by two, stroll by and out on the Battery Green. We can but be impressed by the beauty of the maidens, who, indeed, are celebrated on foreign shores. Carriages filled with ladies and gentlemen roll by, and anon the governor's coach, with the richly dressed ladies of his family within, bowing and smiling. Nor are the commonalty absent. There are laborers in long toil-stained frocks, bare-armed peasant-girls in waist and short gown, turbaned wenches market bent, herdsmen guiding sheep and cattle to the weekly fair, goatherds driving in their flocks to be milked, and outlandish

43

carts, drawn indifferently by horses, donkeys, and oxen, bringing to market the produce of the outlying farms. Anon comes a band of Indians, in single file, moving stolidly, looking neither to right nor left, and clad in array capable of moving even Motley to laughter. One wears a blanket only; another sports a doublet of bear-skin; his fellow a coat of raccoon skins; and, to complete the grotesque array, the last is clad in a long mantle made of the feathers of the wild turkey. The party bear between them two fine bucks, a brace of wild turkeys, and quarters of a bear, and we at once place them as a hunting party coming to market with the fruits of the chase. By and by, in the stone church within the fort, a bell tolls ponderously — one, two, three — up to nine, — the curfew bell, called by the people the " Farmer's bell," probably because at that time the city gates were closed, and none might return to their homes without. As its last notes cease, the lights fade from the stores and houses, the streets become silent, and soon New Amsterdam is lost in slumber. At the same moment Phillis comes to show us to our rooms. She leads the way to a large square room overhead, and in its smooth partition wall lets down a sort of trap-door, which discloses an opening within like a cupboard, in which are placed two great, soft, downy feather-beds. She sets down the tallow dip and departs, whereupon we disrobe and pop into the cupboard between the feather-beds. Phillis then returns, closes the door, and removes the light, leaving the guest to sleep peacefully in his box until morning. As there are several of these cupboards in the guest-chamber, the economy in room of Dutch sleeping arrangements is apparent.

We spend many succeeding days wandering about the city. The Bowling Green pleases us most. It is the " Common " laid out by the City Fathers, at an early day, in memory of the village green of father-land, the scene of public rejoicings and festivities, the parade of the military, and treaty ground of the Indians. Schoolboys are playing there on the morning we first visit it, and dozens of cute little blackamoors are trudging back and forth carrying water from the town pump next the fort. Now and then Gretchen comes with sleeves rolled above her elbows, and stout ankles visible beneath her scant skirt. One day, as we sit beneath a towering elm, we are joined by a lean and withered old man in clerical garb — long black coat, black small clothes, and black stock, — whom we soon discover to be Jan Gillertsen, the " koeck," or bell-ringer. He sits down and converses with us in the grave and formal language of the day, in the course of which we learn that he had been once bell-ringer in the Great Kirk at the Hague, with its carillon of thirty bells, and that love for his daughter, the fair, blue-eyed Judith, wife to one of the city merchants, had brought him thither. By and by he invites us up into his chamber, beneath the belfry of the church in the fort.

Within is a small octagonal chamber barely furnished with a pallet, a large round claw-footed table, a few chairs, a quaintly carved cabinet, which contains, besides the church plate, some old black-letter tomes and illuminated missals. There are besides several engravings of scriptural scenes on the wall, an hourglass, and a fine old Nuremberg clock. The bell rope comes through the ceiling from the belfry overhead, and the flutter of bats and owls in the chamber above easily suggests the presence of uncanny spirits. The old koeck held a grave office.

" He was," says one, "like him set upon a watch-tower of whom the prophet speaks. The city could not well go on without him. He rang the laborers to their tasks, and at night called them to their firesides. He summoned the magistrates to court, the schoolmaster to his classes, the condemned to his doom. He rang the merry marriage peal, the Christmas chimes, tolled for the dead and the solemn funeral, and at nine his bell gave over the city to silence and slumber. On the Sabbath he called men to worship their Maker; and day by day, in the belfry, he watched for the devouring flame that might, God letting, destroy the city."

Another grizzly old mustache whom we sometimes find beneath the elm is the old trumpeter of Stuyvesant's men-at-arms. He has clean-cut features and a sardonic countenance, and when he stands erect it is with the inches and the air of a grenadier. He is full of martial recollections.

" Many a year is buried since I came," he begins. It was in the year 1645. I remember it well, for in that year our Director, Kieft, held on the parade yonder his great council with the chiefs of the wild men. Verily they came in grand array — the chiefs, six of them, Oritany, who spoke for the Hackingsacks; and Sessekennick and Willem, chiefs of the Tappaans; and Rechgawanak, Pacham, and Pennekeck, who spoke for the Onany; Majanwettenemin, Marechawick, and Nyack, and Aepjen, chief of the Mohegans, who stood for the Wappinecks, the Wechquaesqueecks, the Sing Sings, and the Kicktawanks. These came in brave array, as I said, in their head-dresses of turkeys' feathers, and robes of dressed deer's hide, stuck full of eagle quills, with priceless belts of wampum about their necks and ankles; and they sat in a half circle on the green, while the Director and his councilors, likewise clad in their bravest, sat down to fill out the other half. Then the pipe of peace went around to all, and the great treaty was signed, after seven years of war. Afterward the Director thought it seemly to ask the chiefs to a great banquet in the burgomaster's tavern, whereat the Hollands, being ripe and ready, and more potent in heathen stomachs than in our own, the chiefs forsooth were put to bed in the inn, like babies; yet had they the grace next morning to be heartily ashamed, and did hasten to put many miles of forest and river between themselves and the white man's fire-water."

This tale being exceedingly well received, the old soldier is led to tell another.

" I saw a braver sight here, however, under our present puissant Director, whom may the Lord God protect. It was on that Sunday he sailed for his happy victory over the Swedes, in 1655. After the sermon the burgher guard, seven hundred valiant men, mustered at the fort. At roll of drum they gathered before their colors, fully armed with both hand and side arms, their bandoleers well filled with powder and ball, their muskets properly loaded and provided with rests. Then they deployed upon the parade for inspection, while the whole town gazed, and the women pitied the caitiff Swedes. At last, preceded by drummers and trumpeter, the army marched up the ' Heere Straat ' as far as the tavern of Wolfert Webber, who did refresh them with cakes and ale, after which they marched back, and went on board the fleet, which quickly bore them from our sight."

From the Parade we will enter and inspect the fort. It is a quadrangular earthwork, defended by bastions faced with stone, on which are mounted twenty-two of the wide-mouthed guns of the day — bombards, culverins, serpentines, etc. These are of brass or bronze and use stone as well as iron balls for missiles. The interior, or " parade," is a plain surface one hundred and fifty feet square, in the center of which is planted a tall flag-staff with rounds for ascending, and from which floats the orange, white, and blue flag of the West India Company. On the northwest bastion is the quaint wind-mill shown in the engraving, its tower turning on a pivot, such as one may still see in Holland, and on the eastern shore of Albemarle Sound in North Carolina. There is another windmill on the North River shore slightly differing in form. The most prominent object within the fort, however, is the church of " Manhattan stone," built by Kieft in 1642, with its two peaked roofs, between which "the tower loomed aloft," the same tower in which the koeck keeps his lonely vigils. A marble slab in the front wall of the church bears this inscription in Dutch: Ao. Do. MDCXLII. W. Kieft, Dr. Gr. Huft de Gernester dese Tempel doen Bouwen. ("Anno Domini 1642. Wilhelm Kieft, Director General, hath the commonalty caused to build this temple.")

The jail is on one side of the church, and the government house, a plain two-story structure of brick, also built by Kieft, on the other. Low stone barracks and storehouses complete the tale of buildings within the fort. Soldiers in gray jackets and baggy breeches are lounging about, and the towns-people with visiting friends promenade the ramparts or form little groups on the parade — for the fort is the lion of the young city — the seat of government, the church, the signal station and the scene of all military evolutions and displays; a beautiful spot, too, with its views of harbor, rivers, and wooded shores. Sunday comes; we will attend church, being curious to know more of the people and their religious customs. Half-past ten finds us in the fort near the church, just as the first stroke of the bell sounds, so that the church-goers pass in review before us. They come in two great streams, one down Broadway, another up Whitehall, and meet at the fort gate, Bowling Green being soon filled with the wagons and carts of country people, who have come from the green farms miles away, and out-span on the open spaces.

It is a pretty sight, this company of church-goers, for though the age was in many respects crude and hard, in the beauty and variety of costume it far exceeded ours. The ladies' gowns are left open in front to display the quilted petticoat, which in these days is the most important article of female dress. It is of different materials — cloth, silk, satin, camlet, and grosgrain; and of colors to suit the taste of the wearer, red, blue, black, and white predominating. They wear colored hose, and low shoes with high heels, and colored hoods of silk or taffeta, instead of bonnets. Their hair is frizzled and curled and sprinkled with powder; they wear gold and diamond rings, on their fingers, and gold lockets on their bosoms, but greater attention seems to have been paid to their Bibles and psalm-books, which are richly bound in gold and silver, and attached by gold chains to their girdles. The gentlemen are elegantly attired in the costume of father-land. Their heads are covered with soft-felt hats, with wide brims looped up with rosettes, and with powdered " full bottom " wigs. Their long coats are adorned with silver buttons, and the capacious pockets trimmed with silver lace. In material, there is colored stuff, red, blue, and buff; black velvet, broadcloth, and silk. Their waistcoats, or doublets, are of velvet or cloth of brightest colors, and richly embroidered with silver lace. Their breeches, generally of the same material as their coats, end at the knee in black-silk stockings. Their shoes are low and adorned with large silver buckles.

The worshippers have nearly all passed in when a carriage drives up to the fort entrance, and Governor Stuyvesant and his party alight. There is the Governor, his wife, and his widowed sister, Mrs. Bayard. The Governor bears himself with a military air, despite the wooden leg, bound with silver bands, which replaced the one lost in honorable fight at St. Martins. His wife, a beautiful French lady, daughter of a famous Parisian divine, is worshipped by the gentlemen for her beauty, and envied by all the ladies for the Parisian elegance of her toilettes. We will follow the Governor's party into the church. It is a plain, bare edifice, with a very high pulpit, and above that a huge sounding-board. Scarcely are we seated when the tall forms of the burgomasters and schepens in their black official robes appear, preceded by the koeck and his assistants bearing the cushions for the official pew. At the same time Domine Megapolensis enters by the chancel door. At the foot of the pulpit stairs he pauses, and with hat raised before his face, offers a silent invocation, while the people bow before him. As he seats himself in the pulpit, the zeikintrooster rises, and, facing the congregation, reads the morning lesson. The service proceeds. When the good domine's sermon has exceeded the hour limit marked by the sands in the hour-glass before him, the zeikintrooster announces the fact by three raps of his cane, and the sermon is brought to an end. Then the koeck inserts the public notices to be read in the end of his mace, and hands them up to the minister. The reading being done, the deacons rise in their pews, while the domine delivers a short homily on the duty of remembering the poor, and then pass through the congregation, each bearing a long pole, to which a black velvet bag with a little bell is suspended, to receive the alms of the charitable. Service over, the people disperse to their homes, and the poor schout-fiscal is relieved of his irksome task of patrolling the streets, wand of office in hand, closing the doors of all tap-rooms, and chastising such negro slaves as he finds indulging in games, for although these people had holiday on Sunday, they were sternly prohibited from playing or gaming " during the hours of morning service." Having nothing better to do, we will follow one of the wagon parties which has come from the Walloon settlement on the Long Island shore — the nucleus of the present great city of Brooklyn. The wagon passes out of the water-gate before described, and along the river road to the ferry, which is near the present site of Fulton Ferry. There is a little house here — an open shed roofed with thatch, — a large flatboat worked with sweeps, and several rude skiffs for conveying single passengers. A huge fish-horn hangs upon a tree nearby, and seizing this, the Walloon blows a blast as loud as that which summoned Charlemagne at Roncesvalles. The old ferry-master and his slaves, away back in the forest, are a long time coming, and the traveler, to kill time, begins reading a placard which is affixed to the shed, and which, with many other rules and regulations, contains the primitive ferriage fees.

One of the items provided that the lessee should be bound to accommodate passengers in the summer only from five o'clock in the morning till eight o'clock in the evening, " provided the windmill hath not taken in its sail."

The ferry-boat is an hour crossing. When it comes clumsily up to the other shore we find there a ferry-house and tavern, and little else. The site of the second greatest city of the Union is still covered with forest. There are a few farms here and there in the sheltered hollows, and considerable villages at the Wallabout, Hempstead, and Flatbush, but the Heights are silent and solitary.

One day we saunter round to the city court, which holds its sessions in the Stadt Huys every Monday in the year, except that it takes a recess from December 14th until three weeks after Christmas. It is ten minutes of nine. Citizens are wending their way toward the Stadt Huys. Solomon La Chair, the notary, comes arm and arm with his confrere. Van der Veere, each with his *Marsenaer's Praxis* in hand. On the green before the City Hall, caressing his " cat," loiters " Big Pieter," the negro whipper and

47

executioner. On the *puy*, or platform, on one side of the stoep stands a gray-haired old man, with a sort of skull-cap on his head and a bell in his hand — Stoffel Mighielsen, the town-crier. As we look he rings his bell three times, and reads a high-sounding proclamation from their High Mightinesses, the Director and Council at the fort. We will enter with the little stream of litigants and witnesses pouring in. It is a large square room, with the arms of New Amsterdam engraved on the lozenge-shaped window panes. Over the judge's bench are wreathed the orange, blue, and white colors of the West India Company, and the tricolor of father-land. On the bench are the stuffed red cushions we saw carried to the church on Sunday. The leather buckets kept by the city for putting out fires are hung on the sides of the room. Johannes Nevins, court secretary, is already at his desk turning the leaves of his book of minutes. On his right is a box containing the seal of New Amsterdam, on his left the half-hour glass which is turned precisely at nine, that all tardy members may be fined, — one half hour late, six stivers; one hour late, twelve stivers; and whoever is wholly late, without reasonable excuse, forty stivers. Next to the secretary sits the Gerechts Boode, or court messenger. Pieter Schaffbauck, the jailer, is busy assigning seats to the visitors, and looks after a prisoner he has brought in from jail. There is one other court officer, Matthew de Vos, the bailiff, who is conversing with some clients. On a rack nearby are the law books, the court armory, " The Placards, Ordinances, and Octroys of the Honorable, Great, and Mighty Lords of the States of Holland and West Friesland," " Dutch Court Practice and Laws," the " Practigke ende Hande Bouck in Crimineele Zoacken," by Dr. Van Brugghe, and others, heavy leather-bound tomes. Nine o'clock is struck. The court-house bell rings. Silence is proclaimed by the court messenger, and the judges enter at a side door in solemn procession, Nicasius de Sille leading, then the Heeren Burgomasters, Martin Cregier and Oloff Stevenson Cortlandt; the schepens, Pieter Van Cowenhoven, Johannes Van Brugh, Jacob Kip, and Cornells Steenwyck. The court is opened by Domine Megapolensis, who arises and offers a long and impressive prayer, of which we will quote the more material portion.

"We beseech Thee, O Fountain of all good gifts, qualify us by thy grace, that we may with fidelity and righteousness serve in our respective offices. To this end enlighten our darkened understandings that we may be able to distinguish the right from the wrong, the truth from the falsehood, and that we may give pure and uncorrupted decisions; having an eye upon thy word, a sure guide, giving to the simple wisdom and knowledge. Let thy law be a light unto our feet, and a lamp to our path, so that we may never turn away from the path of righteousness. Deeply impress on all our minds that we are not accountable unto men, but unto God, who seeth and heareth all things. Let all respect of persons be far removed from us, that we may award justice unto the rich and the poor, unto friends and foes alike, to residents and to strangers according to the law of truth, and that not one of us may swerve therefrom. And since gifts do blind the eyes of the wise, and destroy the heart, therefore keep our hearts aright. Grant unto us also, that we may not rashly prejudge anyone without a fair hearing, but that we patiently hear the parties, and give them time and opportunity for defending themselves; in all things looking up to thee for thy word and direction."

Without further formality, the court proceeds to business. A large legal-appearing docunment, superscribed "Worshipful, Right Beloved Schout, Burgomasters, and

Schepens of the City Amsterdam in New Netherland," is handed in by the court messenger, and opened by the schout, who reads:

" Worshipful, Right Beloved:

" Considering, on the one hand, God's manifold mercies and benefits which in his bounty he hath from time to time not only exhibited, but also continued to this budding province; and on the other hand, the resolution and order of the supreme authority of this province, adopted and executed for the further benefit and security of this province: We, the Director General and Council of this province, have, above all things, deemed it necessary to order and prescribe a general day of fasting, prayer, and thanksgiving, which order we hereby send to your Worship, according to the form of our father-land, to the end that it shall be proclaimed and observed in your Worship's city, whereunto confiding we are, and remain,

" Your Worship's good friends,

" The Director General and

" Council of New Netherland,

" P. Stuyvesant."

The letter is ordered to be proclaimed from the *puy* after previous ringing of the bell. Several cases of assault, petty thieving, slander, and tapping on the Lord's Day are then disposed of, the schout fiscal appearing as prosecuting attorney and examining both prisoner and witnesses. At last the court comes to the case of Hend. Jansen Clarbout, on trial for a capital offence.

The secretary reads the Herr Schout's demand against the prisoner, that the burgomasters and schepens vote each for himself for the conclusion of his sentence. The magistrates therefore write their judgment upon pieces of paper, which are collected by the secretary, who opens and reads them as follows:

" The Herr Burgomaster, Martin Cregier — ' That he shall be whipped and branded, and banished for all his life out of the province of New Netherland.'

" The Herr Burgomaster, Oloff Stevenson Cortlandt — ' Though he be worthy of death, yet from special grace he adjudges that he be whipped and branded and banished.'

" The Herr Schepen, Pieter Van Cowenhoven — ' He shall be put to death.'

" The Herr Schepen Johannes Van Brugh ' decides that he shall be whipped and branded and banished the country.'

" The Herr Schepen Hend. J. Vander Vin — ' That the offender is worthy of death, and ought, according to the Herr Schout de Sille's demand, be punished until death follow, with the costs and mises of justice.'

The Herr Schepen Jacob Kip — ' The reasons being sufficiently discussed in complete court, and papers and confession being examined, he can, in conscience and conviction, not vote otherwise than that he, Hendrick Jansen Clarbout, ought according to law be executed by death.'

"The Herr Schepen Cornelis Steenwyck — 'Decides that he be whipped and branded under the gallows, the halter being around his neck, and banished forever, and sent hence with his wife and children on pain of the gallows, thanking the magistrates on his bended knees for their merciful and well-deserved justice."

After the reading of these, a second vote is taken, and it is decreed —

"That the offender, Hendrick Jansen Clarbout, shall be brought to the place where justice is usually executed, and with the rope around his neck be whipped and

49

branded, and banished the country, and condemned in the costs and mises of justice."

" I now ask," said the schout, " that the Herr President Burgomaster, Martin Cregier, and the Herr Schepen, Cornelis Steenwyck, be appointed to wait on the Worshipful Director-General and Council to ask permission to erect a gallows before the City Hall, and for power to banish from the District of New Netherlands."

The two messengers file slowly out and return in due time, bearing a written "apostille," which authorizes and qualifies the magistrates, for this time, not only to banish the apprehended Hendrick Jansen Clarbout beyond the city's jurisdiction, but also beyond the province of New Netherland; " and they are likewise permitted to allow a half gallows to be erected before the City Hall, should that be necessary for carrying the judgment into effect."

With the concluding words the twelve great strokes of noon sound from the fort, and court is declared dismissed — dinner, with the burgomasters of New Amsterdam being a sacred ofifice not lightly broken in upon by business or pleasure.

After a time it becomes necessary for us to do a little shopping, and we are directed to the store of the Heer Schepen Cornells Steenwyck, the Macy's of New Amsterdam. The merchant we find a pleasant, agreeable man of the world, with a horizon much wider than most of his class. His career has been full of vicissitude. When quite a young man he had come to the city as mate of a trading vessel and being smitten with the charms of a merchant's daughter, had cast in his fortunes with the young city. "The handsome sailor," the ladies called him for years after his arrival. Perhaps for that reason they did most of their shopping at his store. It was not long before the Herr Steenwyck was known as the best dressed, most polite, and most popular man in New Amsterdam. Then he was made schepen, and, after the English came, mayor. He imported the newest goods from father-land and became rich. In his store, which filled the whole second floor of his dwelling, besides everything in the hardware and grocery line, the fair shoppers might find the latest patterns in blue and red pennistoen, haft tyke, sarge, flannel, fryse, carsay, drugget, mopeling, camersche, canting, calk'o, garelet, hollands, ozenbergs, fouster, neppins cloth, licking, damask, esternyns, galoen, silk crape, callemink, silk-striped stuff, colored silks, bruston-stuff, runell, bangale, colored fustian, buckram, plush, gloves, stockings, tops, blankets, and ribbons.

We shall find the houses of the better class comfortable and some even elegant. A wide, cool hall extending through the center of the house, with doors in front and rear, was a feature of all. These were hung with ancestral portraits, and furnished with a settee, and sometimes with a great Dutch clock with the family arms set in its case. The front room, or parlor, was usually furnished with a marble-topped table covered with a few devotional works and family heir-looms, with Russian-leather arm-chairs, a great square figured rug serving as a carpet, curtains of tabby cloth falling to the floor, a foot bench and cushion. The great chamber, or family room, in the rear was much more richly furnished. In one, we read, there were twelve Russian-leather chairs, two velvet chairs with fine silver lace, a cupboard of French nut-wood, a round table, a square table, a cabinet, a large looking-glass, a bedstead with its two feather-beds and canopy, ten pieces of chinaware, five alabaster images, a piece of tapestry work, a flowered tabby chimney cloth, a pair of flowered tabby curtains, and a dressing-box.

The cabinet was filled with family jewels and with massive silver plate — the latter brought from fatherland and often an heir-loom that had been treasured in the family for generations. Their plate was the pride and glory of the early Dutch families. There were pieces of superb workmanship then in the city, as is seen in the De Peyster family plate illustrated on another page. The " guest chamber," with its canopied bed, and nut-wood dressing-table, its Turkey-leather chairs, and flowered cloth curtains, was also a feature of Dutch domestic arrangements.

The chief social amusements are dancing parties (at which only the decorous square dances are known, and which break up at eleven, after a frugal repast of bread and chocolate is served), and what the young people call " out parties," which are very much like the modern picnic. All along the shores of Manhattan are romantic coves, groves, and glens to which the young people of both sexes are fond of resorting. " The Locust Trees," a beautiful grove of locusts on a knoll near the North River, a little south of Trinity Church; the umbrageous pathway known as the Maagde Paatje, with its attendant hill-side; a little rock glen and clear-water brook on the present line of Gold Street; and the beautiful sylvan lake called the kolch or fresh-water pond, near the present corner of Canal and Broadway, are all favorites with the sylvan excursionists.

We regret that we cannot remain to share in the winter sports, of which our young friends give us sprightly accounts. They have been thus described:

" First, as the weather turns cold, is the skating on the kolch and neighbor ponds. Then comes the snow, and the young men arrange for a sleighing frolic by moonlight. Four horses they get and Jan Dericksen's long sleigh that holdeth ten couples, packed close, as it suiteth young men and maidens to ride, and away they go over the Kissing Bridge, and under the bended pine boughs, often, methinks, as far as to Harlem, where at Mynheer Borsum's tavern they have a dance and a supper, which by our custom may consist of naught but bread and a pot of chocolate.

" Again, though the Dutch be a sober folk, yet do they keep many festivals — Kerstrydt (Christmas), Nieuw Jar (New Year), Paas (Easter), Pinxter (Whitsuntide), and San Claas (St. Nicholas Day). Christmas comes first, and we also observe it as the anniversary of landing day. After the stockings are explored for whatever Santa Claus may have left there, the young people spend the morning skating on the kolch, or turkey-shooting in the forest; at one the great ovens yieldeth up the Christmas feast, which all meet to enjoy. New Year is the greatest day in New Amsterdam. On that day no one does aught but call and receive calls. For days before, the housewives have been brewing, baking, and mixing, and when the day cometh and thou goest to greet thy friend, thou findest the great logs crackling in the twelve-foot fireplace, and in the centre of the table, spread in the middle of the room, a mighty punch-bowl well reinforced by haunches of cold venison and turkeys roasted whole, and ornamented with cakes, comfits, confectionery, silver tankards, and bekers filled with rare Madeira and foaming ale. The good vrouw and her daughters, clad in their best, are there to receive one, and to dispense whole-hearted hospitality, smiles, and good wishes.

" Paas, which we observe on Easter Monday, may be traced back to the early Saxon, from whom the Dutch are sprung. Paas means ' egg cracking,' and a favorite game on that day is called ' playing for eggs.' Thy sweetheart holds an egg in her hand and challenges thee to break it by striking it with thy egg, the broken one belonging to that which remaineth whole. On that day, too, the shops are gay with boiled eggs, tied with red and blue ribbons, or colored by mixing potent pigments in the water which hath boiled them. On Paas Day no true son of St, Nicholas tasteth other food than eggs."

PART II. ENGLISH RULE
VI. THE NEW FLAG.

Returning to take up the thread of our history, we find New Amsterdam under new rulers, with a new name. Henceforth, save for a brief period, she would be called New York, in honor of her new owner, James, Duke of York.

The fort also was given a new name, James; a new flag waved over it, the Union Jack, a standard symbolical of the nation which had come to rule. The red cross on its white ground was derived from a union of the three crosses of St. George, St. Andrew, and St. Patrick, originally emblems of the three kingdoms of England, Scotland, and Ireland, now united in one great nation — a nation of sailors, navigators, pioneers, with such genius for colonization that the sun never sets on its dominions; a nation which, with those that have sprung from it, is now the dominant power on the globe. It must be admitted that the change was in many respects a beneficial one. Instead of a mere trading-post, the slave of a commercial monopoly, surrounded by enemy colonies, each superior to it in numbers and enterprise, New York became one of several provinces, under the same general government, speaking the same language, having to a certain extent the same interests. We shall find that her rate of increase was much more rapid in the one hundred and eleven years of English rule, than during the half century of Dutch domination. Her progress was, however, not so rapid as it should have been, considering the advantages she possessed, for it was the policy of her English rulers to shorten, as far as they dared, that strong arm of her power — her commerce. In treating of this period we shall notice only the more important events and shall strive to give due prominence to its leading principle — the struggle of the people for their rights, and especially for the right to govern themselves.

Twenty royal governors, ruled New York while it remained a colony, under eight kings and queens — Charles II., James II. of the Stuart line, William and Mary of the House of Orange, Queen Anne of the Stuart line again, and lastly, the three Georges of the Brunswick line.

The names of these governors, and their terms of office, were: Richard Nicolls, 1664-1668; Francis Lovelace, 1668-1673; Sir Edmond Andros, 16741682; Thomas Dougan, 1683-1689; Henry Sloughter, 1691, died July 23, 1691; Benjamin Fletcher, 1692-1698; Earl of Bellomont, 1698, died March 5, 1701; Lord Cornbury, 1702-1708; Lord Lovelace, 1708, died May 6, 1709; Robert Hunter, 1710-1719; William Burnet, 1720-1728; Lord John Montgomery, 1728, died July i, 1731; William Cosby, 1732, died March 10, 1736; George Clinton, 1743-1753; Sir Danvers Osborne, 1753, died October 12, 1753; Sir Charles Hardy, 1755-1757; Robert Monckton, 1761-1765; Sir Henry Moore, 1765-1770; Earl of Dunmore, 1770; Sir William Tryon, 1771, deposed in the Revolution.

The interregnum between several of these dates was filled by lieutenant-governors or provisional governors. The average of these rulers in statesmanship and patriotism was not high. Some were politicians merely. Some were old soldiers or sailors, who had to be provided for; and others, younger sons of titled families for whom places were desired. A few were men of sagacity and experience in public affairs, who were appointed for their fitness, or supposed fitness, for the position. Colonel Nicolls the first, was one of the most successful; his position was one of great difficulty and delicacy. The Dutch citizens were to be placated, new and peculiar conditions were to be established, and special laws required to be made. In his treatment of these vexed questions the Governor showed much tact and discretion.

The Dutch were left in possession of their homes, business, religion, and for nearly a year, of their city government. At length the latter was changed to the English form — burgomasters, schepens, and schout giving place to mayor, aldermen, and sheriff. A code of laws was framed, called The Dukes Laws, which were certainly much more liberal in matters of faith and conscience than those of the iron Director, Stuyvesant. Trial by jury was established, a justice court for each town also, with, right of appeal to the Court of Sessions. Treason, murder, denying the true God, kidnapping, striking parents, and some other crimes were punishable by death. Slavery was allowed, but no Christians were to be made slaves except criminals sentenced by the lawful authority. No persons could trade with the Indians without a license. No Indian was allowed to " powwow," or perform incantations to the Devil. Churches were to be built and supported in each parish, but no sect was to be favored above another, and no Christian was to be fined, imprisoned, or molested for his religious opinions.

These were the main provisions of the new laws. There were many others relating to the settlement of estates, anniversary sermons, surgeons, orphans, servants, weights and measures, births, burials, drift whales, wrecks, sailors, laborers, some of which seem very needless and curious in our eyes.

The patents of the great patroonships were confirmed under the titles of " manors." The Dutch still held their title to the old stone church in the fort, and continued to worship there, allowing the English congregation to hold its service in the afternoon. The English service was held on the first Sabbath after the surrender, and this was the first time that that grand liturgy of the Anglican Church, which M. Taine pronounces the " national poem " of England, had been officially heard in New York, though travelling missionaries of the church had undoubtedly read it in the city previous to this time.

Before affairs were fairly settled at home. Governor Nicolls was menaced from abroad. War had broken out between England and Holland because of Nicolls' act, — a war in which France soon joined in favor of Holland, and an attack on New York might be made at any time by the great Dutch admiral De Ruyter, whose fleet was known to be in the West Indies. De Ruyter, however, sailed for the home seas, where he arrived in time to gain fresh laurels in the war, at one time attacking and burning the English fleet in the mouth of the Thames itself. New York escaped for the time; and in 1667 the peace of Breda left the Duke in peaceable possession of his new territory.

In the interim (in 1666) had occurred the terrible plague and great fire of London. One hundred thousand people died by the former in five months; five sixths of the houses in London were swept away by the latter, leaving the people homeless and beggared. These national disasters, by paralyzing trade and emigration, had great influence on the fortunes of New York.

The French, too, who were by this time firmly established in Canada, and laid claim to all the territory west of New York as far south as the Ohio River, required to be closely watched. These continued anxieties, and the financial straits to which his generosity soon brought him, so wore upon the genial Governor that he wrote in 1668 asking to be recalled. The Duke consented, and appointed Colonel Francis Lovelace governor in his place. Everyone had a good word for the retiring Governor. Commissioner Maverick wrote to Lord Arlington: " He has kept persons of different judgments and of diverse nations in peace and quietness during a time when a great part of the world was in wars; and as to the Indians, they were never brought into such peaceable posture and faire correspondence as they now are." As the time for the Governor's departure came a grand dinner was given him at the house of Cornelis Steenwyck; and when on the 28th of August, 1668, he took final leave, a grand procession of military and citizens escorted him to the vessel which was to convey him home.

Colonel Lovelace, his successor, was an amiable, worthy gentleman, a favorite courtier of King Charles II., and one of his Knights of the Order of the Royal Oak. His administration is noteworthy only for the fierce civil and military commotions which disturbed Europe and rolled across the Atlantic with such force as to depose Lovelace from his government, and for the moment even to overthrow British power in New York.

Charles II. had long been restive under the restrictions which his Parliament imposed on his exercise of absolute power. Catholic France, under her able but unscrupulous monarch, Louis XIV., was now the leading power of Europe and the mortal foe of the Netherlands, which was Protestant in religion and republican in government. Charles, ignoring the fact that in 1669 he had formed a league with Holland and Sweden — known in history as "The Triple Alliance," — now proposed to Louis to form an alliance with him against the Dutch, and to maintain Louis' claim to the throne of Spain, on condition that he (Louis) should aid him in establishing an absolute monarchy in England. War was therefore declared by the two nations against the Netherlands. The English engaged the Dutch fleets on the ocean, while Louis marched an army of 200,000 men into the Netherlands. He was, however, defeated and driven back by the Dutch, who cut the dykes and flooded the country with the sea, somewhat as later the Russians repulsed Napoleon by burning the cities their fathers had reared. Meantime the Dutch privateers had nearly swept English commerce from the ocean; while in the spring of 1673 a Dutch squadron, commanded by two brave admirals, Evertsen and Binckes, had been dispatched to recover their lost territory in America, and inflict as much damage on English shipping in those seas as possible. The squadron anchored in the lower bay on the 29th of June with about twenty English prizes in tow.

Governor Lovelace was in Hartford in consultation with Governor Winthop. Captain Manning, in command of Fort James, at once charged his guns, sent a drum through the streets to beat the alarm, and dispatched a messenger post-haste to Hartford for Lovelace. The Dutch commanders, however, knew well the value of time, and moved their fleet to within musket-shot of the fort, while they sent to Manning a laconic summons to surrender. " We have come for our own," they added grimly, " and our own we will have." Manning sought to parley and secure terms, but Evertsen replied that he had already promised protection to citizens and property and added that unless the Dutch flag was hoisted in half an hour he should fire on the fort, " and the glass is already turned up," he added significantly. Manning stood to his guns, and when the half hour had expired the fleet fired a broadside into the fort, killing several men and wounding more. At the same time, the Dutch commander threw six hundred men ashore at a point just back of the present Trinity Church and assailed his enemy in the rear. Manning, finding the odds too great, surrendered on conditions. He was allowed to march out through the gates at the head of his garrison with drums beating and colors flying. In the fort, the red-cross flag was pulled down, while the blue, white, and orange again floated triumphantly. The fort took a new name, William Hendrick, the province was called New Orange, after the young Prince of Orange, now the hope and pride of the Dutch State. The Dutch occupation was of short duration, however, and had little effect on the fortunes of the city. On the 9th of February, 1674, a treaty between Holland and England was signed at Westminster, by the terms of which Holland relinquished forever all claims to her former colony of New Netherlands. Governor Lovelace, however, was not restored to office, Sir Edmond Andros being appointed in his place. Lovelace returned to England, where he learned that his predecessor, the gallant and generous Nicolls, had been killed in one of the first battles of the war.

Andros, the new Governor, was a courtier by birth as well as by training. His father had been Master of Ceremonies to Charles II., and he himself had been trained in the king's household. He was also a good soldier, and a man of title and estate, having recently become, by the death of his father, bailiff of Guernsey and hereditary seigneur of the fief of Sausmarez. He was a scholar, and a patron of art, something of a statesman, but harsh and imperious in temperament. His lovely and accomplished wife, Lady Mary, daughter of Sir Thomas Craven, accompanied him.

The frigates Castle and Diamond, with the distinguished party on board, arrived on the 22nd of October, 1674. Anthony Colve, the Dutch Governor, received them with stately ceremony, and after the proper amount of speech-making and letter-writing had been done, delivered over the government. Before embarking for Holland, Colve performed an act of courtesy greatly to his credit: he sent Sir Edmond as a present the elegant coach and three broad backed Flemish horses which he had used in his official journeys.

Few events of sufficient importance to be included in our story occurred during the reign of Governor Andros. He had many vexatious disputes with New Jersey and Connecticut over the question of boundaries, and some trouble with the people he governed, who wished their laws made by an assembly of men chosen by the people, as was the case with their sister colonies.

With the capture of the city by Nicolls, the English-speaking people in New York, together with the more progressive Dutch citizens, had expected a more liberal form of government than they had enjoyed under the West India Company, but, instead, they found the one-man power still paramount; they had exchanged the rule of a company of merchants for the rule of a duke. True, they had been given concessions, but still they were allowed no voice in the management of their affairs. At length, in the summer of 1681, under their leader, John Younge, high sheriff of Long Island, they drew up a monster petition to the Duke, reciting their grievances, which were: the exaction of a revenue without their consent, and the enthralling of their liberties and burdening of their trade by an arbitrary power exercised over them; and praying that the Duke would henceforth govern his province through a governor, council, and assembly, as was done by the king in his plantations. James gave careful attention to this petition. Dyer, his Collector of Customs in New York, had written him that the merchants had refused to pay the duties levied under his laws, alleging that they were illegal and unconstitutional; in fact, that he, Dyer, had already been indicted by the colonial court "for traitorously exercising regal power and authority over the king's subjects." Fortunately for New York, James had two excellent advisers — his brother, King Charles, and the illustrious William Penn, who had recently drafted, with the aid of the republican statesman Algernon Sidney, a wise and liberal form of government for his new province of Pennsylvania. King Charles said it was evident that, in order to collect a revenue, an assembly must be granted. Penn exhibited his system of laws as a model, and, resting his hand lovingly on the Duke's shoulder, advised him to give the province the franchise. The Duke, after debating for some time the question of selling his American estate — for which large offers had been made, — decided to retain it and give it the franchise; but as Andros had become obnoxious to the people, he decided to recall him, and appoint in his place Thomas Dougan, a gentleman who had distinguished himself in many battles, and who had served creditably as Lieutenant-Governor of Tangiers, in Africa.

Dougan arrived at Nantasket, near Boston, in August, 1683, and came on to New York by way of Connecticut and Long Island, everywhere received with respect and affection by the people, who were pleased by the affability of his manners, and by the news he bore, that the Duke had granted their petition. One of Dougan's first acts was to issue writs for an election of representatives to the long-desired Provincial Assembly. By these writs we find that New York then extended eastward on the mainland as far as the west bank of the Connecticut River, and included Long Island, Martha's Vineyard, and Nantucket; at least the Duke claimed this under his patent, although Connecticut disputed his claim to the territory between the Connecticut River and the Hudson.

New York, Albany, Rensselaerswyck, Esopus, Long Island, Staten Island, Pemaquid, and Martha's Vineyard sent deputies in answer to the writs, the whole number amounting to eighteen; most of these were Dutch. This first Assembly of New York convened on October 17, 1683, with Matthias Nicolls as Speaker, and sat for three weeks. The first act passed by it was a Charter of Liberties and Privileges," granted by the Duke. This charter recognized the principles of self-government and self-taxation which the people had long contended for, and secured freedom of conscience and religion to all. It also provided for the levying of duties on goods imported. Another act of Assembly divided the province into twelve counties. A third established court of justice, of which there were four distinct classes: town courts; county courts, or courts of sessions; a general court of oyer and terminer; and a court of chancery, or supreme court, — the latter composed of the governor and council. From the judgment of this court, however, any aggrieved citizen might appeal to the king.

This charter was quite an advance on that of 1664 and is interesting as a landmark in the long-continued struggle of the people for their rights. We must not forget to mention, too, among the laws of this Assembly, a naturalization act, by which all persons, except slaves, residing in the colony, of whatever race or tongue, were accounted citizens, provided they professed Christianity and took the oath of allegiance to the king. In the same manner, others seeking the city in time to come might also be made citizens. This act was intended largely to benefit the Huguenots, whom the merciless persecution of King Louis XIV. of France was driving from that country by tens of thousands. But before the Charter of Liberties and Privileges could be ratified by James, and forwarded to New York, an event occurred in England which prevented it from ever being transferred. This event was the death — February 3, 1684 — of Charles II., and the elevation of James to the throne. James Rex, the colonists soon found, was quite a different person from James the Duke. Religious bigotry was his bane. He was also narrow and illiberal, and sadly lacking intact and judgment. The first time the affairs of New York came before him as king, he discovered that the Charter of Liberties and Privileges, which had never been sent to the colony, was too liberal, and he declined to "confirm it, but allowed it to continue in force until he should otherwise direct, so that the colonists still continued to enjoy its privileges. He also at this meeting broached the project of uniting New York and New England under one government. A letter was also written and dispatched to New York, having the royal signature, providing that all men then in office should be continued in power until further orders. The cry, " The king is dead — Long live the king," caused little commotion in New York. As nothing was said in the letter about an Assembly, one was called by Governor Dougan in October, 1684, the appointed time. It was the last held, however, during the reign of James 11. That reign was brief and inglorious. James was a Catholic and attempted to re-establish the Catholic religion in his realm. But his Protestant subjects rose in revolt, and called the Dutch prince, William of Orange, who was a Protestant, and who had married Mary, the daughter of James, to lead them and be their king. William consented and, as we know, landed at Torbay, November 5, 1688, and was greeted with so popular an uprising that James hastened to abdicate in favor of his son and daughter. Some things he had done before this, which have special interest for us, since they refer to New York. The most interesting of these was the grant in 1686 of a charter to the city. This should not be confounded with the Charter of Liberties and Privileges, which was granted the province. It was a broad and liberal instrument, and the wonder is that James, who was at this moment plotting to deprive the American colonies of their charters, should ever have granted it. The influence of Governor Dougan at court, and the high character of such citizens as Mayor Nicholas Bayard, Recorder James Graham, and others, was no doubt largely responsible for it. It was the great charter, the foundation on which the subsequent charters of 1708 and 1730 were laid. It confirmed all previous " rights and privileges " granted the city, and gave it in addition, by name, the City Hall, the great dock and bridge, the ferry, the two market-houses, and the waste, vacant, unpatented lands on the island above low -water mark, with the coves, rivulets, creeks, ponds, etc., not before granted. Some of these granted rights yield the city a large revenue today, while others have been appropriated to the use of the people.

Soon after a new city seal was presented. The beaver of the old Dutch seal was retained, and a flour barrel and the arms of a windmill were added, the whole being significant of the trade in beaver and other furs, and the bolting of flour, the two leading industries of the city at this time. By the spring of 1688, James' great plot against the chartered rights of the American colonies was fully matured, and he issued a decree uniting all the colonies north of the fortieth degree of latitude into one great province, to be called New England. Pennsylvania alone was excepted. New Jersey, New York, and New England were merged into one; and the charters they had so long and jealously guarded were swept away in an instant. New York was especially unfortunate; she lost not only her Provincial Assembly and her Charter of Rights and Privileges, but her name and identity even.

Sir Edmond Andros, who has been introduced to us as Governor of New York, was made Governor of the United Province, with head-quarters at Boston. Andros came to New York in August, 1688, to receive the submission of the people. The occasion is described as being a brilliant event. A large and imposing retinue accompanied him. The City Guard — a regiment of foot and a troop of horse in showy, shining regimentals — received him and conducted him to Fort James, where his commission was read to the assembled people; later it was read in the City Hall; the seal of New York was brought into his presence, broken and defaced by order of the king, and the Great Seal of New England adopted in its place. Andros' rule, however, was of short duration. In the spring of 1689 news reached Boston of the abdication of James and the accession of William and Mary, and the people very quickly disposed of the hated Governor by seizing him and sending him to prison.

VII. REBELLION.

An exciting and instructive chapter in the city's history follows this act of New England in deposing her Governor. New York, too, was deprived of a ruler, and indeed of any government that all parties would recognize. A chaotic condition of affairs followed and continued for two years. Two factions at once arose: composed as to race, of the English against the Dutch; as to class, of the aristocrats against the common people; as to religion, of the Church of England against the Dutch Reformed Church.

The strife was as to who should rule the city. The English party held that the officers appointed by James should continue in power until their successors should appear armed with authority from William and Mary; in other words, that the former government should stand. The Dutch party held that with the flight of James his authority ceased as much in the colonies as in England, and that therefore the people should appoint officers to enforce the laws and maintain the peace until the pleasure of William should be known. There was a precedent for this view in the case of the New England colonies, which had set up their former governments on the overthrow of James. Both parties made out plausible cases, but neither would be convinced by the arguments of the other.

The leaders of the English party were Lieutenant Governor Nicholson and the three members of the deposed Governor's council, Frederick Phillipse, Stephanus Van Cortlandt, and Nicholas Bayard. The councilors were men of the highest repute in the city, Frederick Phillipse was known as the richest man in New York. He was a native of Friesland, of high birth, who had come to the city in youth poor and friendless and had attained his present position largely through his address and ability as a merchant. He had an immense estate between the Spuyten Duyvil and the Croton River, which had been erected into a manor in 1693, under the title of Phillipseborough. The old manor-house you may still see in the heart of the city of Yonkers, transformed into the City Hall. Van Cortlandt was Mayor and had been Judge of the Admiralty; a man of wealth and education. Bayard was a nephew of Governor Stuyvesant. He had been Surveyor and Secretary of the Province, Alderman, and Mayor of the city, and was now Colonel of the regiment of City Militia. All were learned, courtly, patriotic men, whose counsels in ordinary times would have been treated with the greatest respect and deference. The leaders of the democratic party were Jacob Leisler and his friend Jacob Milborne. Leisler was a German, born at Frankfort-on-the-Main, and had been a resident of New York about thirty years. He was a prosperous merchant, a deacon in the Dutch Reformed Church, but had never held public office, nor was he well versed in public affairs. He was at this time captain of one of the six train bands which comprised Colonel Bayard's regiment of militia. He was a man of great energy and force, and of much native quickness and sagacity, but entirely uneducated, coarse and violent, in speech and manner, self-willed, arrogant, passionate, and of unbalanced judgment; a fanatic on the subject of popery, a stern hater of the English, their church, and institutions. Milborne was Leisler's son-in-law; a man of better education, but of far less principle.

The struggle for power began April 29, 1689, by Leisler's refusing to pay the duties on a cargo of wine he had imported, on the plea that the Collector, Ploughman, was a Catholic, and therefore not qualified to perform his duties under the Protestant sovereigns. There was a heated discussion over it in the City Hall, between the councilors and the merchant, which was ended by Leisler's falling into a passion and declaring he would never pay a penny to Ploughman. From this moment strange stories and whisperings were put into circulation and were caught up and eagerly retailed by the ignorant peasantry, who being without schools, books, or newspapers, and most of them unable to read, were quite at the mercy of the demagogues. Lieutenant-Governor Nicholson, it was whispered, was plotting to betray the city into the hands of the French. The woods on Staten Island were said to be filled with Papist emissaries, whom Nicholson was in the habit of meeting to concert plots against the city. Another rumor was, that King James, who had fled to France, was on the seas with a powerful French fleet, intending to reduce the city. Others told how the leading Dutch citizens were fast being won over to popery. Again, ex-Governor Dougan, who was still a resident of the city, was said to have concocted a plot to murder the Protestants and deliver the town to the Catholics. Some even came to Colonel Bayard and asked him to dismiss the Catholics on the militia force lest they should turn their arms on the citizens. " Dismiss the Catholics! " said the colonel; " why, there are not above twenty on the force, and they are old cripples "; and he had to send for Captain Leisler to reassure them.

We must take into consideration this condition of the public mind in order to understand how the usurpation we are about to describe could have been effected. A very little thing at last precipitated revolution. Governor Nicholson lived in considerable state at his house in the fort, which at this moment was defended only by a sergeant's guard of regular troops, most of the garrison being employed on detached duty in Maine. To reinforce the sergeant's squad, a company of the city militia was detailed each night to mount guard at the fort. One night Nicholson coming home late found a militiaman stationed as sentinel in a sally-port and sharply reprimanded the sergeant in command, as only the regulars were detailed for sentinels. The man said it was by order of Lieutenant Cuyler, of the militia company. Nicholson ordered the offending officer before him, and put the question " Who commands this fort, you or I? Cuyler laid the responsibility on his superior officer, Captain De Peyster. Nicholson, who seems to have felt that he was being watched by the militia captains, in a gust of passion drove them from the room, saying that he would rather see the town on fire than be commanded by them.

The soldiers and gossips tortured this expression into a threat to burn the town: and they said the Governor had laid a plot to murder all the Dutch inhabitants the next Sunday as they went to church in the fort. Towards noon of that day. May 31st, a single drum-beat was heard. At once, as if by concerted signal, laborers dropped their implements, mechanics their tools, and rushed into the streets. The city stood affrighted. Shopkeepers put up their shutters: householders barred doors and windows. Captain Leisler's company was observed to muster before his house in the strand. Gathered there, they were harangued by Sergeant Joost Stoll, who at last exclaimed, " We are sold, we are betrayed, we are going to be murdered," and led his company to the fort, attended by the mob. Probably there was not one of the commonalty from Leisler down, who did not honestly believe that his life and property were in jeopardy. Lieutenant Cuyler was at the fort and admitted the soldiers, and in a few moments Leisler appeared and took command. Soon after Colonel Bayard, by command of the council, went to the fort and ordered the soldiers to disperse, but Stoll coolly told him that they disowned all authority of the government. A little inquiry convinced Bayard that the entire City Guard was in open rebellion. When this fact was reported to Governor Nicholson, he called a meeting of the council at the City Hall: but while they were deliberating there came a sound of marching men, and Captain Loedwyck at the head of his company appeared in the chamber and demanded the keys of the fort. To prevent bloodshed, and being without soldiers to defend his authority, Nicholson yielded them up under protest. And so the popular party, or Leislerites, came into possession of the city. For a time Leisler governed with some show of moderation. He wrote an address to William and Mary in behalf of the " militia and inhabitants of New York," in which he described at length, the revolution and the causes which had led to it and promised most loyal submission for himself and those acting with him. In June, however. Governor Nicholson sailed for England, intending to lay his case before the king, leaving affairs in charge of three councilors, and from this time on Leisler grew more and more arrogant and dictatorial. He compared himself to Cromwell and spoke often of his patriotism and address in saving the city from pillage and massacre. He declared that the sword must now rule in New York, and behaved with great insolence, and after a time with great cruelty, toward those opposed to him; in fact, he behaved quite like a man whose head was turned by rank egotism, and the possession of unlimited power.

Soon news came that William and Mary had been proclaimed in Barbados, and, soon after, in Boston. They were proclaimed in Hartford on the 13th of June, and two envoys, Major Gold and Captain Fitch, were dispatched to New York with the orders for proclaiming them there. They also bore a royal proclamation confirming all Protestant officers in the colonies in their places. Leisler managed to secure both proclamations in advance of Mayor Van Cortlandt — although the latter rode far out into Westchester to intercept the envoys; and, on the 22nd, read the former in the fort. Afterward it was given to Mayor Van Cortlandt to be read in the City Hall, and was so read, after many angry words had passed between Leisler and Van Cortlandt over the former's unwarranted act. Two days later Van Cortlandt obtained a copy of the proclamation confirming all Protestant officers in their places. We can imagine his elation; it ratified all he and his party had done; it constituted himself and his colleagues, Phillips and Bayard, the only legal government for the province, since they had received their commission from the crown. Leisler and his party, on the other hand, were filled with rage and dismay. Perhaps they feared for their lives if such bitter enemies as the councilors came into authority; perhaps they were simply intoxicated with the lust of power: at any rate they determined to resist. Of course such an act would be high treason and punishable with death; but they do not seem to have thought of that. Mayor Van Cortlandt had the proclamation read to the aldermen and the citizens in the City Hall the same day it was received. The next morning, June 25th, he invited the other councilors and the Common Council to his house, and the two bodies conferred long and earnestly as to how lawful authority should be restored to the city, and the people quieted. One of their first acts was to remove the Collector of Customs — Ploughman, — who was a Catholic, and therefore ineligible, and to appoint in his place four commissioners, worthy and reputable citizens, Protestants all, Nicholas Bayard heading the list. These gentlemen, after taking the oath of office, received the keys and began their duties. They had barely time to change the first letter in the king's arms, however, when the clank of sabers and tread of armed men was heard, and Leisler, at the head of a body of militia, marched in, and savagely ordered them out of the room. Bayard sternly reminded him that they were there by authority of the king and warned him against offering violence to his Majesty's officers. Leisler, in reply, began a long tirade, in which the epithets " rogues, traitors, and devils," were freely applied to the commissioners. In the midst of it, a soldier seized Wenham, one of the commissioners, and dragged him into the street, where he was sadly battered by the mob. Bayard himself was struck at fiercely, but warded off the blows, and succeeded in escaping to a house nearby, which was at once besieged by the rabble. He, however, escaped to his own house. Meantime a mob filled the street and clamored for the blood of the aristocrats. They had but one rallying cry: " The rogues have sixty men ready to kill Captain Leisler! "

Next morning friends of Colonel Bayard, including the aldermen, came to him with the warning that his life was in danger, and besought him to flee the city. Bayard at last consented. Horses were provided outside the city limits, and in disguise, accompanied by two negro servants, he succeeded in leaving the city, and in reaching Albany. He returned secretly in October, having learned that a favorite son was at the point of death. His presence was quickly discovered, however, and an armed posse was sent to the house of death to arrest him. The men searched the house from top to bottom with oaths and ribald shouts, swearing they would fetch their victim " from the gates of hell," but failed to find him. They next attacked the house of Mayor Van Cortlandt, threatening to take his life, but were held at bay by Mrs. Van Cortlandt until her husband could make his escape. Fleeing from the city. Van Cortlandt passed up into Connecticut, and took refuge with Governor Treat, at Hartford.

It is not necessary to detail the various acts of violence and usurpation committed by Leisler from this time forward. Let us see how retribution finally came to him.

Shakespeare's Ariel must have written the first state paper intended to regulate affairs at New York. Nicholson had not then reached London, and the ministry, supposing him to be still in power, addressed a letter to him ordering him to assume the government, call the chief citizens to his aid, and " do and perform all the requirements of the office." By some fatuity, this letter was not addressed to Nicholson by name, but to " Our Lieutenant-Governor and Commander-in-Chief of our Province of New York in America, and in his absence to such as for the time being take care for preserving the peace and administering the laws in our said province of New York in America."

When John Riggs, the messenger bearing this letter, reached New York, Leisler sent an armed force to conduct him to the fort. Next morning the councilors, summoned by Riggs, met in the fort to receive the letter, but were not allowed to accept it by Leisler. " The king," he said, " knew that he was at the head of the government and intended the letter for him." The councilors protested, but Leisler's show of force overawed the messenger, and the packet was delivered to him, whereupon he turned upon the councilors, and calling them " popishly-affected dogs and rogues," bade them " begone." Leisler now told the people that the king had named him Lieutenant-Governor, and at once entered on the duties of the office — appointed a council and other officials, had William and Mary proclaimed a second time, and when the Sabbath came, rode to the Dutch Church and sat in the Governor's pew, while his council walked gravely in and seated themselves in the pew reserved for magistrates.

One can imagine the feelings of the aristocrats. No doubt they prayed heartily that this rogue might soon come to the end of his tether. Meantime Governor Nicholson had reached London and had laid his case before the king and the Plantation Committee. They sustained him in all his acts, and at once appointed a new governor. Colonel Henry Sloughter, while Nicholson was rewarded by being made Lieutenant-Governor of Virginia. The Irish and other internal troubles, however, prevented Sloughter from at once setting out, and for some time longer the Lord of Misrule continued to play his pranks with the colony. In the winter of 1690, Leisler learned that Sir Edmond Andros, who had lain in jail in Boston since his arrest, was about to be sent to England for trial, and apprehensive that the councilors would send letters to the king by him, he caused sturdy John Perry, the Boston post rider, to be closely watched. The house of Colonel Lewis Morris, in Westchester, was the last place where Perry received letters for Boston, and one day, after leaving it, he was seized by Leisler's men-at-arms, brought to the city, and thrown into prison. In his mail-bag were found, as Leisler had suspected, letters to the king from Bayard, Van Cortlandt, and others of their party, complaining bitterly of the acts of the usurper. Leisler at once proclaimed that he had discovered a " hellish conspiracy " against the government, and that Colonel Bayard was the ringleader in it. A file of soldiers, therefore, seized that gentleman, loaded him with chains, and cast him into the common goal, where he received the treatment accorded the worst malefactors. Van Cortlandt escaped the soldiers and became again a fugitive, but William Nicolls, the Attorney-General of the province, was captured and lodged in the same prison with Colonel Bayard.

In the spring of 1690 Leisler called a congress of all the colonies, to meet at New York, and deliberate on the threatening attitude of the French in Canada. This was the first American Colonial Congress, and met in New York May 1, 1690.

Tyranny often works its own cure; and the weakest of all governments is that based on the ignorance and superstition of the governed. Leisler had by this time become very unpopular with the people. His imprisonment of so many leading citizens shocked their sense of justice, and to many other odious and arbitrary acts he now added that of seizing estates and personal property to satisfy taxes. The right of his Assembly to lay such taxes was denied by many, and refusal to pay was often followed by confiscation. " Governor Dog-driver," " Lieutenant Blockhead," " Deacon Jailer," were the epithets now conferred upon him. Once, in May, 1690, he was assaulted in the streets.

An address to William and Mary, written about this time, and signed by the French and Dutch domines and leading citizens of New York, describes the city as being at the sole will of an insolent alien, assisted by those who formerly were not thought fit to bear the meanest office, several of whom can be proved guilty of enormous crimes. . . . They imprison at will, open letters, seize estates, plunder houses, and abuse the clergymen."

Some six months later, after a series of fresh outrages, the people of Jamaica, Hempstead, Flushing, and Newtown addressed a yet more piteous appeal to the king's secretary.

Milborne, they charged, famous for nothing but cruelty, had " in a barbarous and inhuman manner plundered houses, stripped women of their apparel, and sequestered estates," and they besought the king to relieve them of this oppressor, all of whose acts seemed based on Catiline's maxim: " The ills that I have done cannot be safe but by attempting greater." The king seems to have been brought to a lively sense of the situation by these petitions, and Governor Sloughter was ordered to proceed to his government at once. The Archangel, the Beaver, and two smaller vessels were gotten ready, two companies of soldiers were placed on board, and early in December, 1690, the fleet set sail, Sloughter and his staff in the Archangel, Major Richard Ingoldsby, the Lieutenant-Governor, in the Beaver. The instructions, commissions, Leisler's letters, and the petitions of the people were given to Sloughter, with instructions to inquire carefully into the whole story of Leisler's rule. Sloughter was given also a system of government for the colony, which continued in force until the close of the Revolution. It differed little from that of James. There was to be a governor and council appointed by the king and an assembly elected by the people. Liberty of conscience was assured all peaceable citizens " except Papists"; but the Church of England was made the State church and placed under the jurisdiction of the Bishop of London. The former members of the council were re-appointed with scarcely an exception, thus condemning Leisler in advance. News reached New York, by way of Boston, that the Governor was on the way, long before the ships arrived. Both parties watched breathlessly, as one might say, the day of reckoning. At length, on the 29th of January, 1691, a vessel was signaled from the Battery, and as she came on it was seen that it was one of the Governor's fleet. One, two, three soon appeared, but the fourth could nowhere be discovered. By strange mischance the absent vessel proved to be the Archangel, the one which bore the Governor. Had it been either of the others, the crimes of treason and murder might not have been fixed on Leisler, and the city would have been spared scenes of riot and bloodshed. As the Beaver came to anchor she was boarded by Phillipse, Van Cortlandt, and others, to whom Ingoldsby explained that the fleet had been separated by a great storm, and that, for aught he knew, the Archangel might be at the bottom of the sea.

The councilors then briefly acquainted him with the position of affairs and urged that he make an immediate demand for the possession of the fort and government. A strange scene ensued — one of the last acts in this tragedy of errors.

Ingoldsby sent a messenger to Leisler demanding the fort for the king's soldiers and their stores. Leisler, in reply, demanded to be shown Ingoldsby's commission and authority. The Lieutenant-Governor had nothing of the sort; everything was with Governor Sloughter in the Archangel. Leisler then replied, emphasizing his loyalty to the king, and tendering the City Hall for the troops, but refusing to yield the fort until Ingoldsby could produce written orders from the king or Governor. Ingoldsby was afraid to land and remained cooped up in his ship for several days; but at last, being assured that the great body of the people were with him, he landed his soldiers as cautiously, he wrote home, as though making " a descent into the country of an enemy," and took post in the City Hall. Next he sent a letter to Leisler, ordering him to release Bayard and Nicolls — still confined in the fort, — since they were named councilors to the king. This demand threw Leisler into a paroxysm of rage. . " What! " he cried, " those popish dogs and rogues! " and he returned word that he should hold the prisoners until his Majesty's further orders arrived. This was the situation from day to day for six weeks: the king's Lieutenant-Governor cooped up in the City Hall, practically a prisoner; the king's councilors confined in the common goal; both controlled and dictated to by a citizen whose power consisted only in his supposed hold on the people and his command of the city militia. Perhaps if Ingoldsby, who was a brave soldier, could have produced his commission, he would have adopted a bolder policy.

It is charitable to suppose that Leisler was at this time really insane. He now committed the overt act.

Hearing that Ingoldsby and the councilors had gathered a force of several hundred men in the city, he sent orders to them to disperse under pain of being attacked and destroyed. Two hours for a reply was the ultimatum. It came in less time. It said that the Lieutenant-Governor proposed to preserve the peace, and that whoever should attack him would render themselves "public enemies to the crown of England." Some of Ingoldsby's soldiers were drawn up on parade, probably on the Bowling Green, as Leisler received the message. A gun from the fort was at once turned on them and fired. A house in which the soldiers lodged was also fired into. Two British soldiers were killed and several wounded. The fire was returned without injuring any of Leisler's men. Next day, March 19th, as both parties stood at bay confronting each other, the Archangel was signaled in the Narrows. Had she been really a celestial visitant, she could not have been more welcome. Governor Sloughter, being informed of the condition of affairs, hurried in a pinnace to the city. Night fell ere he arrived, but he went at once to the City Hall, where his commission was read to the people. Their joyous shouts and acclamations, we are told, were heard by Leisler in the fort. The Governor and the councilors then took the oath of office. It was eleven o'clock at night; nevertheless, Ingoldsby and his soldiers were dispatched to the fort to demand it in the name of the king. Leisler would not comply until he had sent Sergeant Stoll, who had met the Governor abroad, to make sure of him as the real Sloughter. Stoll told Governor Sloughter that he was glad to find him the same man he had known in England. "Yes," was the quick retort, "I have been seen in England, and intend now to be seen in New York." Stoll, as an envoy, was ignored, however, and Ingoldsby was again sent to the fort with orders for Leisler and those calling themselves his council to report to the Governor at once, and to bring Bayard and Nicolls, the prisoners, with them. But Leisler was fruitful in expedients and urged that it would be against all military precedent to surrender a fort at night. A third time Ingoldsby was sent, and a third time he was " contemptuously " refused. Then, it being past midnight, Governor, councilors, and messengers retired with an agreement to meet at an early hour next morning. The morning came, and Governor and council met promptly at the City Hall. In the interim Sloughter had matured his plans. Taking no notice of a humble letter from Leisler, asserting his loyalty, and offering to give " an exact account of all his actions and conduct," he ordered Ingoldsby to go to the fort and command the men to lay down their arms, offering pardon to all save Leisler and his council. Ingoldsby did so. Leisler and his councilors were given up to the guards and led prisoners to the City Hall. Then the heavy doors of the dungeons were thrown open, and Bayard and Nicolls, aged and emaciated almost beyond recognition, tottered out into the sunlight. They were met with congratulations mingled with exclamations of pity. For thirteen months they had languished in prison, their estates plundered by a military despot, and their families exposed to the fury of a mob. Bayard and Nicolls were conducted to the City Hall, where they took the oath of office amid the cheers of the people. Leisler and his councilors were then led through the street to the fort and thrust into the cells just vacated by their victims; the chain that Bayard had worn was even put upon Leisler's leg. A popular demand at once arose for the speedy trial and punishment of Leisler and his council. Sloughter, quite willing to escape the ordeal of sitting in judgment on them, agreed that a civil trial should be had. On Monday, March 23rd, three days after the surrender, the prisoners were examined and bound over for trial. The case was next given to the grand jury, which found a true bill against Leisler, Milborne, and eight others, and indicted them for treason and murder, " for holding by force the king's fort against the king's Governor, after the publication of his commission, and after demand had been made in the king's name, and in the reducing of which lives had been lost." Many other crimes might have been charged against the prisoners, but the prosecution wisely decided to bring only this, the penalty of which, if proven, was death.

The court sat March 30th, and the trial proceeded with that solemnity and stately ceremonial which then characterized English court procedure. It was a special court of Oyer and Terminer. The judges, too, had been specially appointed, and a very august tribunal they were, as they sat there clad in their black robes and full-bottomed wigs — Chief-Justice Dudley, Thomas Johnson, Sir Robert Robinson, former Governor of Bermuda, Jasper Hicks, Captain of the Archangel frigate, Lieutenant-Governor Ingoldsby. Colonel William Smith, Major John Lawrence, Recorder Pinhorn, John Younge, and Isaac Arnold. They were gentlemen who had suffered little or nothing from the prisoners and were considered least prejudiced against them. The trial lasted eight days and was watched with intense interest by every class of citizens. Not for sixty years would the city see another trial of such absorbing interest. The eight lesser prisoners pleaded not guilty to the charge. Leisler and Milborne declined to plead at all until the court should decide whether the king's letter to Nicholson had conferred the government on Leisler. The court referred the question to Governor Sloughter and his councilors, and their prompt reply was that neither in the king's letter, nor in the papers of the Privy Council, was there any authority for the prisoner to seize upon the government. This swept away any defense the prisoners may have hoped to make. Unless they could prove authority for their acts they stood convicted. Leisler and Milborne did the best that could be done under the circumstances. They refused to plead and appealed to the king. They were therefore tried as " mutes." Leisler, Milborne and six of the eight other prisoners were found guilty; two were acquitted. Chief-Justice Dudley at once passed sentence of death upon the eight, there being but short shift in those days between trial and execution. The prisoners pleaded for a reprieve until the king's pleasure should be known, and the petition was for a time entertained, Sloughter having doubts as to his authority for signing the death-warrant in case of an appeal to the king. In his letter to William accompanying the petition, Sloughter wrote: " Never greater villains lived, but I am resolved to wait your pleasure, if by any other means than hanging I can keep the country quiet."

It was soon impressed upon him, however, that there was no security for the country's peace until the leaders, at least, were executed. The Dutch clergymen, it is said, openly advocated from the pulpit the death of Leisler and Milborne. Ladies of the highest station, who had suffered from Leisler's acts, earnestly pleaded with the Governor to sign the death-warrant. The most loyal and eminent men of the province came to him, declaring that there was no security for life or property while the leaders lived, as they could at any moment be rescued by a mob; they even said that they would remove from the country unless the sentence was carried out. There were counter-petitions, too, from the friends and families of the condemned, praying for clemency. At length news came from Albany that the Mohawks, incensed by certain acts of Leisler and his lieutenants while in power, were on the point of joining the French, and that nothing would have greater influence in quieting them than the death of their enemy.

At a meeting of the Governor and council held May 14th, it was " unanimously resolved " that, for the satisfaction of the Indians, and the assertion of the government and authority, and the prevention of insurrections and disorders for the future, it is absolutely necessary that the sentence pronounced against the principal offenders be forthwith put in execution." A minute of this action was sent to the Provincial Assembly — which the Governor had convened, — and returned with this endorsement: "This House, according to their opinion given, do approve of what his Excellency and Council have done."

Upon this grave counsel and advice, the Governor signed the death-warrant. On a dismal, rainy Saturday morning Leisler and Milborne were brought out to die. The gallows had been erected on what is now the east side of the City Hall Park, near the present site of the Sun newspaper office. A motley crowd assembled, and greeted the condemned, as they appeared, with oaths and ribald shouts, and were only prevented from doing them bodily harm by a strong guard of soldiers. Leisler met his fate with firmness and dignity. He made a long speech on the scaffold, from which we extract two sentences:

" So far from revenge do we depart this world, that we require and make it our dying request to all our relations and friends, that they should in time to come be forgetful of any injury done to us, or either of us, so that on both sides the discord and dissension (which were created by the Devil in the beginning) may, with our ashes, be buried in oblivion, never more to rise up for the trouble of future posterity." And again: " All that for our dying comfort we can say concerning the point for which we are condemned, is to declare as our last words, before that God whom we hope before long to see, that our sole aim and object in the conduct of the government was to maintain the interest of our sovereign Lord and Lady and the reformed Protestant churches of these parts."

Perhaps the justest judgment that could be passed over this man is, that he was of unsound mind, crazed by religious fanaticism, fear of Popish plots, and unwonted possession of unlimited power. His earnest prayer that dissension should end with his death was not however fulfilled; his faction continued to survive for generations and was a thorn in the side of royal governors for half a century. When the appeal of Leisler came before King William, he declared that the sentence was a righteous one and sustained the judges. He restored the estates of the deceased to their heirs, however, on the ground of loyal services rendered by Leisler, and four years later, in 1695, Parliament, on petition, reversed the decree of attainder, thus removing the stigma of treason. The six minor prisoners condemned with Leisler and Milborne, were eventually released.

VIII. THE ROMANTIC AGE.

A LITTLE more than two months after the execution of Leisler, Governor Sloughter died suddenly, not without suspicion of having been poisoned. Lieutenant-Governor Ingoldsby took the helm of government for a brief period — from July, 1691, to August, 1692, — when he was succeeded by Colonel Benjamin Fletcher. This gentleman was a soldier, who had been advanced by brave service done their Majesties in the Low Countries. He was a courtier, too, a politic man, shrewd, pliant, persuasive, possessing many of the characteristics of the modern politician — not to be commended for everything he did, but perhaps the best man for the place that could have been found; for he came to the government in " very troublous days " indeed. The French and Indians were pressing hard his northern frontiers, and the spirit of faction was rife in the city. The Leislerites, having recovered from their panic, were engaged in constant intrigues and collisions with the aristocratic party, so-called, the issue being the execution, or "murder," as the former called it, of Leisler and Milborne.

Governor Fletcher's reign may be termed the romantic age of the city — the age of tradition and story, of privateer and pirate, of Captain Kidd and the Red Sea Men. We will consider this subject of piracy somewhat at length, from its rare literary interest, and because former historians have dwelt but briefly upon it. The privateers were successors of the " buccaneers," bodies of adventurers who, early in the sixteenth century, under the patronage of the English and French courts, established themselves on the islands of the Caribbean Sea, and waged bitter war against the common enemy, the Spaniards, whose many rich and populous cities scattered along the Mexican and South American Coasts of that sea invited to attack. The privateer, who succeeded them, was more regular. He was a private citizen, owner of a swift merchant-vessel, whom his government in time of war commissioned to proceed against the enemy and kill, burn, and capture wherever he might meet him. If captured, the privateer's commission entitled him to be treated as a prisoner of war. The English, Dutch, and French were the first to adopt this arm of war, and it continued to be used by them until abolished by the treaty of Paris in 1856. If, however, a privateer turned his guns upon peaceful nations not named in his commission, he became a pirate, and the common enemy of mankind. A Captain Petersen was the first American privateer of whom we have an account, and we know of him only from the fact that with his barque of twenty-two guns and seventy men he captured two French vessels off the Canadian coast, and not content with that exploit, attacked and carried the French fort Chibocoton nearby, the commander of which had put off in a small boat to learn the cause of the firing.

The war between France and England, known in history as King William's war, which broke out in 1688-9, greatly increased the number of these privateers, not a few of whom became pirates. If they adopted piracy, their method was to bear away for the Red Sea, the Arabian Gulf, and that part of the Indian Ocean which washes the southern shore of Asia. The rich argosies of the Dutch and British East India Companies then traversed those seas, and there was also a rich coasting trade between the opulent cities of Arabia and the adjoining countries and India. These coasters were generally unarmed, and no match for the fierce, swift, corsairs which darted on them like a falcon on its prey. The booty secured, there were two ways of disposing of it. Sometimes the pirate himself returned to New York as an honest

69

privateer and entered his cargo in the Admiralty Court, where it was sold by due process of law. Again he ran down with his plunder to the island of Madagascar, where the pirates had a grand rendezvous — a village with warehouses and magazines filled with gold and East India goods, and defended by a fort and stockade. Here he usually found a merchant-ship in waiting, sent out by some firm in New York with which he had an understanding, and which was ready to exchange the goods she had brought out for those taken by the pirates, or to purchase the latter for cash. This done, the merchant vessel sailed for New York, where her cargo was entered as East India goods secured in the regular way, the pirate meanwhile setting forth in quest of fresh victims.

This trade with the pirates soon came to be a regularly organized traffic, and enormous fortunes were made and lost in it. The fate of four vessels which all sailed from New York in July, 1698, for Madagascar, may be taken as an illustration. The first, the Nassau, Captain Giles Shelley, was laden with Jamaica rum, Madeira wine, and gunpowder. The rum cost in New York two shillings per gallon, and was sold in Madagascar for three pounds per gallon. The wine cost nineteen pounds per pipe and was sold for three hundred pounds; and the gunpowder we may suppose at a similar advance. In return, the Nassau purchased East India goods and slaves of the pirates, and taking twenty-nine of the latter as passengers, sailed for home. The pirates paid four thousand pounds for their passage, and the voyage is said to have netted the owners thirty thousand pounds.

A sister ship, the Prophet Daniel, was not so fortunate. She too cleared for Madagascar, ostensibly for slaves. Her supercargo, John Cruger, a young man of spirit and enterprise, who later became a great merchant, and mayor of the city, in his logbook of the voyage, gives this unique account of the fate of the vessel:

" 24th August (1699), arrived at Fort Dolphin (a famous pirate haunt on the African coast). I acquainted Mr. Abraham Samuel, the king of that place, of my arrival, and came with him to a trade. 12th September, I went with Mr. Samuel twenty-five miles up in the country, and on the second day after, I got the miserable news that our ship was taken by a vessel that came into the harbor the night before, whereupon I made all the haste down I could. We got some of the subjects of Mr. Samuel to assist us, and fired upon the pirate for two days, but could do no good. Then I hired two men to swim off in the night to cut their cables, but Mr. Samuel charged his men not to meddle with them (as I was informed); said Samuel having got a letter from on board the pirate, in which, I suppose, they made great promises, so that he forbade us on our lives to meddle with any of the said pirates. It appears that the manner in which they took us was as follows: When their ship came to an anchor in the harbor, they desired our boat to give them a cast on shore, they having lost their boat, and pretended to be a merchant-ship, and had about fifty negroes on board. At night the captain of the pirate desired that our boat might give him a cast on board of his ship, which was done; and coming on board he desired the men to drink with him; and when our men were going on board their ship again he stopped them by violence; and at about 9 o'clock at night they manned the boat, and took our ship, and presently carried away all the money that was on board, rigging, and other things, and then gave the ship and negroes and other things that were on board to Mr. Samuel.

" Mr. Samuel took likewise away from me twenty-two casks of powder, and forty-nine small arms; likewise all the sails belonging to the Prophet, which were on shore, and. then sold the ship again to Isaac Ruff, Thomas Wells, Edmond Conklin, and Edward Woodman, as it was reported, for fourteen hundred pieces of eight. The purchasers designed to go from Fort Dolphin to the island of Don Mascourena, thence to Mattatana upon Madagascar, and so for America. Some days after there arrived at Fort Dolphin a small pinke called the Vine, from London, which took in slaves for Barbados, in which I took my passage, and was forced to pay for the same sixty-six pieces of eight and two slaves."

The captain of the pirate, Evan Jones, and several of the crew were known to Cruger, who records that they were from " Westchester, New York." Of the two other ships that sailed on the same errand — slaves and East India goods, — one was captured by an East India Company's frigate, and the other by New York pirates — so we see that this questionable trade was not always prosperous. For it was a questionable trade. True, the merchants of New York were not supposed to know that these goods were obtained by piracy: they simply sent their cargoes to Madagascar and purchased of factors these East India goods in return. Yet there were few in New York so simple as not to know whence these rich cargoes were derived.

While the trade lasted, it lent a sort of picturesque and Oriental magnificence to the city. Rare fabrics of Teheran and Samarkand, costly perfumes, spices, ointments, and precious woods filled her warehouses; Arabian gold was current coin; her women were arrayed in robes woven for Eastern queens; jewels and gems of costliest workmanship in gold, silver, ivory, and pearl sparkled on their fingers and bosoms; and in the merchants' houses were the Persian rugs and carpets, the bizarre bric-a-brac and curiously carved furniture of the East. New York was never so near the Orient as in those days. The pirate captains were notable persons at this time. People pointed them out on the streets as now we point out a visiting magnate or literary celebrity. They were not termed pirates, but privateers; and as they dressed well, spent money freely, and were men of infinite jest, excellent story-tellers, they were freely invited to the tables of the resident gentry, and even to that of the governor himself. Indeed, his commerce with the pirates was the scandal of Governor Fletcher's reign; but as he afterward cleared himself in an examination before the Commissioners of Trade in England, it is probable that his relations with them were not so bad as painted.

Edward Coates was one of the first of these freebooters of whom we have any account. In 1694, his ship appeared off the east coast of Long Island, having a few days previously divided eighteen hundred pieces of eight among her crew. Coates entered into negotiations with the authorities for permission to come up to the city. The Governor, it was charged, was given the ship, which he afterward sold for £800. Madam Fletcher was presented with chains of Arabian gold, rare gems, and precious silks and cashmeres from Indian looms. The councilors, too, were handsomely feed, and then the pirate ship ventured to come up to her dock. Coates afterward averred that the ransom cost himself and his men £1,800.

Thomas Tew was another of these famous sea rovers. He came to New York in the November of 1694 with "great wealth from the Indian seas." We have a description of this worthy. He was a slight, dark man of about forty who dressed

71

richly and scattered gold profusely. His uniform was a blue cap with a band of cloth of silver. His blue jacket was bordered with gold lace, and further garnished with large pearl buttons. Loose trunks of white linen covered his lower limbs as far as the knee, where they gave place to curiously worked stockings. A rich chain of Arabian gold hung from his neck, and through the meshes of a curiously knit belt gleamed a dagger, its hilt set with the rarest of gems. This person, dispensing draughts of Sopus ale to whoever would drink, and throwing golden louis d' or about as carelessly as though they were stuyvers, soon became a familiar object in the streets and taverns of New York.

But this influx of ill-gotten wealth did not really benefit the city. Riches thus acquired never benefit in 'the end; the sum of human experience is and always will be, that honesty is the best policy. In this case, these fortunes, quickly won, created a distaste for the slower methods of legitimate trade; they fostered rash enterprises and hazardous ventures, and very soon brought punishment and disgrace. It was not to be expected that the powerful East India Company would long submit to such depredations on its property. It called the attention of the king and Privy Council to them, and again and again urged that a suitable naval force should be sent into the Indian seas to protect its property and capture the marauders. But alas, all the ship's frigates were engaged in the war with France; and then again, there was the difficulty of catching the freebooters, who sailed in swift ships, and had a thousand hiding-places along the savage coasts.

This scarcity of ships and urgency of the merchants introduces one of the most striking and dramatic chapters in the history of New York, and also that most notorious character of his age. Captain William Kidd. This person is a striking example of the power of a nation's ballad-makers. English minstrels have made his name a household word. Our own Poe and Irving have conjured with him most effectively. Fortune-hunters have prodded the sands of the Atlantic coast from Montauk Point to the Florida reefs in search of his buried treasure, while Sound skippers still see his low, black, rakish craft flying down the Sound in the scud of the departing storms. So much has been said of him in song and story, that the reader will no doubt be glad to know something of his actual career. When history takes him up. Captain Kidd was master of the trading barque Antigua, sailing between New York and London, and well known to the merchants of both cities as a bold and skillful navigator. In his certificate of marriage to Sarah Oort, widow, in 1691, he is styled " Captain William Kidd, Gentleman." He had a house and lot on Tienhoven Street (now Liberty), where his wife and their only child (a daughter) lived and was a man of wealth and consideration. While the king and his ministers were considering the demands of the East India Company, Kidd was on the Atlantic bound to London. With him, as a passenger, sailed Robert Livingston, a leading character in the province of New York, well born in England, Town Clerk of Albany, Secretary of Indian Affairs, Commissary of the Provincial Army, and founder of the manor of Livingston. The two men knew of the king's strait, and over the Antigua s dinner-table formed a plan which, on their arrival in London, was pressed on the ministers and the king with all the influence they could command. The plan was, in brief, that Kidd, who knew most of the pirates frequenting New York and their haunts, should be given an armed vessel well manned, and, furnished with a private commission from the king, should go in pursuit of the pirates, and capture them wherever they could be found. Five of the leading noblemen of the realm — Somers the Lord Chancellor, the Earl of Bellomont, the Earl of Romney, the Duke of Shrewsbury, and the Earl of Oxford, with Livingston and Kidd, agreed to furnish the funds for the enterprise, and were to be repaid by a certain share of the property taken from the pirates. The king also was made a partner in the enterprise, receiving a share of the profits. The Adventure Galley, a large ship, was provided and manned with seventy men, and in her Kidd set sail, arriving in New York in the spring of 1696. He soon filled the city with placards asking for men to engage in his adventure and beat up the town for recruits. Captain Kidd and his novel design of pirate-hunting became the talk of the day, and the army of nondescripts that then filled the city — pirates, privateersmen, ne'er-do-wells, young men from the country eager for adventure and booty — hastened to enroll themselves under his banner. One hundred more men were secured in this way; but the wiseacres of the port shook their heads over the affair. They said that when Captain Kidd put to sea, if he failed to capture any pirates to provide prize-money for his crew, they would mutiny and turn pirates themselves— which was, in fact, what happened. After patrolling the American coast for a while without result, Kidd bore up for the Red Sea, and nothing was seen of him in New York for nearly three years. Meantime, Colonel Fletcher had been recalled, chiefly because of his supposed collusion with pirates, and Richard, Earl of Bellomont, an Irish nobleman of the highest character, who had been very active against the freebooters, was appointed Captain-General of New York and New England, with special instructions to suppress piracy and smuggling in the colonies. Bellomont reached New York April 2, 1698 and was received with much rejoicing and stately ceremonial.

IX. THE EARLIER CHURCHES OF NEW YORK.

In the period covered by the preceding chapter some interesting and even historic church edifices were built in New York. The first of these was the Dutch Reformed Church of St. Nicholas, on Garden Street. In 1691 the congregation became dissatisfied with the stone church in the fort. It was growing small for their numbers, and besides, it seemed unseemly that the temple of the Prince of Peace should be placed in the midst of warlike armament and preparations. They decided, therefore, to build a new church. On what is now Exchange Place — the narrow street whose towering buildings cast the shadows of late afternoon at mid-day — Mother Drisius then owned an extensive peach orchard, and she, on being appealed to, consented to sell it to the Consistory for a church site. The new building was completed and dedicated in 1693 and was much the finest church edifice then in the country. It was built of brick, in the form of an oblong square, with a large steeple in front, in the base of which was a room large enough for the Consistory to hold its meetings. The windows were long and narrow, with small panes, on which Master Gerard Duykinck had burned the arms of the principal families of the congregation. The bell, pulpit, and other furniture of the old church were transferred to the new, and many painted family escutcheons were afterwards added. In 1694, the silver workers of Amsterdam wrought out for it a silver baptismal bowl, on which were engraved sentences from the pen of Domine Selyns, indicating its spiritual significance. This interesting relic is still in use in Dr. Terry's church, corner of Fifth Avenue and Twenty-First Street, the lineal descendant of the Garden Street church.

This church also enjoys the distinction of having been the first religious society chartered in the colony, its charter taking precedence of Trinity's by some months. The instrument gave it legal power to call its minister, to hold property acquired by gift or devise, and made payment of church rates compulsory on its members. Meantime the members of the Church of England had been worshipping in the chapel in the fort. In 1696 they too became dissatisfied with the chapel, and decided to erect a church of their own. Governor Fletcher was warmly in favor of the project, and gave them the revenue of the King's Farm, which was one of the Governor's perquisites, for the term of seven years. This farm consisted of a garden, an orchard, pasturage for horses and cows, and a triangular grave-yard in one corner. The site of the present Trinity was chosen for the new church. Great interest in its erection seems to have been taken by all classes of people. Gifts of money and material were brought. Governor Fletcher, in addition to other gifts, gave it a Bible; the Earl of Bellomont some books of divinity; Lord Cornbury, a black pall, on condition that no one belonging to the city should be denied the use of it. " For building the steeple," Lewis Gomez gave 2s.; Abraham Luilna £1, Rodrego Pacheco, £1; Moses Levy, 11d.; Mordecan Nathan, 11d.; Jacob Franks, £1; and Moses Michael, 8s 3d. The building was completed in 1696. It is said to have been one hundred and forty-eight feet long and seventy-two feet wide and fronted toward the west. Its steeple, the pride of the city, was one hundred and seventy-five feet high. Over the main entrance was a Latin inscription, "Per augustam Hoc Trinitatis Templum Fundatum est anno regni illustrissimi," etc., the full inscription in English being as follows:

" This Trinity Church was founded in the 8th year of the Most Illustrious Sovereign Lord William the Third, by the Grace of God King of England, Scotland, France, and Ireland, Defender of the Faith, and in the year of our Lord 1696, and was built by the voluntary contributions and gifts of some persons, and chiefly enriched and promoted by the bounty of his Excellency, Colonel Benjamin Fletcher, Captain-General and Governor-in-Chief of this Province, in the time of whose government the inhabitants of this city, of the Protestant religion of the Church of England, as now established by law, were incorporated by a charter under the seal of the province, and many other valuable gifts he gave to it of his private fortune."

Within, on the walls, were the arms and escutcheons of the principal families. Nearest the chancel, a pew was set apart for the governor, and known as the " Governor's Pew," and which continued to be occupied by the chief magistrate so long as New York remained a colony. The first Trinity was enlarged and improved in 1737 and was destroyed by the great fire of 1776. The following description of the remodeled church, as it appeared in 1750, is given by William Smith, the historian of New York:

" It stands very pleasantly on the banks of the Hudson, and has a large cemetery open on each side, enclosed in front by a painted paled fence. Before it a long walk is railed off from Broadway, the pleasantest street in town. . . . The church within is ornamented beyond any other place of worship among us. The head is adorned with an altar-piece, and opposite is the organ. The tops of the pillars which support the galleries are decked with gilt busts of angels winged. From the ceiling are suspended two glass branches, and on the walls hang the arms of some of the principal benefactors. The alleys are paved with flat stones. The rector is Rev. Henry Barclay, who has a salary of £100 a year, levied on all the other clergy and laity of the city, by virtue of an Act of Assembly procured by Governor Fletcher."

Another interesting church of that day was that of the French Huguenots — Eglise Françoise a la Nouvelle York — which began its organized existence in 1688, although, it is said, sermons were preached in the French tongue as early as 1628. Its members were chiefly Huguenots — Protestants of France who had been driven from their homes and firesides by the cruel persecution of Louis XIV. Their history is a very interesting one, although we can refer to it but briefly. In 1598, Henry IV. of France issued his " Edict of Nantes " (so called because first published in the city of Nantes), which, in large measure, granted religious liberty to his Protestant subjects. In 1785, this edict was revoked by Louis XIV., and all persons were required to conform to the Catholic faith on pain of death or banishment. Rather than obey this despotic act, 400,000 people of the best blood of France left their homes and took refuge in Holland, England, Prussia, and other Protestant countries. Thousands came to New York and held here their ancient worship. November 10, 1687, Rev. Pierre Peiret, of the county of Foix in Southern France, arrived, and the scattered sheep found in him a shepherd. He organized the church at once. October 10, 1788, Domine Selyns wrote: "Our French brethren are doing well, and their congregations increase remarkably by the daily arrival of French refugees." In that year they built a small church which stood on the site of the present Produce Exchange. It was the only Huguenot Church in the colony, and the people used to come in covered wagons on a Saturday from Long Island, Staten Island, New Rochelle, and other places, outspan their horses, and spend the night in their wagons that they might be ready for service in the morning. On the 8th of July, 1704, Lord Cornbury laid the corner-stone of a new church for them, called Le Temple du St. Esprit. This church stood for years on the northeast side of Pine Street and is still remembered by older

75

citizens. By 1710 it had become one of the wealthiest and strongest in the city. John Fontaine, a traveler, who visited New York in 1716, speaks of attending service there, and observes that "it is very large and beautiful, and within it there was a very great congregation." The same traveler tells us that there was then a French Club in New York. The old church was taken down in 1831, and its bell, the gift of Sir Henry Anhurst, was given to the French church at New Rochelle (now Trinity Episcopal), which, it is said, still retains possession of it.

The first Presbyterian Church in New York was erected in Wall Street in 1719 and is identical with that which now worships in Dr. Van Dyke's stone church on Fifth Avenue, near Eleventh Street. The first Baptist Church in the city was built in 1760, on Gold Street, near John. The Methodists held services in New York as early as 1766, under the leadership of Philip Embury, a local preacher; but their first house of worship, the present John Street church, on John, near Nassau, was not built until 1768.

X. LORD BELLOMONT'S STORMY REIGN.

Not long after Governor Bellomont's arrival, it became apparent that his selection was a very unwise one. He was a cold, austere, somewhat bigoted man, of excellent intentions, but lacking intact, pliancy, and the personal magnetism so necessary in a ruler of men. He was prejudiced against Governor Fletcher and his friends, the chief men of the city, and took no pains to conceal his belief that they were in league with thieves and pirates. His first public act was an exceedingly impolitic one — he espoused the cause of the Leislerites, which had been held in abeyance under Governor Fletcher, and so fomented the faction that it was roused into activity again and became a disturbing and dangerous element. He issued a writ restoring to their families the estates of Leisler and Milborne, and as these had by this time passed into the hands of innocent parties, the injustice of it nearly provoked a riot in the city. His attempts to suppress piracy, smuggling, and the " manors," or great landed estates, which had been granted by Governor Fletcher and his predecessors, were equally unwise and futile. These were admittedly great evils; but an entrenched evil cannot be swept away in a moment, and the attempt if made is apt to provoke a revolution. The new Governor ordered summary seizures of goods, and arbitrary arrests of persons on suspicion; he dismissed high officers of government without a hearing and removed members of the council to supply their places with his partisans; he also prepared a bill for vacating the lands granted by former governors and prohibiting any one person from holding more than one thousand acres in the province. One of the land grants aimed at was that of Domine Dellius, of Albany, which had been, purchased by him of the Indians, and had been confirmed by Fletcher. Another was a grant made by Fletcher to Trinity Church. Thus in a brief period Lord Bellomont found arrayed against him in defense of their rights the clergy, the landed aristocracy, the merchants, and the king's officers. The province was torn with the dissensions of the factions thus created. Domine Dellius sailed for England to lay his grievances before the king. Rev. William Vesey, Rector of Trinity Church, left the Governor out in his prayers on the Sabbath, and openly prayed that Domine Dellius might have a prosperous voyage and be successful with the king. The Governor seems to have had no friends, except the reinstated Leislerites. Meantime Colonel Fletcher, smarting under the imputations cast upon him, had been clamoring to have his accounts with the government settled that he might proceed to England, armed with his vouchers, and have his accounts investigated by the Lords of Trade. Having, he said held a commission under the crown for thirty-five years without reproach, " he did not think he should become a castaway in the rear of his days." It is proper to add that in a subsequent examination before the above-named body the charges against him were dismissed as groundless.

In 1699, Bellomont proceeded to Boston to attend to affairs of government in that quarter, and while there had the pleasure of arresting his former friend and whilom associate, Captain Kidd. This personage was either a very great rascal, or a man greatly wronged, probably the latter. On leaving New York in quest of pirates, he had proceeded to the Indian seas, where, as he declared, his men mutinied and forced him to embark in a course of piracy. While the Governor was in Boston, Kidd came into Gardiner's Bay, on the eastern coast of Long Island, with a sloop, having left his " great Moorish ship," the Quidah Merchant, in the West Indies, and from that point dispatched a message to Lord Bellomont, saying that his men had forced him into piracy, and offering to give up all his treasure, of which he had a large amount, if he could be assured a free pardon. Bellomont said in reply that if Kidd would deliver himself up, and could establish his innocence, he should not be molested. Kidd accordingly came to Boston, where he was arrested and thrown into prison, and on examination was remanded to England for trial. He was hanged on Execution Dock in 1701.

On the 5th of March, 1701, Governor Bellomont died suddenly, and was buried with due honors in the chapel of the fort. When the latter was levelled in 1790, his leaden coffin was removed, it is said, to St. Paul's Churchyard, although no monument marks his grave. What the outcome of his government would have been had he lived, it is impossible to say, but as it was, he left the colony in a much more unsatisfactory condition than he found it.

XI. MIDDLE COLONIAL PERIOD.

The period between 1701 and 1764 is barren of events of great importance and may be passed over with brief reference to events of special significance. During this period the French and Indian wars troubled the peace of the city, and more than once she was called upon to furnish men and money for the protection of her northern frontiers. For some time, the Leislerites also made much trouble, but in time the bitterness of the quarrel subsided. On the 7th of March, 1702, King William III. died, after a reign of thirteen years, and Queen Anne was at once proclaimed. So excellent a ruler was she that her subjects called her " good Queen Anne." She gave many gifts to struggling churches, and among others, in 1705, Lord Cornbury being Governor, bestowed on Trinity Church the Annetje Jans estate, a tract of some sixty acres above Chambers Street on the west side of Broadway. This was in addition to the King's Farm, before mentioned, and although at that time of little value, now yields large revenues. Lord Lovelace succeeded Lord Cornbury as Governor, and on the former's death, in 1709, Colonel Robert Hunter was appointed Governor. This gentleman was a man of culture and refinement, who, in England, had enjoyed the friendship of Swift, Addison, Steele, and other wits of Queen Anne's reign, and who corresponded with them while in this country. He was accompanied by quite a fleet of vessels bearing three thousand Palatines, Protestant Germans who had been forced from their homes on the Rhine by the French armies and had sought refuge in England. It was the design of the English minister to plant them on the colony's northern frontiers to serve as a barrier against the French and Indians, and also to employ them in producing naval stores which were then much in demand. And as the poor people were utterly penniless, Queen Anne agreed to give them a free passage to this country, and to maintain them for a specified time until they should be in a position to support themselves. Newburgh, Germantown, the valleys of the Schoharie and Mohawk, and a portion of Pennsylvania, were largely settled by these people.

During Governor Hunter's reign, a serious uprising of the negro slaves occurred. These were mostly Africans, as barbarous as when in their native wilds; and in 1712, a few of them, who had been badly treated by their masters, formed a plot to massacre the people indiscriminately. They met at midnight in an orchard not far from the present Maiden Lane, armed with guns, swords, butcher's knives, and other weapons, and, setting fire to an out-house, struck down the citizens who came running to put it out. Nine men were thus murdered and six severely wounded before any could escape and give the alarm but at length the news reached the fort, and the Governor sent a detachment of soldiers to the scene, at the sight of whom the conspirators fled to the forests on the northern part of the island. Sentries were stationed at the ferries that night, and next day the militia was called out, and by beating the wood, succeeded in capturing all but six of the criminals, who committed suicide rather than suffer the vengeance of the whites. Those taken, twenty-one in number, were condemned and executed, several being burned at the stake. A similar plot was discovered in 1741, of which the reader will find an extended account in the chapter on colonial manners and customs.

In 1725 quite an event occurred in the birth of the first newspaper, the New York Gazette. It was, indeed, an infant when compared with our present mammoth dailies, being printed on a half sheet of foolscap. It was filled with custom-house entries and foreign news and appeared weekly. William Bradford, the government printer, was the editor and publisher.

In 1730 another event occurred in the granting of a new city charter, giving increased privileges, which, from the fact of its having been granted during Governor Montgomery's term of office, is known as the Montgomery Charter.

Nine years after its inception the Gazette found a rival in a new paper, called the Weekly Journal. The Journal was edited by John Peter Zenger, one of the Palatines who had come over with Governor Hunter in 1710, and who had been apprenticed to Bradford the printer. The new paper supported the party opposed to the Governor; in fact, it had been established as the organ of the Whig or popular party. There was nothing that the Journal could do to bring the " aristocrats," as it called the Governor's party, into contempt that it did not do. It criticized Governor, Councilors, Assemblymen, everybody and everything connected with the ruling class. It made use of squibs, lampoons, ballads, witticisms, satire, when such would serve its ends, and is noteworthy as furnishing the first instance where the power of the press was invoked in aid of or against a political party. Bradford, who, as the State printer, espoused the Governor's cause, replied in his Gazette, but his articles lacked the pith and vigor of those in the Journal, some of which were written by the ablest men of the city. At length the Governor's council pronounced four issues of the Weekly Journal " libelous," as containing many things " tending to sedition and faction, and to bring his Majesty's government into contempt," and ordered them burned by the public hangman, at the same time directing that the mayor and other city magistrates should attend the ceremony; but the magistrates declined to obey the council's behest, declaring it to be an arbitrary and illegal act, an opinion which was shared by most of the citizens. But when, a few days later, Zenger was seized and thrown into prison on a charge of libel, the city was wild with excitement. The same spirit which thirty years later resisted the Stamp Act, was exhibited then. Men clearly perceived that the right of the public press to openly criticize measures of government was in danger, and rallied, not so much to the support of Zenger as to the defense of a free press. The tidings created the greatest excitement throughout the colonies, and the issue of the trial was awaited with the deepest interest.

If Governor Cosby had been a wise man, able to gauge the popular feeling, he would not have forced the issue; but he was not wise, and the trial of Zenger for libel was decided on. The leaders of the popular party in New York at this time, were two lawyers — William Smith and James Alexander. Smith had been Recorder of the city, and had filled other offices with credit, and was noted for his captivating eloquence. Alexander had been Surveyor General and had also a great reputation as a lawyer. These two gentlemen now volunteered as counsel for Zenger, but at the outset were betrayed into an indiscretion which led to their removal from the bar. They boldly questioned the legality of the commissions of Chief-Justice De Lancey and of Justice Phillipse, the two judges composing the court, on the ground that they were not worded in the usual form and had been issued by the Governor without consent of the council. The judges considered this act gross contempt of court and excluded the offenders from further practice. " You have brought it to that point, sirs," said Judge De Lancey, " that either we must go from the bench or you from the bar." John Chambers was assigned as counsel for Zenger; at the same time the disbarred attorneys hastened to Philadelphia, and secured for the defense Andrew Hamilton, who was reputed the greatest and most eloquent lawyer of his day. At the same time through the press, at clubs, and by private conversation they made the public fully acquainted with the merits and demerits of the case.

When the trial came on, in July, 1735, Hamilton appeared armed for the fray, and was greeted by the crowded court-room as the champion of popular rights. His first contention was that the newspaper articles charged as false, scandalous, malicious, and seditious libels, contained only the truth, and could not, therefore, be libelous. Bradley, the king's Attorney-General, took exception to this, and quoted the old English law, that even the truth, if repeated maliciously, with intent to defame and injure another, became a libel, and was punishable as such. The legal battle raged all summer, with varying fortunes for the combatants. At length there came a day when the case was given to the jury. The court's charge had been against the prisoner, but after a few moments' deliberation the jury returned a verdict of " not guilty." It was received with the wildest expressions of delight by the crowds within and without the court-house. Hamilton became the hero of the hour and would have been borne to his hotel on the shoulders of the people but for his emphatic protest. As it was, the corporation of the city tendered him a public dinner, at which he was presented by the mayor with the freedom of the city in a gold box; the same evening a grand ball was given in his honor. This trial is generally regarded as having secured the freedom of the press in America; it is also interesting to us, as tending to create and sharply define the two great parties of a generation later.

The event of the year 1752 was the building, by subscription, at the foot of Broad Street, of the Royal Exchange, for merchants. The building was supported on arches, the lower story being open — much as markets in southern cities now are. One room in the upper story was set apart as a meeting room for the merchants; a coffee-room, which later became a famous resort, was opened in one end. The Exchange stood until 1827, when it was succeeded by a finer building on Wall Street. It was the home of the first organization of merchants in the port, the present Chamber of Commerce not having been founded until 1769.

The closing days of British rule in New York were marked by the founding of the city's noblest institution of learning — Columbia College. For several years prior to 1751, sums of money had been raised by public lotteries and other means for the founding of a college in the city. In that year it was learned that £3,443 had been raised, and a bill was passed by the Assembly naming ten trustees to take charge-of it. The next year the vestry of Trinity Church offered to donate from the estate granted them by Queen Anne a site and the necessary grounds for a campus. This offer was accepted by the trustees, and in 1753 they invited the Rev. Dr. Samuel Johnson, a clergyman possessing excellent qualifications for the place, to be the first president. His salary was £250 per annum. The vestry gave to the college the use of their large room in the church building, and here in the autumn of 1753 the college was opened with an entering class of ten. The charter, signed by Acting Governor De-Lancey, October 31, 1754, named the new college " King's" after the venerable institution on the banks of the Cam. On August 23, 1756, the corner-stone of the new building was laid by Governor Hardy with appropriate ceremonies. Its site included the whole block now bounded by College Place, Barclay, Church, and Murray streets — a beautiful situation at that time, with its surroundings of groves and green fields, and its fine view of the Hudson.

The first Commencement was held in June, 1758, and the new building was first opened to the students in May, 1760. In 1763 Dr. Johnson resigned, and Dr. Myles Cooper, a fellow of Queens College, Oxford, who had accepted a professorship in the college the preceding year, succeeded to the presidency. During the Revolution the college was dismissed and its building used as a hospital. On its reorganization in 1787, it was given the name Columbia, anything savoring of royalty being then exceedingly odious to American ears.

XII. THE PEOPLE DURING THE COLONIAL PERIOD.

Quite a number of distinguished gentlemen accompanied Sir Edmond Andros to New York in 1678. Among them was the Rev. James Wooley, a recent graduate of Cambridge University, -who came as chaplain to the king's forces in New York. On returning to England, Mr. Wooley published a little book called, "A Two Years' Journal in New York," which was eagerly read by the public of that day, curious to know something of the Duke's new possessions. We transcribe from this book some pleasant descriptions of the city and its domestic life in 1678-80, preserving the quaint English in which they were written.

" The country," he says, " is of a sweet and wholesome breath, free from those annoyances which are commonly ascribed by naturalists for the insalubrity of any country, viz., south or southeast winds, stagnant waters, lowness of shoals, inconstancy of weather, and the excessive heat of the summer; it is gently refreshed, fanned, and allayed by constant breezes from the sea. It does not welcome guests and strangers with the seasoning distempers of fevers and fluxes, like Virginia, Maryland, and other plantations. Nature kindly drains and purgeth it by fontanels and issues of running waters in its irriguous valleys, and shelters it with the umbrellas of all sorts of trees from pernicious lakes, which trees and plants do undoubtedly, tho' insensibly, suck in and digest into their own growth and composition those subterranean particles and exhalations which otherwise would be attracted by the heat of the sun, and so become matter for infections, clouds, and malign atmospheres. ... I myself, a person seemingly of a weakly stamen, and a valetudinary constitution, was not in the least indisposed in that climate during my residence there the space of three years."

The people he found very hospitable, though " a clan of high-flown religionists." The two clergymen — the Lutheran and the Dutch Reformed — he criticized as severely as the Labadists did him.

"They behaved themselves one toward another so shily and uncharitably, as if Luther and Calvin had bequeathed and entailed their virulent and bigoted spirits upon them and their heirs forever. They had not visited or spoken to each other with any respect for six years together before my being there, with whom I being much acquainted, I invited them both, with their vrows, to a supper one night unknown to each other, with an obligation that they should not speak one word in Dutch, under the penalty of a bottle of Madeira, alleging I was so imperfect in that language that we could not manage a sociable discourse. So accordingly they came, and at the first interview they stood so appalled, as if the ghosts of Luther and Calvin had suffered a transmigration, but the amaze soon went off with a salve tu quoque and a bottle of wine, of which the Calvinist dominie was a true carouser, and so we continued our mensalia the whole evening in Latin, which they both spoke so fluently and promptly that I blushed at myself, with a passionate regret, that I could not keep pace with them. The inhabitants," he continues, "both English and Dutch, were very civil, amongst whom I have often wished myself and family, to whose tables I was frequently invited, and always concluded with a generous bottle of Madeira."

And he has this account of one of the amusements of the day:

"We had very good diversion in an orchard of Mr. John Robinson, of New York, where we followed a bear from tree to tree, upon which he could swarm like a cat, and when he was got to his resting-place, perched upon a high branch, we dispatched a youth after him with a club to an opposite bough, who, knocking his paws, he comes grumbling down backwards with a thump, so we after him again."

It seems scarcely credible that only two hundred years ago, between Cedar Street and Maiden Lane, men took bears by shaking them, like fruit, from the orchard trees.

Every New Year's Day, our author goes on to say, the English observed "a neighborly commerce of presents." Some sent him " a sugar loaf," some " a pair of gloves," some " a bottle or two of wine." One day he saw two " Dutch boors " grappling each other under his windows.

" I called up an acquaintance and asked him to fetch a kit full of water and discharge it at them, which immersion cooled their courage and loosed their grapples. So," he adds, " we used to part our mastiffs in England. The city of New York," he goes on to say, " in my time was as large as some market towns with us, and all built the London way: the garrison side of a high situation and a pleasant prospect; the island it stands on all a level and champain. The diversion, especially in the winter season, used by the Dutch, is aurigation, i. e., riding about in wagons. . . . And, upon the ice it is admirable to see men and women as it were flying upon their skates from place to place with markets upon their heads and backs."

When our author returned home he took with him as mementoes of the country, " a gray squirrel, a parrot, and a raccoon." While Mr. Wooley was preaching in New York, two young travelers from Germany, in queer scallop hats and long cloaks, came to the city — members of a sect of German pietists, called the Labadists, deputed by their coreligionists to seek a location in this country for a community. These men had sharp eyes, and went prying all about the colony, picturing the things they saw with both pen and pencil. Among other things, they heard Mr. Wooley preach at the fort, and were no better pleased with him than he was with the Dutch domines.

"After the prayers and ceremonies," they wrote, "a young man went into the pulpit, who thought he was performing wonders; he had a little book in his hand, out of which he read his sermon, which was about a quarter of an hour long. With this the services were concluded, at which we could not be sufficiently astonished."

The Labadists spent some time in New York with kind friends, who regaled them on " milk and peaches, fish and fruit." One day, they called on Jean Vigne, the ancient miller, who was the first male child born of European parents in New York. On September 29, 1679, they set out for a journey through Long Island. Crossing the ferry, they went up a hill, " along open roads and woody places, and through a village called Breucklen, which has a small ugly church standing in the middle of the road." At the farm-house of Simon de Hart, where they spent the night, they had for supper, a roasted haunch of venison, a goose, a wild turkey, and oysters, both raw and roasted; and sat up with their host late into the night, before a hickory fire that roared half-way up the chimney. They visited New Utrecht, and were entertained by Jacques Cortelyou, who lived in a large stone house, one of several in the village, and was a Doctor of Medicine, a land surveyor, and mathematician. Owing to sickness in his family, they were obliged to sleep in the barn, which they did on straw spread with sheepskins, " in the midst of the continual grunting of hogs, squealing of pigs, bleating and coughing of sheep, barking of dogs, crowing of cocks, and cackling of hens." Afterward they returned slowly to New York, noting the Indian villages, the wild grapes, peach orchards, and fields of watermelons by the way, and finished their travels by a journey up the Hudson and through New Jersey.

From the statements of these travelers it would appear that at that time a primitive state of affairs existed. But with the advent of the English the order of society gradually changed. Dutch social life was democratic in tone, simple, domestic, unostentatious. The English social structure, however, was founded on caste. There was a lower, middle, and upper class, each with separating walls so strong that few could break them down. Some of the wealthier Dutch families held strictly aloof from the strangers, and formed a distinct class, but the majority met the English officers and attaches in polite entertainments and came soon to adopt the ideas of the courtly strangers as to social strata and etiquette; so that ill a few years, among both the English, French, and Dutch — the three ruling social elements, — there came to be an aristocracy and classes. London fashions soon became popular, although, as William Smith, a resident historian, observed, " by the time we adopt them they become disused in England." London teachers, tailors, peruke makers, tradesmen, came over in numbers, and an increased display and elegance in dress, equipage, furniture, and dwellings was the result. This display and extravagance probably reached its height between 1700-1705, when the ventures of the privateers and Red Sea men had flooded the city with Arabian gold and East India goods.

Broadway on a Sabbath morning, as the bells were ringing for church, must then have presented an animated and even brilliant spectacle, far exceeding that which modern beaux and belles present, for although on Fifth Avenue, of a Sunday after service, the ladies give us here and there a touch of color, the men are sober-suited as monks: in those days, however, both ladies and gentlemen shone rich as emperor moths. These worshippers, whom we imagine ourselves as watching, come in groups moving down the wide, shaded streets, some entering Trinity, others turning down into Garden Street, and passing into the new Dutch Church on that thoroughfare.

Both places of worship are equally fashionable: The Dutch Church is the wealthier, but then Trinity has the governor's pew, and the prestige that comes of state patronage and emolument. Let us describe, as showing the fashions of the day, the dress of this group of five bearing down abreast of the churchyard. They are Nicholas Bayard and Madam Bayard, William Merritt, Alderman, and Madam Merritt, and Isaac De Riemer, Mayor. Bayard, who has been Secretary of the province, Major and Colonel of the city militia, wears a cinnamon-colored cloth coat with skirts reaching quite to the knee, embroidered four or five inches deep with silver lace, and lined with sky-blue silk; his waistcoat is of red satin woven in with gold; his breeches, of the same color and material as his coat are trimmed with silver at the pockets and knees; dove-colored stockings of silk, and low shoes adorned with large silver buckles, cover his nether extremities. His hat, of black felt, has a wide flapping brim, and is adorned with a band of gold lace. His "full bottomed " wig is plentifully powdered with starch finely ground and sifted, to which burnt alabaster or whiting has been added to give it body and is scented with ambergris. A "steinkirk" of fine muslin encircles his neck, the ends of which are laced and tucked into his expansive shirt bosom: the latter is of fine Holland adorned with colebatteen ruffles, the waistcoat being left open the better to display them. His gloved hands hold an ivory snuff-box, having an invisible hinge and a looking-glass in the lid, and well filled with sweet-scented snuff. After taking a dainty sniff at the snuff he applies to his nose a handkerchief of silk ornamented with the arms of Britain; printed on its folds are the ensigns and standards captured from the French. He pulls out his watch to note the time, and we find that it is enclosed in a beautiful shagreen case studded with gold and has his seal and a large silver key attached to it by a wide silk ribbon. He carries a cane, too, with a gold head elegantly engraved in cypher and crown, but the diamond-hilted sword with its gay sword knot, then an almost indispensable adjunct to a gentleman's dress, in deference to the day has been left behind. The two other gentlemen are dressed much in the same style, except that there is a pleasing variety in style and color. Merritt, for instance, wears a salmon-colored silk drugget coat, with silver brocade waistcoat and small-clothes while De Riemer has a sagathie cloth coat, with waistcoat and breeches of *drop du Barre*.

But if the gentlemen are thus brilliant, what is to be said of the ladies, who are apt to lead the sterner sex in matters of personal adornment. Instead of a bonnet, Madam Bayard wears a " frontage," — a sort of headdress formed of rows of plaited muslin, stiffened with wire, one above the other, and diminishing in size as they rise. She, too, wears the "steinkirk," or neckcloth. The bodice of her purple-and-gold atlas gown is laced over very tight stays, and the gown itself is open in front to display the black-velvet petticoat edged with two silver orrices and high enough to show the green-silk stockings and beautifully embroidered shoes of fine Morocco with red clocks. Her coiffure is also powdered; her complexion has been " aided " with French red and pearl powder, and she is perfumed with rose-water and Eau de Came. Some of the ladies moving down the street are even more brilliantly attired. What do you think of this kincob, Isabella-colored gown, flowered with green and gold over a scarlet-and-gold atlas petticoat edged with silver, or of this blue-and-gold atlas gown; or of that stately East India princess in purple and gold, or of this pretty little lady in a satin gown over an Alijah petticoat, striped with green, gold, and white? There are some notable people, too, amid the throng. Lord Bellomont, tall and courtly, never losing the royal governor in the man; James De Lancey, later Chief-Justice and Lieutenant-Governor, even now invested with a judicial air; Dr. Samuel Staats, who, after a brief residence in India, has returned with a beautiful Indian " Begum," or princess, for his wife; Frederick Phillipse, Gabriel Minvielle, Thomas Willett, Richard Townley, and John Lawrence, king's councilors; James Graham and James Emott, eminent lawyers; Abraham Gouverneur, George Heathcote, Johannes and Abraham De Peyster, and other famous men of that day.

The period preceding the Revolution — from 1740 to 1770 — was perhaps the most picturesque and interesting in the city's history. New York was then a British town, a London in miniature, yet much more cosmopolitan than London, for among her inhabitants were numbered every race, class, sect, and condition — except the Catholic. It was an offence punishable with life imprisonment for a Jesuit priest to enter New York at this time.

"Let us view the city as it appears about this time, 1730-65. Along the East River shore, at the former date, it was laid out as far north as the present Catherine Street. West of Broadway cross streets had been opened as far north as the present Chambers Street. Along the line of the latter was a wall of stout palisades defended by block-houses at intervals, extending across the island as a defense against the French and Indians. An old print of Fulton Ferry in 1746 (see illustration), shows the quaint Dutch ferry-house on the New York side, and wide fields and clusters of cottages on the Brooklyn shore, but no city. By 1763, as appears by Maerfchalckm's map of that date (see illustration), the city had crept north as far as Warren Street on the west and Chatham on the east, while a village plot had been laid out on the west of the " High Road to Boston," the present Bowery. The Collect and the marshes in its vicinity (now Canal Street and adjacent blocks) were then in their primitive state. A distant view of the city from the high land on the north, about 1760, shows how little of the island was then built upon. In the view from the harbor, however, the city appears as a considerable town.

Most of the streets are paved, and lighted by lanterns suspended from every seventh house. There is a rattle watch that patrols the city at night, and a fire company, of " four and twenty able-bodied men and, two fire-engines of Mr. Newsham's patent," recently imported from London.

We will begin our walk this time with the fort on the Battery — Fort George, — so called because of the pleasant custom the people have of naming their fort after the reigning sovereign. As in the old Dutch time, the fort is the capitol, the seat of government. The governor still lives within. The colonial records are kept here; it is the scene of all military displays and social festivities on fete days. A royal governor, in the palmy days of the colony, lived in considerable state, maintained a chaplain and secretary, besides aides in brilliant uniform, and servants in livery, and when he appeared in public, rode in a coach-and-four with coachman and footmen, and his arms emblazoned on the panels. He had to garrison the fort and maintain his authority two lieutenants at four shillings per day, one ensign at three shillings, three sergeants at one shilling and sixpence, two drummers at one shilling, a master gunner, one hundred privates at eight pence, four " mattrosses " at one shilling, a "chirurgeon " at two shillings, a store-keeper at two shillings, and a chaplain at six shillings. The governor, as commander-in-chief, received the munificent salary of eight shillings per day, although, of course, there were perquisites. The governor's residence, known as the " Government House," was also the social center. There were " high doings " there, often, in those far-off days of the colony. No fete day — whether of the coming of an heir to the throne, or the birthday anniversary of the king, queen, or Prince of Wales, or the advent of a new governor, or the anniversary of a national event — could be observed without the holding of a grand ball in the Government House, at which the beauty and the chivalry of the town were gathered. Thus we read that on October 30, 1734, on the anniversary of his Majesty's birthday, " in the evening the whole city was illuminated. His Excellency and Lady gave a splendid ball and supper at the Fort, where was the most numerous and fine appearance of Ladies and Gentlemen that had ever been known upon the like occasion." And on January 21st, of the same year, being the anniversary of the birthday of His Royal Highness, Frederic, Prince of Wales: "In the evening there was a splendid and numerous appearance of Gentlemen and Ladies at the Fort, where they were received by His Excellency and Lady, and the Honorable Family. The night concluded with a splendid supper and ball, which lasted till four o'clock in the morning."

Imposing ceremonies often preceded the ball, as on the anniversary of the king's birthday in 1734.

" Between the hours of eleven and twelve in the forenoon His Excellency, our Governor, was attended at his House in Fort George by the Council, Assembly, Merchants, and other Principal Gentlemen and Inhabitants of this and adjacent places. The Independent Companies posted here being under Arms, and the Cannon round the Ramparts firing while His Majesty's, the Queen's, the Prince's, and the

Royal Families', and their Royal Highnesses the Prince and Princess of Orange's Healths were drunk, and then followed the Healths of His Grace the Duke of Newcastle, of the Duke of Grafton, of the Right Honorable Sir Robert Walpole, and many other Royal Healths."

And on the anniversary of the Coronation, June 11. 1734:

" At twelve at noon the Gentlemen of the Council, Assembly, and the City waited upon His Excellency, the Governor, at the Fort, where their Majesties', the Royal Family's, and the Prince and Princess of Orange's Healths were drunk under the discharge of the Cannon, the regular troops in their new clothing all the while standing under arms, who made a fine appearance. Afterwards His Excellency, attended by the Gentlemen of the Council, etc., went into the Field, and received the Militia of the City drawn up there, and expressed great satisfaction at their order, discipline, and appearance, and was pleased to order twelve barrels of beer to be distributed among them to drink their Majesties' and the Royal Healths."

One can imagine much more than the staid old chronicler describes. The long procession of gentlemen, splendidly attired, with the city fathers in their silken robes of office at their head; the stately governor in full uniform, perhaps with the orders of chivalry blazing on his breast; the grave courtesies and interchange of stately compliment as the wine goes round; the thunder of the cannon; and in the afternoon the streets filled with citizens in gala dress, and the parade of the militia. In the evening at the governor's house, which is aglow with light, the scene is still more brilliant, for there ladies and gentlemen, clothed like Solomon in his glory, float up and down the long ball-room, balance, turn, lead down the middle, cast off, to the music of the contra dance, or La Belle Kathrine. The coming of a new Governor to the province — which, as we have seen, was pretty often — was also a great occasion. When Governor William Cosby arrived, for instance, in July, 1732, he landed " about ten o'clock in the evening, and was received at the Water side by several Gentlemen, who attended him to the Fort. The next day, between the Hours of eleven and twelve, His Excellency walked to the City Hall (a Company of Halberdiers and a Troop of Horse marching before, and the Gentlemen of His Majesty's Council, the Corporation, and a great number of Gentlemen and merchants of this city following, the streets being lined on each side with the Militia), where his Commission was published, and then His Excellency returned, attended, as before, back to the Fort. The Militia then drew up upon the Parade and saluted him with three vollies."

A pleasant little episode occurred at the Government House while Sir William Cosby occupied it, although the dry old chronicler from whom we have quoted nowhere refers to it. The Governor was blessed with two fair daughters, in whom wit and beauty combined to render them the belles of the city. The younger had left a lover in England, no less a personage than Lord Augustus Fitz Roy, son of the famous Charles, Duke of Grafton. According to the English social code the match was beneath the lover and could not be allowed. It is even hinted that Sir William was given the governorship in order to separate the young people and cure the future duke of his infatuation. If so, the scheme signally failed, for the lover followed his mistress to New York, and during his visit the pair were secretly married, it is said, through the connivance of Madam Cosby, the Governor's lady. One night the English chaplain, Domine Campbell, was assisted to scale the rear wall of the fort, and in the chapel married the lovers secretly and without a license. To avert suspicion from Governor Cosby, the clergyman was prosecuted for the offence, but it was observed by the gossips that no serious punishment followed. Under date of August 12th, our chronicler gives the denouement of the affair: " On Saturday morning sailed from hence Captain Stephens, for London, having on board my Lord Augustus and his Lady, Governor Cosby's daughter."

The next winter a second wedding occurred at the Government House, Miss Grace Cosby being married to Mr. Thomas Freeman, of London. It would seem that there were astute politicians at the City Hall at that time, for, three days after, the Common Council and other officials waited upon the Governor, and the Recorder in a neat speech informed them that the Corporation, desirous of proving the deference they entertained for the Governor and his noble family, had ordered that the Honorable Major Alexander Cosby, brother to his Excellency, recently arrived, and Thomas Freeman, the Governor's son-in-law, be presented with the freedom of the city in gold boxes. The boxes were, however, of silver, gilded, as is proved by this entry in the council minutes of March 15, 1733-4: "Ordered the Mayor issue his warrant ... to pay to Mr. Charles Le Roux, Goldsmith, or order, the sum of seven pounds, one shilling, eleven pence half penny . . . for two silver Guilt Boxes for the Freedoms of the Honorable Major Alexander Cosby and Thomas Freeman, Esq."

Lady readers are no doubt curious to know just how the governor's mansion was furnished. Of its furniture in the time of Governor John Montgomery, Cosby's immediate predecessor, we have an official description, Governor Montgomery having died in 1730, and an inventory of his effects having been taken. It was as follows:

A bed with China curtains $7 50
Twelve leather chairs 18 00
Two dozen ivory-handled knives and forks . . . 4 00
Four pair crimson barreline window curtains . . . 15 00
Six yellow chairs ....
Five pair yellow canalet curtains 20 00
A large looking-glass with gilt frame 20 00
Cloth housing with silver lace 13 00
A fine yellow camlet bed 75 00
Water and champaigne glasses ......
A very large quantity of wine and different sorts of liquor
in the cellar 2,500 00

and silverware, comprising candlesticks, coffee-pots, knives and forks, spoons, salvers, tea-trays, casters, etc., to a large amount. He had also one saddle horse, eight coach horses, two common horses, two breeding mares, two colts, a natural pacing mare, a four-wheeled chaise and harness, a servant's saddle, a coach with set of fine harness, two sets of travelling harness, brass-mounted, with postilion's coat and cap; saddles with holsters, caps, and housings; a fine suit of embroidered horse furniture with bridles, etc. The inventory continues:

A negro musician $225 00
A negro boy 115 00
Two negro boys 250 00
A mulatto woman 100 00
Negro woman called Betty 150 00

Negro woman called Jenny 80 00
Negro woman 90 00
Three white servants apprenticed .....
Six new black cotton chairs, $5 each 30 00
Japanned tea-table ....
Complete set of China ware 15 60
A repeating table clock 40 00
A pair of gilded frame sconces .....
A large chimney glass . .....
Twelve new-fashioned matted chairs 24 00
A walnut card-table ....
A pair of large sconces with gilt frames 45 00
Walnut-framed sconces and branches 45 00
An eight-day clock 40 00
Japanned fruit-plates, cut-glass cruets ....
Gold lace and gold buttons 50 00
Gilt leather screen 15 00

Pictures of Greenwich Park, $1.18; of a vineyard, $2.00; of goats, $1.50; a landscape, $1.30; sheep-shearing, $1.40; a winter piece, 70 cts.; a parrot cage, and " Tycken " umbrella.

A barge with accoutrements 125 00
A small four-oared boat ....
A library 1,000 00

The governor's wardrobe comprised " cambric shirts ruffled," dimity vests, silk stockings, a scarlet cloak, a laced hat, a scarlet coat and breeches with gold lace, a cloth suit with open silver lace, silk stockings with embroidered clocks, gold-headed cane, " bob-tail " wig, periwig, and other articles.

On the very spot now occupied by the Sub-Treasury, with its grand statue of Washington looking calmly on the hurrying crowds, stood at the period we are describing the second City Hall, known after Washington's inauguration as Federal Hall. The city had built it in 1700 at a cost of £3000, the old City Hall, or Stadt Huys, built by Kieft, having been sold for £920, and partly defraying the cost. Here the Common Council and the Provincial Assembly held their sessions, and the Supreme Court and the Mayor's and Admiralty Courts met. It was also the City Prison, and was trebly honored in later years as the place where the first Congress of the United States held its first session, and where its first President took the oath of office. It was notable in old colony times as the rostrum where the royal governors published their commissions. It was also a central figure in the inauguration of a new Mayor, as is shown by the following extract from the journal of Mayor Thomas Noell, who took the oath in 1701:

"On Tuesday, the 14th day of October, 1701, I was commissioned and sworn Mayor of the City of New York before the Honorable John Nanfan, Esq., Lieutenant Governor of this Province and Council in his Majesty's, Fort William Henry, and from thence, according to the usual solemnity, I went to Trinity Church, where was a sermon preached by Mr. Vesey, which, ended, I went to the City Hall, attended by the Recorder, Aldermen, and assistants, and other officers, where, after the ringing of three bells, I published my Commission, and then went up into the Court-house

90

and took the chair, where Isaac De Riemer, Esq., the late Mayor, delivered to me the charter and seals of this city."

In the City Hall, too, visitors of distinction were usually received, and sometimes granted the freedom of the city. Thus when, in 1732, the Lord Augustus Fitz Roy arrived in pursuit of his bride, the mayor, aldermen, and assistants waited on his lordship

" in a full body, attended by the principal officers of the City Regiment; and being introduced to his Lordship in the Council Chamber, the Recorder addressed himself to him in the name of the Corporation, congratulating his Lordship on his safe arrival, and returning the thanks of the City for the Honor they received by his Lordship's presence, as also for his Lordship's condescension in being pleased to become a member thereof. Then the Worshipful, the Mayor, presented his Lordship with the Copy of his Freedom, to which was annexed the City Seal enclosed in a curious Gold Box, with the Arms of the City thereon neatly engraved; which his Lordship was pleased to receive with the greatest Goodness and Complaisance, and likewise to assure the Corporation that he should always entertain the kindest sentiments of this Expression of their Regard and Esteem for him."

This " gold box " was made by Mr. Charles Le Roux, the Tiffany of those days.

At this early day the corporation evinced an aldermanic fondness for good dinners. Every great event and fete day, as we have seen, was celebrated by a grand dinner given by the corporation, to which the governor and principal inhabitants were invited. One day, mousing over some musty old records, we had the good fortune to find the bill of the caterer for one of these banquets — that given in 1704 in honor of Lord Cornbury's advent as Governor.

It would seem that the dinner was a part of the anniversary celebrations also, for in the records of the Common Council of Dec. 21, 1717, we have this entry: "Ordered, the Mayor issue his warrant to the Treasurer to pay to Mr. John Parminter or order, the sum of five pounds, seventeen shillings, and three pence, current money of New York, it being for expenses of this corporation at his house on the 20th day of October last, being the anniversary of his Majesty's Coronation."

Turning eastward from the City Hall, a few steps down Wall Street bring us to the water-front, then, as now, the most interesting portion of the city. Make the tour of the city docks to-day, and you will have studied the products of the known world, heard the tones of every civilized tongue, learned the cut of every civilized jib. They were quite as interesting in colonial times. Throughout that period, the privateers, and their next of kin, the pirates, furnished the romance and interest. The privateersmen were a brave and gallant class and formed an effective arm of the colonial naval service. Their vessels were generally small, swift, graceful craft, well-armed and well manned, and pounced on the unprotected French merchantmen like falcon on the dove. Privateersmen were fond of giving their vessels high-sounding or sentimental names. There were the Sea Flower, the Dragon, the Castor and Pollux, the Sturdy Beggar, the Charming Peggy, the Bachelors, the Dolphin, the Brave Hawk, the Charming Polly, the Rainbow, the Speedwell, the Dreadnaught, the Hornet, the Decoy, the Tyger, the Royal Hunter, the King William III., the Duke of Marlborough, the Charming Sally, the Hope, the Wheel of Fortune, the Flying Harlequin, the Little Bob, the Revolution, the Two Friends, the True Briton, the Tartar, the Charming Fanny, the Happy Return, the Irish Gimblet, the Royal

American, the Lovely Martha, the Terrible, the Nebuchadnezzar , the Fame, the Lively, the Impertinent, the Tory's Revenge, the Musquito, the Eagle, the Surprise, the Spitfire, the Experiment, the Golden Pippin, the Norfolk Revenge, the Game Cock, the Try All, Favorite Betsey, the Hook-Him-Snivey, the Who'd-have-Thought-it, and others equally *outre*. Their number was large, A list from 1704 to 1763 enumerates one hundred and eighty-five, with guns ranging from six to twenty-six each. A letter written at New York Jan. 5, 1757, to a merchant in London, says: " There are now thirty Privateers out of this Place, and ten more on the Stocks and launched." And in the London Magazine of September, 1757, we have a list of privateers fitted out at New York " since the beginning of the war " (old French and Indian war, 1755-63), which gives 39 vessels, 128 guns, and 1,050 men. Their gains were often enormous. The letter from New York above quoted, says that up to that time (1757) the privateers had brought in fourteen prizes, valued in the aggregate at 100,000. From the beginning of the war in 1755 to Jan. 9, 1758, fifty-nine prizes were sent into the port of New York by these vessels, together with twenty-six condemned in other ports. As we come out on the " New Dock " we see a long-roofed, low-porched tavern — that of Capt. Benjamin Kierstede —a favorite resort of the privateersmen of the day. We enter and find half a score of old sea-dogs —

" Salt as the sea wind, tough and dried

As a lean cusk from Labrador," —

sitting around the box stove spinning yarns after the manner of sailor men. It will be interesting to put on record some of their accounts of their exploits, as their truth can be proven by letters and documents. There was the French ship La Pomine, of 180 tons burden, 14 carriage guns, 43 men, and a commission from the Due de Penhievre, Admiral of France, from St. Marks, Hispaniola, bound to Rochelle, France, taken by the privateer brig Clinton, of New York, about fifteen leagues north of Cape Nicola without the loss of a man. Her cargo invoiced 88 casks sugar, 237 casks indigo of 87,500 cwt., and 15 bales of cotton; valued at £40,000. Every man of the Clinton received £160 prize-money — the result of a six weeks' cruise. Captain Be van, of the Clinton, seems to have done the handsome thing by his crew, for we read that he gave them a hogshead of punch and an ox roasted whole in the fields. Then there was the Spanish ship that the William and the Greyhound took in concert, — cleared £90) per man; the Rising Sun, of Marseilles, taken by the Prince Charles, with 1,117 hogsheads of sugar, 458 casks of coffee, cash, and "small plunder" worth 1,000; the St. Joseph taken by the brig William, with 614 hogsheads of sugar and 200 bags and 20 casks of coffee; the Le Boice taken by the brig Triton, with 20 tuns of wine and 15 tons of flour, besides soap, candles, and dry goods. Captain Troup, of the brig Hester, was chief of the privateersmen. He was roving about in West India waters, in the spring of 1747, when he overhauled a' Danish craft. We were then at peace with Denmark, but something prompted him to board the stranger, on whom he found a Spanish merchant bound to Cordova, with several strong boxes in his keeping. These he seized and, on opening them, found 8,000 pieces of eight. Captain Troup made sure of the gold, but he paid the Danish captain the freight agreed on by the merchant for carrying the specie. No wonder when riches were thus easily won that Governor Hamilton, of New Jersey, should complain that the privateersmen were sweeping into their ranks the flower of the youth of his province. Not all the prizes were taken so easily, however. Conflicts, often against fearful odds, were frequent, and hand-to-hand fights in which prodigies of valor were performed. We instance the case of the privateer Dragon and the brig Greyhound, which, in 1746, were cruising in the Bay of Mexico, having with them the sloop Grand Diable, which they had captured a few days before. On the 2nd of May, they fell in with a Spanish frigate of 36 guns and 300 men,

"with whom," says the old chronicler, "they all engaged for the greatest part of two days; but were at last obliged to leave her, after expending most of their ammunition. They did all that was possible for men to do with a superior force, and left her a perfect wreck, but were not in a better condition themselves, having almost all their masts so much wounded that they every moment apprehended their going overboard, and, after fishing them, were obliged to make the best of their way home. . . . Of the enemy they saw many fall, and their colors were three times shot away, but always hoisted again immediately."

Not all the voyages were prosperous. Thus we read: " The privateer ship Lincoln, Captain John Jauncey, of New York, was lost on the Spanish coast, December 11, 1745. She sunk while the crew were 'putting the vessel on the careen.' "

We will set out now for a desultory stroll about the city; and first, let us visit the shopping center, which we shall find in Pearl Street, and in the short streets leading from Broadway to the water front. The stores are plain and unpretentious. Many occupy the first floors of the dwelling-houses. They have all sorts of wares for sale, like modern country stores, — dry goods, wet goods, hardware, — all under the same roof. At present Mr. Adolph Phillipse is the leading merchant in New York. He is a man of great wealth, with a town-house and manor at Phillipseborough, has been King's Councilor, Master in Chancery, Judge, and Speaker of the Assembly, and although a bachelor is a favorite with the ladies. Mr. Phillipse is an importer and has also a wholesale and retail department. His store is a brick building, three stories high. On the first floor is the wholesale department, filled at this moment with country merchants in broad-brimmed hats and homespun clothes, inspecting, weighing, tasting, and purchasing. On this floor is also kept the great chest, in which, in the absence of banks, are stored the money, wampum, pearls, silver-ware, and jewelry of the establishment. On the floor above, dry goods, wet goods, and hardware, for retail, are kept. It is filled with fair shoppers as we enter, and the clerks are busy indeed, hearing and answering requests in three languages — English, Dutch, and French, — the three tongues being in common use in New York at this time. The shoppers are buying white Paduasoy at $1.87 per yard, of our money; taffety at 87 cents, silk tabby at 63 cents, widows' crape at 50 cents, brocaded lutestring at $1.12, and " hoop petticoats " of five rows at $1.25, of six rows at $1.56; whalebone hoop petticoats are worth $3.75; India brocade is $1.00 per yard; flowered Spanish silk, 75 cents; scarlet stockings, 75 cents; black-silk do., $1.50; India dimity, 63 cents per yard; men's velvet, $3.00 per yard; cherry derry, 33 cents, and so on through a long line of rich East India stuffs — chilloes, betelees, seersuckers, deribands, tapsiels, surbettees, sannoes, gilongs, mulmuls, cushlashes, and other fabrics that the shoppers of that day had at their tongue's end.

" Sedan chairs " are a favorite means of locomotion. Fine ladies drive up in their carriages, with negro coachmen and footmen. One, just alighting as we pass out, is Mrs. Dr. De Lange, wife of the leading physician, and reputed one of the handsomest and best-dressed matrons of the city. Poor lady! One hundred and fifty years after

93

she was dust, and when her gowns had been packed away in camphor and lavender as precious heirlooms, we came upon the inventory of her wardrobe, from which we take this tale of her jewels, which were contained in a " silver, thread-wrought small trunk," worth three pounds:

" One pair black pendants, with gold hooks, valued at 10s.; one gold boat, wherein were thirteen diamonds to one white coral chain;, £16; one pair gold ' stucks,' or pendants, in each ten diamonds,;£25; one gold ring, with a clasp back, worth 12s.; one gold ring, or 'hoop,' bound round with diamonds, 10s."

Dr. De Lange's arms, we find, comprised a sword, with silver handle, valued at £2 2s.; another, with an iron handle, two cutlers' edges, a carbine, a pistol, and two " keanes," one with silver " knot," or head, and one with ivory.

But let us continue our walk. Down Pearl Street we go, flourishing our ivory-headed " keanes," after the manner of men about town. The first thing noticeable here is the great number of markets — long, low, open buildings, roofed with tiles. There is one at the foot of Broad Street, another at Coenties Slip, a third at the foot of Wall Street, another at " Burgher's Path," the present Old Slip, — the Fly Market; another at the foot of Maiden Lane, another at Rodman's Slip, just above. At the foot of every street is a market, while on Broad Street, from Wall to Exchange Place, is a public stand for country wagons, which come in heavily laden with all manner of produce. The markets are well-stocked with beef, pork, mutton, poultry, wild-fowl, venison, fish, roots, and herbs of all kinds in their season. Oysters, too, are a prominent feature; a fleet of two hundred sail is constantly employed in catching them on beds within view of the town.

The " Slips," and the side streets leading off from Pearl, are the haunts of many quaint craftsmen. This shop of John Wallace, for instance, " at the Sign of the Cross Swords, next door to Mrs. Byfield, near the Fly Market," who " makes, mends, and grinds all sorts of knives, razors, scissors, and pen-knives."

" Surgeons," he advertises, " may be supplied with very good lancets, and other surgeons' instruments. Gentlemen may be furnished with all sorts of kitchen furniture, that belongs to a smith's trade. Barbers may have their razors ground for four-pence a piece. He puts up and mends all sorts of jacks and makes multiplying wheels for jacks. He mends locks and makes keys and stillards also. He also sells all sorts of cutlery ware, and all at reasonable rates."

Right here by the Fly Market, too, at the house of William Bradford, "next door but one to the Treasurer's," is lodged " Moses Slaughter, staymaker," from London, who has brought with him, as he has been careful to inform the town:

"A parcel of extraordinary good and fashionable stays of his own making, of several sizes and prices. Slaughter is anxious to suit those that want with extraordinary good stays. Or he is ready to wait upon any ladies or gentlewomen that please to send for him to their houses. And if any wish references, he refers to Mrs. Elliston, in the Broad Street, and to Mrs. Nichols, in the Broadway, who have had his work."

Another quaint craftsman has his shop in Old Slip — Anthony Lamb, mathematical instrument maker, " at the Sign of the Quadrant and Surveying Compass." How many of the following list, one is tempted to ask, are now in use by the profession:

" Quadrants, forestaffs, nocturnals, rectifiers, universal scales, gunters, sliding gunters, gauging rods, rulers, wood or brass box compasses for sea use, pocket compasses, surveying compasses, surveying chains, waterlevels, senecal quadrants, protractors, parallel rulers, trunk telescopes, walking-stick spy-glasses, universal or equinoctial ring or horizontal brass dials, steel or brass jointed compasses, drawing pens, three-legged stoves, shipwright's draught, bows, bevels, squares, walking sticks, and other small work."

Here, at the corner house at Old Slip (John Cruger's), we can secure passage on Mr. Silvanus Seaman's Staten Island " Passage Boat," which leaves here each Tuesday and Friday for the island, and at any other time if passage or freight presents." Here, " at the northwest corner of the Great Dock, next door to the Sign of the Leopard," Simon Franks, from London, has a little shop, " where he makes and sells all sorts of perukes, after the best and newest fashion, and cuts and dresses lady's wigs and towers after a manner performed much better than is pretended to be done by some others."

In Robert Crommelius' little shop " near the Meal Market in Wall Street," one may buy all sorts of " writing paper, superfine Post Paper, ready cut by the half ream, blank books, sail duck. Powder-blue, copper tea kettles and Pye-pans, Ivory combs, sewing and" darning needles, spectacles, all sorts of shot, small bar-lead, sash leads, wine glasses, wafel Irons," etc. At the corner of Beekman's Slip Abraham Bamper sells fine clocks, watches and ear-rings. Another out-of-the-way tradesman is Joseph Seddell, " Pewterer," at the sign of the Platter, at the lower end of Wall Street, near the Meal Market, " in the house where Mr. Joseph Sackett lately lived, where he sells Pewter ware of all sorts, cannons, — six and four pounders, and swivel guns, cannon shot, iron pots and kettles, cart and wagon boxes, backs for chimneys, Fuller plates, pig and bar iron, etc. He will pay you hard money for old bars and pewter." Most gruesome and picturesque of all is the undertaker. In 1740, people were not so finical, and little attempt was made by the tradesman to relieve the ghastliness of death. Coffins, some quite magnificent in silver and lace trimmings stood on end around his wareroom. On a bier in the rear were the Parish Palls, two of them, one of black velvet designed for general use, the other of cloth, with an edging of white silk a foot broad, which could only be used for unmarried men and maidens. Flannel shrouds with gloves, scarfs, hat bands, and other mourning paraphernalia filled shelves ranged around the sides of the room. On the counter, painted a funeral black, was a tray of lacquer-work, holding the shopman's cards, and samples of the " invitations to funerals " it was then customary to send to relatives of the deceased. By these cards the public was informed that the undertaker " hath a velvet pall, a good hears, mourning cloaks, and black hangings for rooms to be let at reasonable rates. He hath also for sale all sorts of mourning and half mourning, white silk for scarfs and hat bands at funerals, with coffins, shrouds and all sorts of burying cloaths for the dead."

In this connection we will speak of a beautiful custom practiced by young maidens of visiting the graves of their deceased companions on each anniversary of death and strewing them with the flowers of remembrance. Trinity being the English churchyard was the one generally sought. It was much more impressive in that day than now, with its groves of forest giants and numerous somber yews, "the cheerless, unsocial plant" of the poet.

To this solemn abode of the dead the maidens came, clad in white, and bearing baskets of flowers, and as they performed their pious office they sang pathetic little songs, one of which we reproduce:

" Come with heavy mourning,
And on her grave
Let her have
Sacrifice of sighs and mourning.
Let her have fair flowers enough,
White and purple, green and yellow.
For her that was of maids most true,
For her that was of maids most true."

The street signs please us by their number and variety. Very few of the commonalty can read, and so in place of letters the tradesmen have a distinguishing sign. Three sugar loaves and a tea-canister indicate the shop of a grocer near Coenties Market. Patrick Carryl sells " good raisins of the sun," cheap at the sign of the Unicorn and Mortar in Hanover Square. The chair-maker on Golden Hill has the sign of the Chair Wheel, a vender of clocks the sign of the Dial. The Exchange Coffee house and Tavern the sign of the " King' s Arms." Another tavern sign is the Scotch Anns. Thomas Lepper's Ordinary, opposite the Merchants' Coffee-house, has the sign of the Duke of Cumberland. He advertises that dinner will be ready at half an hour after one. The Boston Post puts up at Mr. Jonathan Ogden's, the sign of the Black Horse, in upper Queen (Pearl) Street. George Burns keeps one of the most popular taverns of the city at the sign of the Cart and Horse, and constantly takes in the " Boston, Philadelphia, and New York newspapers." There is a newly-opened tavern at the sign of the Bunch of Grapes, near the Widow Rutger's beer-house, going up towards the Cart and Horse. " John Reed, Taylor," is to be found at the sign of the Blue Ball in Wall Street. The stables of George Goodwin are at the sign of the Dolphin, facing the Common. Looking glasses are new-silvered, and pictures made and sold at the sign of the Two Cupids, near the Old Slip Market, and so on. " Jamaica Pilot Boat," " Rose and Crown," " The Bible," Fighting Cocks," " Cross Swords," " Platter," " Quadrant and Compass," " Spread Eagle," " White Swan," " The Sun," " The Leopard," " Horse and Manger," are favorite signs.

The coffee-houses on the London plan are favorite resorts for all classes. As one wrote of them about this time: " You have all manner of news there. You have a good fire, which you may sit by as long as you please. You have a dish of coffee. You meet your friends for the transaction of business, and all for a penny if you don't care to spend more." We will enter the Exchange Coffee-house, the principal one in the city. Bare sanded floor, plain pine tables and seats, a roaring fire, a perpetual supply of hot water, and the coffee and tea-pots set close by to keep warm, comprise the furniture.

Quite a number of gentlemen are present; some drinking at the bar, some exchanging the news, some reading the weekly newspapers. One of the latter looks up with a smile as we enter, and then reads aloud to his companion:

"We hear from Ridgefield, near the county of Westchester, that one William Drinkwater, late an inhabitant there, proving quarrelsome with his neighbors and abusive to his wife, the good women of the place took the matter into consideration, and laid hold of an opportunity to get him tied to a cart, and there with rods belabored him on his back, till, in striving to get away, he pulled one of his arms out of joint, and then they untied him. Mr. Drinkwater complained to sundry magistrates of this usage but all he got by it was to be laughed at, whereupon he removed to New Milford, where, we hear, he proves a good neighbor and a loving husband; a remarkable reformation arising from the justice of the good women."

" Served him right," his friend remarks, and then reads an item that has interested him:

" Last Thursday morning a creature of an uncommon size and shape was observed to break through a window of a store-house of this city, and jump into the street, where was suddenly a number of spectators, who followed it till it jumped over several high fences, and at last stuck between two houses, where they shot it. Many had the curiosity to view it, and say it was 7 feet long. Most of them say it is a panther, but whence it came or how it got into the store-house, we are at a loss to know."

The taverns, we notice, are quite numerous and of various grades. Let us stop at the " Black Horse," where the Boston Post, which runs weekly in summer and fortnightly in winter, "puts up." It is a traveler's inn, the favorite of the commonalty, while the " King's Arms " is patronized by the patrician class. As we push open the two-leaved door and enter, a strange and picturesque scene greets us. A huge fire of logs burns in the red-tiled fireplace, the white, sanded floor is stained with splotches of tobacco juice and discarded quids, while an odor of vile tobacco fills the air. Quite a number of the frequenters of the place are present — the smith in his leathern apron, the butcher in his long frock, laborers in soil-stained smocks and homespun breeches, a jockey in cap and feather, farmers in camlet coats and sheepskin breeches — all leisurely draining from long pewter mugs their mid-day dram of Sopus ale. One of " His Majesty's players " is singing a " catch " as we enter, and we stop to listen:

" Under the trees in sunny weather,
Just try a cup of ale together.
And if in tempest or in storm
A couple then to make you warm,
But when the day is very cold
Then taste a mug of twelve months' old " —

which sentiment is heartily applauded. There are a number of placards on the walls — a schedule of ferry charges and regulations, notices of auction sales, fairs, horse races, and among them a paper that interests us very much. It is entitled " The Several Stages from the City of New York to Boston, and where Travelers may be Accommodated."

" From New York to Boston," we read, " is accounted 274 miles. From the Post Office in New York to Joe Clapp's in the Bouwerie is 2 miles (which generally is the bating place, where gentlemen take leave of their friends going so long a journey), and where a parting glass of generous wine,"

" ' If well applied, makes their dull horses feel
One spur in the head 's worth two in the heel.'

By and by a shouting and hubbub without draws everyone to the door, and the fire engines and firemen dash by. There is a fire in Henry Riker's blacksmith shop in the crowded part of the city. At the fire the engines attract our attention. They are

97

known as the Newnham engine, after the inventor, and were patented in England early in the century. Each required twelve men to work it; it took water from a cistern or failing that from a wooden trough into which water was poured, and it could throw a continuous jet of water seventy feet high, and with such velocity as to break windows. In 1736 the corporation built a house for its engines contiguous to the Watch House in Broad Street, having appointed the year before one " Jacobus Turk, gunsmith," to keep them clean and in good repair upon his own cost for the sum of ten pounds per annum. It was not until September 19, 1738, that the first twenty-four firemen were appointed under Act of Assembly, their only salary or emolument being exemption from serving as constable, surveyor of highways, jurors on inquests, or as militia. The different trades and races seem to have been well represented, for we read of John Tiebout, blockmaker, Hercules Windover, blacksmith, Jacobus Delamontaigne, blockmaker, Thomas Brown, cutler, Abraham Van Gelder, gunsmith, Jacobus Stoutenburgh, gunsmith, Wm. Roome, Jr., carpenter, Walter Hyer, Sr., bricklayer, Johannes Alstein, blacksmith, Everet Pells, Jr., ropemaker, Peter Lott, carman, Peter Brower, bricklayer, Albertus Tiebout, carpenter, John Vredenburg, carpenter, John Dunscomb, cooper, Johannes Roome, carpenter, Peter Maeschalck, baker, Petrus Kip, baker, Andrew Myer, Jr., cordwainer, Robert Richardson, cooper, Rymer Broger, blacksmith, Barnet Bush, cooper, David Van Gelder, blacksmith, Johannes Van Duersen, cordwainer, Martinus Bogert, carman, Johannes Vredenbergh, cord, wainer, Johannes Van Sys, carpenter, Adolph Brase, cordwainer, and John Man, cooper, " all strong, able, discreet, honest, and sober men!'

The same act defined the firemen's duties. On the first alarm they were to drag the engines to the fire and there under direction of the magistrates, engineer, or overseer, "with their utmost diligence, manage, work, and play the said fire engines and all other tools and instruments, at such fire with all their power, skill, strength, and understanding, and when the fire is out shall draw the engine back." The city firemen were chartered in 1798 as the Volunteer Fire Department, and continued as such until 1865, when the present efficient system of a paid force took its place. In the early days of the volunteer force great care was taken in the selection of the men. They passed an examination before being accepted, and were given a certificate of membership, which was framed and handed down as a precious heirloom.

We have so far omitted to notice a very numerous class — the servants or slaves. We meet them everywhere — on the streets, bringing water, selling pies, giving the babies an airing, doing the family marketing; indeed they perform most of the menial work in the houses, stores, and fields. There are three classes of them — negroes held as slaves, Indians, and European immigrants. Most of the negroes are native Africans, imported direct from Angola and Madagascar in the colony vessels — a savage, brutal, and heathen race. We have not been able to determine the status of the Indian slaves; probably they were prisoners of war, or criminals condemned to servitude. The European servants were those " indentured " or bound out until such time as their wages should discharge their passage money. These three classes are proved to have existed from certain items in the newspapers of the day, as when we read in 1732: "Just arrived from Great Britain and to be sold on board the ship Alice and Elizabeth, Captain Paine, Commander, several likely Welch and English servant men, most of them tradesmen." Again in 1751: " Likely Negroes, men and women, imported from the coast of Africa, ... to be sold by Thomas Greenell "; and in 1759: " On board the ship Charming Polly, Captain Edward Bayley, Master, now riding at anchor in the harbor of New York, are several Palatine and Switzer servants to be sold; some are farmers and some tradesmen." Again, in 1747: " Run away on April the 25th, from Capt. Abraham Kip, in New York, an Indian man about eighteen years old, and speaks good English." Twenty shillings' reward was offered for his return. The servants, whether white or black, had a great propensity for running away, and it was rarely they went emptyhanded. The Indian tribes and the colonies of Connecticut and New Jersey on either hand offered safe refuge. Colonial newspapers did a thriving business in publishing advertisements of runaway slaves, and from their descriptions of the truants may be gained vivid pictures of colonial costumes and customs. Here are a few specimens:

" Run away from Richard Bishop, a servant man named John Farrant about nineteen years of age, of a fresh complexion, about five feet and a half high; he had on when he went away a brown livery coat and breeches: the coat lined and cuffed with blue; a blue shoulder knot, a black natural wig, and a pair of red stockings."

" Run away from Joseph Reade, of the city of New York, merchant, a likely mulatto servant woman named Sarah. She is about 24 years of age and has taken with her a calico suit of clothes, a striped satteen silk waistcoat, a striped Calliminco waistcoat and petty-coat, two homespun waistcoats and petty-coats, and a negro man's light-colored coat with brass buttons."

William Bradford advertises his " apprentice boy," James Parker, who had " a fresh complexion and short yellowish hair," and wore a yellowish Bengali coat, jacket, and breeches lined with the same, and had taken with him " a brown colored coarse coat with flat metal buttons, two frocks, two shirts, one pair of striped ticken jackets and breeches."

The number of these slaves owned in a family was considered an index of its wealth and social position. Thus, of the aristocracy of New York, in 1704, Colonel De Peyster owned five male slaves, two females, and two children. Widow Van Cortlandt had the same. Rip Van Dam had three negroes, two negresses, and a child. The Widow Phillipse, with but herself and child to be cared for, owned one man, three women, and three children. Balthazar Bayard had six slave domestics; Mrs. Stuyvesant, four male negroes and a negress. Captain Morris, with only himself and wife, maintained seven slaves. William Smith, of the manor of St. George, employed twelve.

The great body of servants, as has been said, were Africans. They were rude, savage, lazy, and inefficient, and a constant source of fear and uneasiness to their masters. Indeed, between the French and Indians, Popish plots, and uprisings of his slaves, the colonial gentleman deemed himself in constant danger of assault. In 1741, out of a population of twelve thousand, two thousand were negro slaves. The latter had become very much disaffected at this time, partly, no doubt, because they were subject to such strict regulations. Not above four were allowed to meet together on the Sabbath, which was their holiday. No negro or Indian slave could appear in the streets after nightfall without a " lantern and a lighted candle in it," under penalty of forty lashes at the whipping-post. Gaming was visited by the same penalty. A slave must be buried by daylight; no pall or pall-bearers were allowed at the funeral, and not more than twelve slaves were permitted to attend.

These restrictions, added to the hardships of their lot, led to several uprisings among them, one of which, that of 1741, we will consider somewhat at length, since it will introduce to us an interesting colonial court scene.

In February, 1740-1, numerous robberies were committed in the city, and several negro slaves, with one John Hughson, at whose tavern they were wont to congregate, were suspected of being concerned in it. Some of the suspected slaves were arrested and tried for the offence. This was on March 4th. On the 18th, the wind blowing a gale, the roof of the governor's house in Fort George was discovered to be on fire. At once the church bells rang, and the people, with the fire engines and the twenty-four firemen, hurried to the fort. It was soon seen, however, that no earthly power could save the governor's house and the chapel beside it, and the people turned their attention to the secretary's office over the fort gate, in which the records of the colony were kept. The office was consumed, however, in spite of their efforts. The barracks opposite caught next, and in an hour and a quarter everything combustible within the fort was in ruins. The heavy timbers of the chapel belfry burned all night long, lighting town and bay with a fitful glare, while the hand grenades stored in the fort kept up a continual fusillade, as the flames reached them. The excitement in the city was intense. The wildest rumors were current. Some thought that a Popish plot to burn the city was on foot, others that it was a negro uprising. To quiet the people, Captain Cornelius Van Home's militia company, seventy strong, was called out, and patrolled the streets until day broke. Wednesday, March 25th, another fire broke out at Captain Warren's, near the Long Bridge, in the extreme southern part of the town, but the fire engines put it out. A week later, fire was discovered in the store-house of the merchant Van Zandt, in the eastern end of the city, but the engines confined the fire to the building.

April 4th, at night, a fire broke out in a cow stable near the Fly Market, in the most thickly settled portion of the town. Everybody ran with their buckets, the fire engines rattled down, and the flames were quenched. On their way home the people were startled by another cry of fire, which proved to be in the loft of the house of Benjamin Thomas on the west side. When extinguished, it was found that an incendiary had been at work, for coals had been placed between two straw beds, on which a negro slept. The next day, Sunday, another attempt was discovered—coals had been placed under a hay stack near the coach house and stables of John Murray, Esq., in the Broadway, near his house, and these coals, by cinders spilled in carrying them, were traced to the house of a negro nearby. The same day a Mrs. Earle, remaining home from church, heard three negroes, walking by her house, threaten to burn the town, and recognized one of them " as Mr. Walter's Quaco," All doubt that a plot to burn the city existed was banished when, next morning at ten, a fire broke out in the house of Sergeant Burns, and another, about the same time, in a cluster of buildings near the Fly Market. There were some Spanish negroes, recently captured, in the city, who had been muttering and threatening the whites ever since their arrival, and these were now seized and haled before the magistrates, who, after examination, committed them to prison.

Other fires occurred, and many negroes, with several white people were arrested. On April 21, 1741, the Supreme Court of Judicature of the colony came in and sat in the City Hall, " His Honor James De Lancey, Esq., Chief Justice, absent, Frederick Phillipse, Esq., Second Justice, and Daniel Horsmanden, Esq., Third Justice, present." The prisoners having been duly indicted by the Grand Jury, were brought before the court. A description of the trial, taken from an account by one of the judges, Mr. Daniel Horsmanden, we present, as giving the reader an excellent idea of the stately and solemn ceremonial of the colonial courts.

The judges sat on the bench in heavy black robes and full-bottomed wigs. The prisoners being marshalled before it, the court rose and Judge Phillipse said: " The King against the same on trial upon three indictments." They then sat down and the clerk said: " Cryer, make proclamation."

Cryer — " Oyez! Our Sovereign Lord the King doth strictly charge and command all manner of persons to keep silence upon pain of imprisonment. If anyone can inform the King's Justices or Attorney-General for this province on the inquest now to be taken on the behalf of our Sovereign Lord the King, of any treason, murder, felony, or any other misdemeanor committed or done by the prisoners at the bar, let them come forth, and they shall be heard, for the prisoners stand upon their deliverance."

Clerk — "Cryer, make proclamation."

Cryer — " Oyez! You good men that are impaneled to inquire between our Sovereign Lord the King and John Hughson, Sarah his wife, Sarah Hughson the daughter, Margaret Sorubiero, alias Kerry, the prisoners at the bar, answer to your names."

Clerk — "John Hughson, Sarah the wife of John Hughson, Sarah the daughter of John Hughson, Margaret Sorubiero, hold up your hands:

" These good men that are now called, and here appear, are those which are to pass between you and our Sovereign Lord the King upon your lives or deaths; if you, or any, or either of you challenge any of them, you must speak as they come to the book to be sworn and before they are sworn."

Judge Phillipse — "You, the prisoners at the bar, we must inform you that the law allows you the liberty of challenging peremptorily twenty of the jurors, if you have any dislike to them, and you need not give your reasons for so doing; and you may likewise challenge as many more as you can give sufficient reasons for; and you may either all join in your challenges or make them separately."

John Hughson, for the prisoners and himself, challenged sixteen. The twelve selected were then sworn.

Clerk — Cryer, make proclamation "; after which the clerk, turning to the jury, continued:

"You gentlemen of the jury, that are sworn, look upon the prisoners and hearken to this charge."

Three indictments were then read, and the clerk, turning to the jury, said: Upon this indictment they have been arraigned, and hath pleaded themselves ' not guilty,' and for their trial hath put themselves upon God and their country, which country you are."

The Attorney-General then opened for the king, and the trial proceeded. It is not necessary to follow it in detail. After hearing the testimony and the pleadings, the jury returned a verdict of "guilty," and Judge Phillipse, after a solemn and impressive address, sentenced them as follows:

. . . " I must now proceed to the duty the law requires of me, which is to tell you that you, the prisoners now at the bar, be removed to the place from whence you came, and from thence to the place of execution, and there you, and each of you, are to be hanged by the neck until you are severally dead; and I pray God of his great goodness to have mercy on your souls."

Sarah, the daughter, was finally respited and pardoned. Many others were tried and punished. In all eleven negroes were burned, eighteen hanged, fifty transported, and many more imprisoned. Several white persons were also executed. Business for four months was prostrated. It was a fearful and dramatic chapter in the city's history, and, by general verdict of historians, a quite unnecessary one — that is, it is not now believed that any serious plot to burn the town really existed. These men, whose public acts we have been considering and who have perhaps impressed us with being cold, stern, stately, unapproachable beings, had also their social and domestic life — loved, sorrowed, hated, went the round of fashionable follies and amusements, dressed well, danced well, entertained well, in some respects

" Lived in a nobler way
With grander hospitality,"

than do the men of to-day. The hurry and fever of our modern life was unknown to them. England was two months distant. It took five days' steady travelling to reach Boston, and nearly three to go to Philadelphia. The newspapers came out once a week. There was greater opportunity for social intercourse and interchange of courtly ceremonial. The governor and his lady, the officers of the garrison and of his Majesty's frigates, with visiting noblemen and the resident gentry, formed a minor court circle, that adopted, in a measure, the fashions and amusements of that at home.

Theatre-going, card-playing, horse-racing, dancing, horseback-riding, sails in Captain Rickett's " pleasure boat " were the popular amusements. There was a play-house in the city as early as October, 1733, reference being made to it in an advertisement in the New York Gazette of that date. Perhaps it was to this play house that the following play-bill, cut from the Weekly Post Boy, of March 12, 1750, referred:

BY HIS EXCELLENCY'S PERMISSION.
AT THE THEATRE IN NASSAU STREET,
This Evening will be presented
THE HISTORICAL TRAGEDY OF RICHARD III.
Wrote originally by Shakespeare and altered by Colly Cibber,
Esq. To which will be added a farce called
THE BEAU IN THE SUDDS
AND
On Saturday next will he presented
A TRAGY-COMEDY CALLED
THE SPANISH FRYAR,
OR
THE DOUBLE DISCOVERY,
Wrote by Mr. Dryden.
Tickets to be had of the printer hereof.
Pitt, 5s. Gallery, 3s. To begin, precisely at half an hour after 6 o'clock, and no person to be admitted behind the scenes."

On September loth, a comedy called " The Recruiting Officer" is announced for the same place, and on the 17th the "tragedy called Cato, wrote by Mr. Addison." Quite a long list of " tragedys, comedies, ballad operas, and pastoral dialogues," enacted in the old play-house, might be made from these play bills. There were many other entertainments open to the pleasure-seeker, however. Thus, in the Weekly Post Boy, of December 25, 1749, John Bonnin informs the curious of either sex that he begins that day to exhibit his " Philosophical Optical Machine," " which had given so much satisfaction to all those that had already favored him with their company. He has sundry new additions which he proposes to show all the winter season: to begin at 8 o'clock in the morning and continue showing till nine at night, at the house of Mr. Victor Becket, opposite Mr. Hayne's new buildings in Crown Street. Price, I shilling for grown persons and a sixpence for children." Next is Punch's company of comedians, — which never palls, — with the inevitable " wax figgers." There are fourteen of the latter, comprising the effigies of the royal family of England and the Empress, Queen of Hungaria and Bohemia. " The company will act this week the play of Whittington and his Cat, and next week the Norfolk Tragedy, or the Babes in the Wood. Price, 2 shillings for each ticket."

In " Mr. Holt's Long Room," again, we have the " New Pantomime Entertainment in Grotesque Characters, called the Adventures of Harlequin and Scaramouch, or the Spaniard Tricked "; to which is added an "Optic," wherein is " represented in Perspective several of the most noted cities and remarkable places in Europe and America, and a new Prologue and Epilogue addressed to the town. Tickets, five shillings each." There is also a concert of " vocal and instrumental musick at the house of Robert Tod, to begin precisely at five o'clock. Tickets at 5s." The wonder of its day, however, and the greatest attraction, was the new electrical machine, which was thus announced in the Weekly Post Boy, of May 16, 1748:

" FOR THE ENTERTAINMENT OF THE CURIOUS TO BE SHOWN:

The most surprising effects or Phenomena on Electricity of attracting, repelling, and Flenemies Force, particularly the new way of electrifying several persons at the same time, so that Fire shall dart from all Parts of their Bodies, as has been exhibited to the satisfaction of the Curious in all parts of Europe. Electricity became all the subject in vogue. Princes were willing to see this new fire, which a man produced from himself, and is that to be of service in many ailments. To be seen at any time of the day, from 8 o'clock in the morning till 9 at night, provided the weather proves dry, and no damp air, (a company presenting,) at the House of Mrs. Wilson, near the Weigh House, in New York, where due attendance is given by Mr. Richard Brichell."

The Englishman could not be long in America without importing his own race-horse and hunter. Announcements like the following are often met with: " On Wednesday, the 13th of October next, will be run for on the course at New York, a plate of twenty pounds' value, by any Horse, Mare, or Gelding carrying ten stone (saddle and bridle included) the best of three heats, two miles each heat." The entrance fee was half a pistole each, and the great crowds that "came on horseback and in chaises" were obliged to pay sixpence each as gate money to the owner of the grounds.

There were famous courses too at Greenwich, and on Hempstead Plains, as well as at New York. Thus the Weekly Post Boy of June 4, 1750:

" Last Friday a great horse race was run on Hempstead Plains for a considerable wager, which engaged the attention of so many of this city that upwards of seventy chairs and chaises were carried over the ferry from hence the day before, besides a far greater number of horses; and it was thought that the number of horses on the Plains at the race far exceeded a thousand."

Often individual races and trials of speed were arranged on a wager. Thus we read, under date of April 29, 1759, that " Oliver Delancey's horse ran from one of our Palisade gates (Wall Street and Broadway) to King's Bridge and back again, being upwards of thirty miles, in one hour 47 minutes." Horseback riding through the embowered lanes and by-paths of the island was a favorite amusement. The lady and her escort did not then ride coldly apart, however, but shared the same steed, the fair rider being mounted on a pillion behind, and maintaining her position by passing an arm about her companion's waist; both saddle and pillion were elegantly made and lavishly ornamented. What is now Second 'Avenue was then, according to a naughty chronicler, the favorite drive, the reason being that at the corner of the present Fiftieth Street, a quaint stone bridge, famed as the " Kissing Bridge," spanned a little, clear-water brook that went babbling down to the East River. On crossing this bridge the favored swain was privileged to claim a kiss from his companion — a curious survival of an old Danish custom. If the lady was disposed to be ungracious, however, there were parallel roads she might choose.

Dancing in colony times grew to be one of the fine arts. No merry-making was thought to be complete without one of the stately dances of the day. We have seen how all the king's birthdays and fete days generally concluded with a grand ball in the evening. Sometimes people danced for sweet charity's sake, as they now do. For instance, in the Weekly Post Boy of December 11, 1752, we read:

" A ball on Thursday evening is proposed to be held at the house of Mr. Trotter, in the Broadway, for the benefit of Jacob Leonard, who, by reason of the late sickness in this place, is reduced to low circumstances. Tickets to be had at Mr. Trotter's, or at the said Leonard's, opposite the Presbyterian Church. Price, four shillings."

The dances were mostly those introduced from England, and were, without exception, of a lively character, involving swift motions of the limbs and flying movements of the feet. The modern round dance was unknown. The " country dance " (contra dance?) was the favorite.

These were the duties and diversions of the gentlefolk. The commonalty, too, had their favorite modes of recreation. Athletic sports figured largely in these — foot-racing, jumping, quoit-pitching, climbing the greased pole, " pulling the goose," and others. " Shooting-matches " would seem to have been the favorite, judging from the great number of announcements like the following:

" To be shot for: a lot of land belonging to Robert Bennett, in Sacketts Street. It is to be shot for on Easter Munday, Tuesday, Wednesday, and Thursday, the 7th, 8th, 9th, and loth of April next, with a single ball at 100 yards distance, at the sign of the Marlboroug's Head, in the Bowery Lane. Every person that inclines to shoot for the above-mentioned lot of land is to lay in 5s. before he fires, his price for every shot, and whoever makes the best shot in the four days mentioned shall receive a good and warrantable bill of sale of the afore-mentioned lot of land from Robert Bennett."

Lotteries were popular with all classes, and were generally organized in aid of some charity, church, or benevolent work. Snuff-taking seems to have been the prevalent vice among ladies and formed a favorite subject for the lampooners of the day. This example, from a newspaper of 1731, shows how forced and heavy was colonial wit:

" This silly trick of taking snuff is attended with such a coquetry in some young (as well as older) gentlewomen, and such a sedate masculine one in others, that I cannot tell which most to complain of; but they are to me equally disagreeable. Mrs. Saunter is so impatient of being without it, that she takes it as often as she does salt at meals; and as she affects a wonderful ease and negligence in all her manners, an upper lip, mixed with snuff and the sauce, is what is presented to the observation of all who have the honor to eat with her. The pretty creature, her niece, does all she can to be as disagreeable as her aunt, and if she is not as offensive to the eye, she is quite as much to the ear, and makes up all she wants in a confident air by a nauseous rattle of the nose when the snuff is delivered, and the fingers make the stops and closes on the nostrils. This, perhaps, is not a very courtly usage in speaking of gentlewomen; that is very true, but where arises the offence? Is it in those who commit, or those who observe it 1 As to those who take it for pretty action, or to fill up little intervals of discourse, I can bear with them; but then they must not use it when another is speaking, who ought to be heard with too much respect to admit of offering at that time from hand to hand the snuff-box. But Florilla is so far taken with her behavior in this kind, that she pulls out her box (which is indeed full of good Brazile) in the middle of the sermon, and to show that she has the audacity of the well-bred woman, she offers it to the men as well as to the women who sit next her. But since by this time all the world knows she has a fine hand, I am in hopes she may give herself no further trouble in this matter. On Sunday was sevennight, when they came about for the offering, she gave her charity with a very good air, but at the same time asked the churchwarden if he would take a pinch."

But these merry-makings, and the brilliant society that gave them birth, had their day and passed, — a sterner age succeeding. In 1760 " the times that tried men's souls" were approaching, and it is quite time that, with lofty purpose and pulses stirred, we turned to consider them, — for New York played no insignificant role in the great drama.

XIII. THE HEROIC AGE.

The year 1765 is a red-letter year in American history. In March of that year the Stamp Act was passed, and the Stamp Act was the little entering wedge that first opened the rupture between the colonies and the mother country — a rupture which widened and widened until a great gulf, and at last free national existence for the daughter, was the result. This Stamp Act in itself was not an oppressive measure. It provided simply that all deeds, receipts, and other legal papers, even to marriage licenses, should be written or printed on stamped paper, this paper to be sold by the revenue collectors, and to form part of the revenue collected from the colonies. The difficulty was that a principle, a right, was involved. If there was one thing that the Briton of that day gloried in, jealously guarded, it was the English Constitution. The people had gotten this grand instrument by piecemeal, as it were, through a thousand years of struggle. First, as students of English history know, came Magna Carta, the Great Charter, which the barons forced from King John in 1215. Next, the Petition of Rights, in 1628, one of the conditions of which was that the king should have no power to make " forced loans," that is, levy taxes without the people's consent. Third, the Habeas Corpus Act, in 1679, " for the better securing the liberty of the subject and the prevention of importations beyond the seas." Fourth, the Bill of Rights, of 1689, agreed to when William and Mary came to the throne. And, lastly, the " Act of Settlement," of 1700, which still further limited the prerogatives of the crown. There were, of course, other grants and concessions, but these are generally regarded as the five great pillars of the English Constitution. The way in which British yeomen regarded this grand instrument has been described by M. Taine, in words imbued with the very spirit of the times:

" Everyone, great or small, has his own, which he defends with all his might. My lands, my property, my chartered right, whatsoever it be — ancient, indirect, superfluous, individual, public, — none shall touch it, King, Lords, nor Commons. Is it of the value of five shillings? I will defend it like a million pounds; it is my person which they would fetter. I will leave my business, lose my time, throw away my money, make associations, pay fines, go to jail, perish in the attempt. No matter. I shall show that I am no coward; that I will not bend under injustice, that I will not yield a portion of my right."

This was exactly the position taken by the American colonists when King George and his ministers sought to lay a " forced loan " on them by means of the Stamp Act. They said the tax was illegal, unconstitutional, because levied without their consent; that if the ministry had power to lay this tax, they could go on and levy others, and others, until their property was all swept away. They were willing, they said, to pay their just share of the taxes of the realm; but then they must be allowed to send men to Parliament to defend their rights and look after their interests. A statesman would have foreseen that America must now be made an integral part of the empire, or she would aspire to separate national existence; but, unfortunately. King George and his ministers were not statesmen, and they rushed blindly on to the dismemberment of the empire.

As the time came for the Stamp Act to go into effect New York was on the verge of revolt. The political fabric was mined and honeycombed, the powder laid; it needed but to press the button to produce an explosion that would shatter it to fragments. There were two parties in the field: the royalists, or Tories, who, with blind devotion, supported the king; the Whigs, or " rebels," who were for resisting to the last extremity what they called the " tyranny " of king and Parliament. The strife between the two parties soon became intense; words are powerless to depict it. The very stones seemed to breathe defiance. " Rebellion," " treason," " resistance to tyrants," " confiscation of estates," " imprisonment," " death on the scaffold," were the topics ever in men's thoughts. Pamphlets, broadsides, hand-bills, filled the air; ballads, epigrams, and scurrilous verses were poured forth by the song-writers on both sides. The newspapers — Holt's Journal and Gaines' Mercury for the Whigs, Rivington's Gazette for the royalists, steadily fanned the flame. Read a Whig newspaper of that day, and you find such terms as these: " Tories," " ministerial hirelings," " dependent placemen," " contractors," " informers," " banditti," and the like. Read a Tory newspaper, and it is " rebels," " traitors," " despicable pamphleteers," " liars," " fomenters of sedition," " drunken vagabonds," " mobility," " pulpiteers," " sons of licentiousness." The Tory newspapers averred that Congress took its votes after drinking thirty-two bumpers of Madeira, that the riffraff were hired to insult the soldiers in order to provoke a collision, that Whig meetings were composed of drunken vagabonds, " raisers of riots," whose deity was the liberty pole, whose ever-staunch friend was the mob. They spoke of Holt's Journal as that " fund of lies and sedition "; the Sons of Liberty as being composed of two sorts: those who by their debaucheries and ill conduct had reduced themselves to poverty, and the Puritan ministers " who belched from the pulpit, liberty, independence, and a steady perseverance in shaking off their allegiance to the mother country." They spoke of the " distempered brain," " the violence of the banditti," of liberty as a word they had got " by rote like a parrot," and described the patriots as gathering at a tavern with " a Cooper or an Adams " at their head, where they got drunk, damned the king, ministers, and taxes, and vowed they would follow any ignis fatuiis produced by demagogues."

The Whig writers were even more bitter and sarcastic. They drew parallels between Rome in her decadence and themselves. "The Roman emperors," they said, "held the dignity of government in such open contempt that they frequently made their horses consuls. Ours, in this last point, go beyond them by making asses senators." A Tory they defined as "a thing whose head is in England, its body in America, and whose neck ought to be stretched." A favorite toast was, " Addition to Whigs, subtraction to Tories, multiplication to friends of liberty, division to the enemies of America." They pictured the " ministerial hirelings " as ready to perform any dirty drudgery for the sake of preserving a titled and lucrative place. The British troops, who had been quartered on them to subdue and overawe them, were their pet aversion; the soldiers returned the feeling in kind and improved every chance to insult and annoy them. Naturally men indulging in such abuse soon began to carry arms, their houses became well-stocked arsenals, collisions occurred, women grew pale as their fathers, husbands, brothers, sons, armed for war and took opposite sides.

This talk of resistance and preparations for resisting, it must be remembered, went on in the other colonies as well as in New York, and at last, on the suggestion of the eloquent patriot, James Otis, of Massachusetts, a Congress of the colonies was called to consider the matter. It met in the City Hall in New York on the 7th of October, 1765, nine of the thirteen colonies being represented. Two important state papers — a Declaration of Rights and an address to the king — were the results of this conference. Meanwhile the people were busily talking and acting.

Patriotic men vowed to drink no more wine, to go clad in sheepskins, to purchase no more wares from Great Britain, until the obnoxious act was repealed. Patriotic women agreed to wear only homespun, and thus taboo all British-made goods: while the young ladies vowed "to join hands with none but such as would to the utmost endeavor to abolish the custom of marrying with license." The 1st of November had been appointed as the day when the Stamp Act should go into effect. As the day approaches, it is evident there will be trouble if any attempt is made to enforce it. Threats of resistance are openly made. Lord Grenville, the British Prime Minister, has appointed Americans to sell the stamped paper, thinking thus to placate the colonists. It but adds to their resentment. " If your father must die, will you then become his executioner in order to pocket the hangman's fees? If the ruin of your country is decreed, are you justified in taking part in the plunder?" These questions are asked of the stamp collectors, and they so intimidate them that they flee the country or resign. Oliver, the Massachusetts stamp-master, is hung in effigy on an elm in the outskirts of Boston. The Rhode Island stamp master abdicates at the demand of his infuriated fellow-citizens. Jared Ingersoll, collector for Connecticut, is met by five hundred mounted men as he is riding full speed to Hartford to secure protection from the authorities there, is conducted to the main street of Wethersfield, and there forced to resign, and to throw up his hat and cry " Liberty and Property! " three times. James McEvers, the Hanover Square merchant, appointed for New York, has resigned; so has Coxe, of New Jersey; Hughes, of Pennsylvania, and every collector south of the Potomac. The collector of Maryland is even now in Fort George, hiding from the wrath of his old neighbors and friends. The king is beggared of officers wherewith to enforce his decrees. On October 23rd, the ship Edwards, bearing the stamped paper, arrives from England and, convoyed by a frigate and a tender, comes to her anchorage under the guns of Fort George. The water front is black with citizens, who receive her with menacing gestures, hisses, derisive cheers, while the ships in the harbor fly their colors at half mast in token of grief. That night, men evading the rattle watch steal through the streets and stealthily affix to trees and buildings " hand-bills," on which next morning the people read, written in a bold, free hand:

PRO PATRICI.

The first man that distributes or makes use of stamped paper let him take care of his house, person, and effects.

Vox POPULI.

We Dare!

The Sons of Liberty, it was seen, had been abroad that night. The query next arises, " Who were these Sons of Liberty?" They were members of a great secret order of patriots recently organized in New York, and which soon had its branches in every remote town and hamlet. Its own definition of a Son of Liberty was "a friend and asserter of the rights of the people and the English Constitution, a warm patriot and opposer of the tyrannical acts and pretensions of the British Parliament." In royalist eyes, as we have seen, the Son of Liberty was quite a different person. These hand-bills had their effect. McEvers, to whom the stamped paper was consigned, refused to take it. No one would touch the detested paper. At last, in despair,

108

Lieutenant-Governor Golden had it stored in the fort until the 1st of November should arrive.

That the reader may have a clearer idea of what is to follow, we will pause a moment and consider briefly the theatre and the actors in the drama. The rallying point of the people throughout these troublous days was "the Fields," or "the Common," as it was indifferently called, and which we now know as the City Hall Park. It was the people's Aventine, their Sacred Hill, where they met after each aggression of the ministry, where they were addressed by the tribunes, and where they concerted measures of resistance. These "tribunes" were men singularly well fitted for the responsibility thrust upon them. Among the most active were John Lamb, a New Yorker by birth, an optician by profession, who later became a colonel in the New York Line; Isaac Sears, a merchant in the West India trade, the boldest, most alert, and hot-headed of the patriot leaders; Alexander McDaugall, a Scotchman by birth, who later became a major-general in the Continental army; John Morin Scott, an eminent lawyer; and Marinus Willett, who had marched with Abercrombie to Lake George and Ticonderoga, with Bradstreet to Fort Frontenac, and who later became a lieutenant-colonel in the New York Line, and in 1807 mayor of New York.

Among the more moderate were Oliver Delancey, justice of the king's bench; Robert Livingston, a famous lawyer; Phillip Livingston, " hardware dealer near the Fly Market," later known as one of the signers of the Declaration of Independence; and Peter T. Curtenius, " merchant," later commissary-general of New York in the Revolution. To these were afterwards added, Alexander Hamilton, a student in Columbia College, who later became the greatest statesman of his day; and John Jay, born in New York, December 12, 1745, at this time a law student in the city, later chief-justice of the United States, and a statesman of eminence.

If such were the tribunes, who were the praetors? First in power was Lieutenant-Governor Cadwallader Colden, who, until the newly appointed Governor Sir Henry Moore should arrive, was clothed with supreme authority. He was a man eighty years of age, of the staunchest loyalty, but stubborn, obtuse, who knew of no way of governing except by force. There was General Thomas Gage, irreverently styled " Tom Gage " by the patriots, commander-in-chief of the British forces in America, whose large double house, surrounded by beautiful gardens, stood on the present site of Nos. 67 and 69 Broadway; Major Thomas James, commanding the royal regiment of artillery and owner of " Vauxhall," a beautiful country-seat on the banks of the Hudson, and greatly detested by the people for his arrogance and boastful threats; Rev. Samuel Auchmuty, D.D., rector of Trinity Church; Myles Cooper, D.D,, president of Kings College, later banished for his Tory sentiments and pamphlets; John Antill, postmaster; Daniel Horsmanden, chief-justice of the province; Samuel Bayard, assistant secretary; Colonel William Bayard, the great merchant; John Harris Cruger, treasurer of the city; John Griffiths, master of the port; Thomas Buchanan, to whom later the tea ships were consigned; Daniel Matthews, later mayor, and many others, chiefly those who held office or received emoluments from the king. The fact should be emphasized, however, that there were many among the royalists of the noblest character, who were such purely from loyalty to the crown and from love to their country. The praetors had this advantage over the tribunes, that, quartered in the fort and in wooden barracks on the north side of the Common, were several companies of the 16th and 24th royal regiments, who might be trusted to enforce their commands.

Governor Golden had, in the beginning, greatly incensed the people by repairing and strengthening the fort and by calling in troops from the outposts. " Did he mean to frighten them by this show of force?" the Whig newspapers asked. "Was New York a conquered country to be governed at the point of the bayonet? "

Thursday, the 31st of October, came, the day on which the governor was to take the oath required to carry the Stamp Act into effect. The city awoke in a fever of excitement. " The last day of liberty," it was called; bells tolled; now and then muffled drums were heard beating the funeral march. At an early hour crowds of country people began flocking in. There were, too, many sailors from the ships. The citizens joined them, and all paraded the streets, singing patriotic songs, which mercilessly lampooned the governor, the troops, and the Tories, and threatened dire vengeance on anyone having the hardihood to use the stamped paper. In the evening two hundred of the merchants trading to England proceeded to the City Arms tavern, on lower Broadway, in whose large room the belles and beaux of the day held their " assemblies," and attended concerts and lectures. Here they made brave and patriotic speeches and passed spirited resolutions " to import no goods from England while the Stamp Act remained unrepealed"; "'to countermand all orders for spring goods already sent " to sell no English goods on commission "; and " to buy none from strangers that might be sent out." At the same time, a committee of correspondence, to urge similar action on the part of other cities was appointed. The. merchants of Philadelphia signed this " non-importation agreement," as it was called, on the 14th of November following, the merchants of Boston on December 9th. So we see that both the famous Non-Importation Acts and the Committees of Correspondence of the Revolution all had their origin in New York.

At the same time it was agreed that a grand mass-meeting should be held next evening, November 1st, on the Common. We should have had no stirring, graphic account of what was done at this meeting and afterward, if a young country lad, one E. Carther, had not come to the city from his home in the Highlands, with scores of his neighbors and friends, eager to see and hear all that occurred on this fatal first of November, His letter is one of the classics of the day. It was written, he tells us, when " he was in high spirits and full of old Madeira." First, he informs his parents what the Governor did on this Stamp-Act day, in his contest with the patriots:

" He sent for the soldiers from Tortoise; he planted the cannon against the city; he fixt the cow horns with musket balls. Two cannon were planted against the fort gate for fear the mob should break in loaded with grape shot; he ordered the cannon of the Battery to be spiked up for fear the mob should come so far as to break out a civil war and nock down the fort. Major James had said: ' Never fear; I drive New York with 500 artillery soldiers.' He (Major James) placed soldiers at the Gaol to prevent the Mob letting out the Prisoners. He ordered 15 artillery soldiers at his house near the Coladge where Black Sam formerly dwelt, and the rest of the soldiers he kept within the fort in readiness for an engagement.

" In the evening the citizens began to muster about the streets. About seven in the evening I heard a great Hozaing near the Broadway. I ran that way with a number of others, when the mob first began. They had an ephogy (effigy) of the Governor made of paper, which sat on an old chair that a seaman carried on his head. The mob

110

went from the Fields down the Fly (Pearl Street), Hozaing at every corner, with amazing sight of candles. The mob went from there to Mr. McEvers', who was appointed for stamp master in London. Since he did not accept it, they honored him with three cheers. From thence they went to the fort, that the Governor might see his ephogy if he dare show his face. The mob gave seven Hozas and threatened the officer upon the wall. They jeered Major James for saying that he could drive New York with 500 men. The mob had assurance enough to break open the Governor's coachhouse, and took his coach from under the muzzles of his cannon. They put the ephogy upon the coach, one sat up for coachman with the whip in his hand, whilst others drawed it about the town down to the Coffee House and the Merchants' Exchange."

After being addressed there by their leaders, they turned and marched back to the fort, " with about 500 or 600 candles to alight them."

" I ran down to the fort to hear what they said. As the mob came down it made a beautiful appearance. And, as soon as Major James saw them, I heard him say from off the walls: ' Here they come, by! ' As soon as the mob saw the fort, they gave three cheers and came down to it. They went under the cannon which was planted against them with grape shot. They bid a soldier upon the walls to tell ' the rebel drummer ' (the Governor), or Major James, to give orders to fire. They placed the gallows against the fort gate, and took clubs and beat against it, and then gave three Hozas in defiance. They then concluded to burn the ephogy and the Governor's coach in the Bowling Green before their eyes."

After burning the coach the multitude, which seems to have passed beyond the control of its leaders, went to Major James' house, and destroyed his furniture, saving only one red silk curtain and the colors of the royal regiment, which they carried off in triumph.

" The third day," continues our letter-writer, " they was resolved to have the Governor, dead or alive. The fort got up the fascines in order for battle, and the mob began before dark. The Governor sent for his Council which held about two hours, whilst thousands stood by ready for the word. The Governor consented and promised faithfully to have nothing to do with the stamps, and that he would send them back to London by Captain Davis, of the Edwards."

This account is substantially correct, though written evidently from a royalist standpoint. At the demand of the people, the Governor delivered the stamp paper to the mayor and aldermen, who deposited it in the City Hall, and no further attempt was made to enforce the Stamp Act in New York. The next spring, 1766, a new ministry, with Pitt at its head, having come into power, the odious law was repealed; the Parliament, however, asserted its right to tax the colonies by passing a " Billeting Act," which forced the colonists to maintain the troops quartered among them.

On the arrival of Sir Henry Moore a change was made in the policy of the government. He sought to rule rather by the graces of the courtier and the arts of the diplomatist and succeeded so admirably that the New York Assembly was soon under his control, while the royalist party in the city grew to large proportions. He came as " a friend among friends," he said. The fort was dismantled, the troops dispersed, and the Governor, like a skillful surgeon, devoted himself to healing the wounds his predecessor had made. The earlier part of his reign was marked by one very significant event — a collision between the Sons of Liberty and the soldiers, in which blood was shed, and which antedates by nearly two months the famous Boston massacre, of which so much has been made by historians.

The quarrel arose about a very little matter — a piece of wood called a " Liberty Pole," perhaps forty feet high, standing in the center of the Common, directly abreast of the soldiers' barracks. The soldiers wished very much to cut this pole down; and the patriots were as fully determined that it should stand. Here again a principle was involved. The pole had been erected June 4, 1766, on the anniversary of the king's birthday, to celebrate the repeal of the Stamp Act. Great rejoicings and gratulations attended the act. As day broke, bells pealed and cannon thundered. An ox was "barbecued" on the Common. Twenty-five barrels of beer and a hogshead of punch were provided for the feast. As for the liberty pole, just erected, it flaunted a large banner bearing the electric words: " The King, Pitt, Liberty." Twenty-five cannon were provided to fire a feu de joie, and twenty-five cords of wood were piled about a stout pole, having on its summit a pyramid of tar barrels, which at nightfall would flame into a royal bonfire in honor of His Gracious Majesty and the repeal of the odious act. Now the royalists, and the soldiers especially, were ill-pleased with the repeal of the Stamp Act, which they regarded as a triumph for the people; the liberty pole was to them, therefore, a symbol of defeat. Again, there was bad blood between the soldiers and the citizens, as indeed there ever must be between a spirited people and a body of troops sent out to overawe and coerce them. The soldiers, therefore, determined to destroy the pole which flaunted the " Liberty rag " in their faces. On the 10th of August they succeeded in cutting it down. This created great excitement, and next day a large body of citizens assembled on the Common with the intention of raising the pole again; but they were at once set upon by a detachment of the 24th regiment and dispersed, many being well bruised in the melee. Sears, McDougall, Lamb, and others of the tribunes now collected a little army of the Sons of Liberty, and triumphantly reared the pole. There it remained until the 23rd of September, when the soldiers again destroyed it; but within two days a third was reared in its place. So close a watch was then kept by the patriots, that the soldiers were unable to cut it down by stealth, and it stood in proud defiance until the 18th of March, 1767, when the people celebrated with much spirit the first anniversary of the repeal of the Stamp Act. This enraged the soldiers, and that night the pole was again prostrated. The next day it was raised, and the craft of the ironsmith invoked to secure it with braces and iron bands. At night the soldiers came against it but were unable to destroy it; the next night they attempted in vain to blow it up — an attempt which led the patriots to set a watch to guard their cherished piece of wood. As was expected, the valiant 24th soon came out against it, but were attacked by the guard and so soundly beaten that they fled into their barracks. On the 22nd and 23rd they again attacked the pole, but the whole city having now become aroused. Governor Moore interposed, and commanded the soldiers to cease their aggressions.

The next attempt to destroy the pole occasioned the massacre to which we have referred. Three years had passed, and although several attempts had been made upon it. Liberty's staff still remained erect; but on the 16th of January, 1770, a party of soldiers, by concealing themselves in an old building nearby, succeeded in sallying upon the pole, and cutting it down, and piling it beside the door of Montague's tavern, where the Sons of Liberty were in the habit of holding their meetings. The next day, we are told, nearly the whole city came together in the Common, and, after considering the subject, passed resolutions declaring that all soldiers below the rank of orderly, who appeared armed in the streets, were enemies to the peace of the city, and therefore liable to arrest, as were also those, whether armed or unarmed, who were found out of their barracks after roll-call. This was met with an insulting and taunting placard signed "the 16th Regiment of Foot," which was posted throughout the city by the soldiers. Three of the latter engaged in this work were arrested by two stalwart Sons of Liberty — Isaac Sears and Walter Quackenbos — who attempted to escort them to the mayor's office, but were discovered by a party of soldiers from the lower barracks, who rushed to the rescue. The Liberty boys were on the alert, however, and at once ran to the aid of Sears and Quackenbos, and being armed with canes, bludgeons, knives, paving stones, and whatever else came to hand, a lively skirmish ensued. The soldiers, finding themselves outnumbered, retreated to a small eminence then called Golden Hill, on the present line of John Street between Cliff and William, where, meeting a reinforcement, they made another stand; the bells had by this time alarmed the city; shops were closed; artisans and laborers threw down their tools and rushed by hundreds to the aid of their brethren, and a general melee ensued. The patriots, however, had harder heads and stouter arms than the soldiers, and the latter were forced steadily back and soon found themselves on the summit of the hill tousled and torn, their arms gone, and themselves quite at the mercy of the people, who hemmed them in on every side. The latter had not escaped injury. One had been thrust through with a bayonet. Several were bleeding from wounds. Francis Field, a Quaker, while standing on his own doorstep, had been cut severely in the cheek. At this juncture, another detachment of the 16th came up, and seeing the condition of affairs, called to their fellows to charge through the cordon of people and they would support them by an attack in the rear. Further bloodshed was stopped by the officers of the regiment, who appeared and ordered the soldiers to their barracks. The latter, however, smarted under a sense of defeat, and renewed the fight early next morning by attacking a woman who was returning from market, and who was rescued from her tormentors with a bayonet thrust through her cloak. About noon the military resumed the battle by making a wanton attack on a party of sailors passing through the street. Soon an old man, a sailor, was thrust through and fell, whereupon the mayor tardily appeared and ordered the combatants to disperse. The soldiers derided him, and when a messenger was sent to apprize their officers, they prevented him with drawn swords from proceeding. Fortunately a party of Liberty Boys playing ball nearby heard the shouts and sound of blows and hurrying to the spot drove the assailants off. Still not satisfied, a party of military appeared in the afternoon while a large body of the citizens were gathered in the Common, and charged upon them, though not the slightest provocation had been offered. The crowd opened right and left to give them passage, but, bent on quarrelling, they began snatching canes from the gentlemen present, assailing them meantime with insulting epithets. The gentlemen resisted, however, and so stoutly cudgeled their assailants that they fled in confusion to their barracks. This two days' battle with the military began January 18, 1770. The Boston massacre occurred March 5, 1770, or nearly two months later. The Sons of Liberty, however, erected their pole, which stood until the opening of the great conflict. It was a true liberty pole, far superior to any that had preceded it. It is described as having been " of great length," protected

113

for nearly two thirds its height by iron bands and rivets, and on its topmast was a vane which bore the magic word, " Liberty."

The next event of significance in this epoch was "the Tea Party," which occurred in April, 1774.

We have all read of the famous Boston " Tea Party" of December 16, 1773. New York held hers also, though it did not take place until some three months later, simply because the tea ship destined for New York was driven from her course by a tempest and nearly wrecked, so that she did not reach port until long after due. The Americans were so bitterly opposed to taxation without representation that Parliament decided to abolish nearly all imposts; that on tea and a few other articles was retained in order, as Lord North observed, "to try the question with America." The colonists promptly accepted the gage. When news of the " Tea Act " first reached them (October 20, 1773), the patriots of New York met and " declared that tea commissioners and stamp distributers were alike obnoxious," and passed votes of thanks to the masters of vessels who had refused to charter their ships to convey tea cargoes. The first tea ship was due in New York November 25, 1773, and "The Mohawks," an order identical with that which destroyed the tea in Boston, held themselves in readiness to receive her. At the same time the Sons of Liberty, which as an order had nearly died out, was revived. December 15th news of the arrival of the tea ship at Boston reached New York, and a meeting of the Sons of Liberty was at once held in the City Hall. After letters from the committees of Boston and Philadelphia had been read, and while speakers were urging the union of the colonies for united resistance, the mayor and recorder of the city entered with a proposition from Governor Tryon (who had become governor in 1771), that on the arrival of the tea, it should be taken into the fort at noon-day, where it should remain until disposed of by the king, the council, or the owners; a stern, emphatic " No," three times repeated, negatived the proposition. When the meeting adjourned, it was " until the arrival of the tea ship." By and by (April 18, 1774) the long-expected vessel was reported off Sandy Hook. She was the Nancy, Captain Lockyer, and on the voyage, in a terrible storm, had lost her mizzen-mast and an anchor, sprung her main-top-mast, and sustained other injuries. As Holt's Journal of April 21st wickedly said:

" Ever since her departure from Europe, she has met with a continued succession of misfortunes, having on board something worse than a Jonah, which, after being long tossed in the tempestuous ocean, it is hoped, like him, will be thrown back upon the place from whence it came. May it teach a lesson there as useful as the preaching of Jonah was to the Ninevites."

In this spirit the people received the privileged East India Company's tea.

Although so battered, the New York pilots refused to bring the Nancy farther than Sandy Hook. There, by agreement, a committee of the Sons of Liberty met her, and took possession of her boats that the crew might not escape, and thus prevent her being sent back to England. A part of the committee, however, kindly escorted Captain Lockyer to the city, where, under their guidance, he was permitted to visit his consignee, Mr. Henry White, and was given every facility for repairing his ship and procuring supplies for his return voyage, but under no pretext was he permitted to approach the customhouse to enter his vessel. Three days passed, and the captain was able to say when he would be ready to depart. Next morning (April 21st) the city awoke to find the following placard posted on the doors and street-corners:

" To the Public:

" The sense of the city relative to the landing of the East India Company's tea being signified to Captain Lockyer by the Committee, nevertheless it is the desire of a number of the citizens that at his departure from hence he shall see with his own eyes their detestation of the measures pursued by the ministry and by the East India Company to enslave this country. This will be declared by the convention of the people at his departure from this city, which will be on next Saturday morning at 9 o'clock, when, no doubt, every friend to this country will attend. The bells will give the notice about an hour before he embarks from Murray's Wharf."

Before Captain Lockyer could get away, however, the London, Captain Chambers, was announced. At the Hook the vessel was brought to and boarded by the Liberty Boys, as the Nancy had been, but Captain Chambers positively denied having any tea on board. The Philadelphia committee, however, had sent word to New York that tea was on board, and the committee therefore demanded to see his manifests and cachets. These were shown, but as they mentioned no tea the ship was permitted to come up to the city. The captain's ordeal, however, was not yet over. He had had to deal with only a part of the vigilance committee appointed to watch for the tabooed tea. As the London reached her berth, — about four in the afternoon, — the entire committee marched on board and ordered the hatches opened, declaring their conviction that tea was on board, and assured Captain Chambers that they were ready to open every package in the cargo, if necessary, in order to find it. The captain, seeing that further concealment was impossible, confessed that he had eighteen chests on board; whereupon captain and committee adjourned to the great public room in Fraunces Tavern to deliberate over the matter. They decided, says the chronicler, "to communicate the whole sense of the matter to the people, who were convened near the ship, which was accordingly done. The Mohawks were prepared to do their duty at a proper hour, but the body of the people were so impatient that, before it arrived, a number of them boarded the ship, about 8 p.m., took out the tea, which was at hand, broke the cases and started their contents into the river, without doing any damage to the ship or cargo. Several persons of reputation were placed below to keep tally, and about the companion to prevent ill-disposed persons from going below the deck. At 10 the people all dispersed in good order but in great wrath with the captain; and it was not without some risk of his life that he escaped."

Saturday came, and Captain Lockyer, of the Nancy, made ready to sail on his return voyage to London, his vessel, meantime, having been riding inside the Hook jealously guarded by the Vigilance Committee. As nine o'clock struck, the committee waited on him at his lodgings, at the coffee-house in Wall Street, to escort him to the wharf, while the people, warned an hour before by the sound of bells, assembled in vast crowds to witness the ceremony. The committee began proceedings by leading the captain on to the balcony of the coffee-house, that he might see the people and be seen by them. As he appeared a band struck up " God save the King," and the people greeted him with shouts. Then a procession was formed, with captain and committee at its head, and to the sound of martial music the orderly throng moved down Wall Street to the dock, where a sloop had been provided to convey the captain to the Nancy. Captain and committee filed on board this vessel. Captain Chambers, glad to escape so easily, was also a passenger. As the sloop moved away every bell in the city, except those on the City Hall and Columbia College, rang triumphant peals, the ships in the harbor ran up their gayest colors, the liberty pole on the Common was decked, and the thunder of artillery at its foot proclaimed the triumph of the people.

The last word we have of this brilliant affair is found in one of the newspapers of the day: On Sunday, at lo A.M., the ship and the sloop, with the committee, weighed their anchors and stood to sea; and at 2 p.m. the pilot-boat and the committee's sloop left her at the distance of three leagues from the Hook."

These were the leading incidents in New York of the days immediately preceding the Revolution. During this period, in July, 1771, William Tryon, who had had an inglorious career as Governor of North Carolina, came to the city as Governor, and continued in office until deposed by the Revolution.

XIV. WAR.

Throughout the pregnant period above described, entire separation from the mother-country — independence — had been advocated by none. The colonists still spoke of themselves as Britons, struggling for a Briton's rights. At last came the battle of Lexington, after which they called themselves, not Britons, but Americans. A nation had been born in a moment. This battle of Lexington was fought on Wednesday, April 19, 1775, at four in the morning. On the Sunday following, at four in the afternoon, as Sears, McDougall, Lamb, and other members of the New York Committee of Safety were sitting in the committee-room, a horseman dashed furiously down Broadway and drew rein at their door. Evidently he had ridden far and fast. His horse's eyes were bloodshot, flecks of foam covered his flanks; he trembled and quivered like an aspen. The man bore a paper, which the committeemen opened and read.

" Watertown, " Wednesday morning, near 10 of the clock. " To all friends of American Liberty, be it known that, this morning, before break of day, a brigade, consisting of about 1,000 or 1,200 men, landed at Phip's farm, at Cambridge, and marched to Lexington, where they found a company of our colony militia in arms, upon whom they fired without any provocation, and killed six men and wounded four others. By an express from Boston, we find another brigade are now upon their march from Boston, supposed to be about 1,000. The bearer. Trail Bissel, is charged to alarm the country quite to Connecticut, and all persons are desired to furnish him with fresh horses as they may be needed. I have spoken with several who have seen the dead and wounded. Pray let the delegates from this colony to Connecticut see this: they know Colonel Foster, of Brookfield, one of the Delegates.

"J. Palmer,

" One of the Committee of S. V." (Safety).

There were endorsements by the town clerk of Watertown, and the various Committees of Safety, telling how far and how fast " this messenger of fear and hate " had ridden. The first endorsement was dated at Worcester, April 19th; then followed Brookline, Thursday, 11 A.M.; Norwich, Thursday, 4 P.M.; New London, the same evening, at 7 o'clock; Lyme, Friday morning, 1 o'clock; Saybrook, 4 o'clock the same morning; Killingsworth, at 7 o'clock, A.M.; East Guilford, an hour later; Guilford, at 10 A.M.; Branford, at noon; and Fairfield, Saturday morning, at 8, where the committee added additional intelligence. The New York committee endorsed it on 4 o'clock, Sunday afternoon, and hurried the messenger on. He was at New Brunswick on Monday, at 2 in the morning; in " Princeton," at 6 o'clock; Trenton, 9 o'clock, the same day; and, as appears from an entry in Christopher Marshall's diary, arrived in Philadelphia at 5 P.M. the same day.

As if by magic, behind him the towns and hamlets sprang to arms. So well were the patriots organized in Connecticut that in an instant, as it were, swift riders were spurring with the news to every part of the State. Jonathan Trumbull, her sturdy war governor, at once dispatched an express to Colonel Israel Putnam, hero of the French and Indian wars, whom the messenger found ploughing in his field. He at once dropped the harness from his horse and spurred away to Trumbull, at Lebanon, for orders. " Hurry forward to Concord and organize the army," said the latter; " I will urge forward the troops, arms, munitions." Putnam spurred away, rode all that night, and the next morning at sunrise galloped into Concord, which was filled with

the " train bands " and militia companies of the patriots sadly in need of a leader —
which they found in Putnam. Nearly every town in Massachusetts, Rhode Island, and
Connecticut hurried on its minute men to the seat of war. One old gentlewoman in
Connecticut sent forward her six sons and eleven grandsons, and, like the mother of
the Gracchi, told them to come back with honor or not at all. Over the country roads
of Connecticut marched the quotas of New York, New Jersey, and Pennsylvania,
followed soon by the riflemen of Maryland and Virginia who had been trained to
marksmanship in the Indian wars. Indignation meetings were held in every town,
their united sentiment being voiced in the glowing words of Dr. Joseph Warren, of
Boston: " When liberty is the prize, who would stoop to waste a coward thought on
life? We esteem no sacrifice too great, no conflict too severe, to redeem our
inestimable rights and privileges." Although the government was in the hands of the
Tories, the patriots of New York were no whit behind the other colonies in measures
of resistance. On the same day that the news was received, Colonel Marinus Willett
tells us:

" There was a general insurrection of the population, who assembled, and not
being able to secure the key of the arsenal (in the City Hall) where the colony's arms
were deposited, forced open the door and took 600 muskets, with bayonets, and
cartridge-boxes filled with ball cartridges. These arms were distributed among the
more active citizens, who formed themselves into a volunteer corps and assumed the
government of the city."

Governor Tryon was in England. For Governor Colden the people had a hearty
contempt. The garrison at this time comprised 100 regulars of the 18th Regiment
(Royal Irish) under Major Isaac Hamilton, who confined themselves to their
barracks. Bodies of men went boldly to the customhouse, demanded the keys, and
took possession of the public stores. Two vessels lay at the dock, about to sail with
supplies for General Gage's troops in Boston. Isaac Sears and John Lamb, with their
Liberty Boys, boarded them and quickly unloaded the cargoes, valued at eighty
thousand pounds. Monday came. All business was stopped. Bodies of armed citizens
paraded the streets. The regular authority was overturned. In Paris there would have
been anarchy — the Jacobins and the Commune; but the citizens of New York, eight
days after the overthrow (May 1st), quietly elected a Committee of One Hundred to
govern them until the Continental Congress, which was to meet in Philadelphia in
ten days, should constitute other authority. The tribunes, Sears, Lamb, McDougall,
Curtenius, Scott, Livingston, appear among the One Hundred, but the majority were
either Royalists or moderate Whigs. At the same time, delegates to a Provincial
Congress were elected.

Scarcely were these exciting events over, when it was announced that the
delegates from New England to the Continental Congress were approaching the city,
and almost the entire town turned out to give them a royal welcome. The party
comprised John Hancock, President of Congress, Thomas Cushing, Robert Treat
Paine, and Samuel Adams, of Massachusetts.; and Eliphalet Dyer, Roger Sherman,
and Silas Deane, of Connecticut. As it happened. Miss Dorothy Quincy, of Boston,
the affianced bride of Governor Hancock, had been left behind at the mansion of
his friend, Thaddeus Burr, in Fairfield, and to this fortunate circumstance we are
indebted for the following sprightly letter to her describing the welcome. The letter
is dated at New York, Sabbath evening, May 7, 1775, and proceeds:

118

" At Kingsbridge, I found the delegates of Massachusetts and Connecticut with a number of gentlemen from New York and a guard of the troop. I dined, and then set out in procession for New York, the carriage of your humble servant, of course, being first in the procession. When we arrived within three miles of the city, we were met by the Grenadier Company and regiment of the city militia under arms; gentlemen in carriages and on horseback, and many thousands of persons on foot; the roads filled with people, and the greatest cloud of dust I ever saw. In this situation we entered the city and passing through the principal streets amidst the acclamations of thousands, were set down at Mr. Francis' (the popular tavern of the city). After entering the house three Huzzas were given, and the people by degrees dispersed. When I got within a mile of the city my carriage was stopped, and persons approaching with proper harnesses insisted upon taking out my horses and dragging me into and through the city — a circumstance I would not have had taken place upon any consideration, not being fond of such parade. I begged and entreated that they would suspend the design, and asked it as a favor, and the matter subsided; but. when I got to the entrance of the city, and the number of spectators increased to perhaps seven thousand or more, they declared they would have the horses out, and would drag me themselves through the city. I repeated my request that they would so far oblige me as not to insist upon it. They would not hearken, and I was obliged to apply to the leading gentlemen in the procession to intercede with them. They were at last prevailed upon, and I proceeded. To-morrow morning we propose to cross the ferry. We are to have a large guard in several boats, and a number of the city gentlemen will attend us over. I can't think they will dare to attack us."

The " they " referred to were the Tories. One of the first acts of the Congress to which Governor Hancock and his friends were bound, was to appoint George Washington Commander-in-Chief of the army now gathered about Boston. The latter, as soon as news of Bunker Hill arrived, set out for the seat of war, and reached Hoboken on Sunday, June 25th.

There was in New York at this time quite a corps of delightful letter-writers, of whom Gilbert Livingston, a member of the famous Livingston family; Solomon Drowne, a surgeon in the army; and John Varick, a student of medicine, were chief, who in letters to absent friends gave animated pictures of the scenes transpiring in the city. Livingston, for instance, thus wrote of Washington's entry:

" Last Sunday, about two o'clock, the generals, Washington, Lee, and Schuyler, arrived. They crossed the North River at Hoback (now Hoboken) and landed at Col. Lispenard's. There were eight or ten companies under arms, all in uniform, who marched out to Lispenard's. The procession began from there thus: The companies first, Congress next, two of the Continental Congress next, general officers next, and a company of horse from Philadelphia, who came with the generals, brought up the rear. There was an innumerable company of people — men, women, and children — present."

By a strange coincidence Governor Tryon arrived the same evening from England, and was escorted by the magistrates and militia to the residence of the Hon. Hugh Wallace, where the usual felicitations were indulged in. Washington next morning met the Provincial Congress, then sitting in the city, and conferred with it on military affairs, chiefly no doubt as to the equipping and officering of the three thousand men which the Continental Congress had assigned to New York as her quota for the army about being formed. Four regiments were raised under this call, and Colonels McDougall, Van Schaick, and Holmes were appointed to command them. An artillery company formed part of the force, its captain being John Lamb, whom we have before met. He was soon ordered by the New York Congress to remove the guns in Fort George to the forts that had been raised to guard the passes of the Hudson in the Highlands. While doing this on the night of August 23rd, he was fired on by a sentinel party in a launch belonging to the British frigate Asia stationed nearby. Lamb returned the fire and killed one man and wounded several. The Asia, in return, fired a broadside into the city, her balls ploughing through several houses in the Whitehall and wounding three of Lamb's men. A great panic then ensued. Governor Tryon, writing six days after, observed that at least one third of the inhabitants had left the city. As for the Asia, the provincial authorities ordered that as she had fired upon the city she could no longer be allowed communication with it, and that in future fresh provisions destined for her must be left on Governor's Island. The more ardent patriots deemed this too light a punishment, and they seized and burned several inoffensive milk boats and country sloops that supplied the hated frigate with provisions. " Such is the rage of the present animosity," wrote Tryon in recording the act. A month later he himself was forced to fly from this animosity to the ship Duchess of Gordon, under protection of the Asia.

An incident that occurred in June of this year shows admirably the temper of the men of that day. The one hundred men of the Royal Irish Regiment which had been garrisoning the city, were ordered to Boston to reinforce General Gage, who was closely besieged by the patriot army under Washington and Putnam. The Asia lay at the dock, foot of Broad Street, to receive them. The Committee of One Hundred had consented that the troops should be allowed to embark, against the protest of the Sons of Liberty. On the morning of the 6th, therefore, the column took up its line of march down Broad Street, but a spying Son of Liberty chanced to note that there were six cartloads of spare arms preceding the British column and hurried with the news to Colonel Willett. Now these spare arms belonged to the colony, and the patriots had long cast covetous eyes upon them, arms and munitions of war being the things they then stood most in need of. Colonel Willett, therefore, bade the man alarm the city, and himself hastened to the head of the column and seized the leading horse by the bit. The column stopped and Major Hamilton, commanding, hurried forward and began an angry colloquy with the intruder. Colonel Willett declared that no permission to remove the arms had been granted, and continued arguing until a great crowd, including many of his fellow-leaders, had collected; when he turned the cart to the right and told the carman to drive up Beaver Street. The other five -carts were made to follow amid the huzzas of the people, while the despoiled British were allowed to file on board the Asia These arms were later used in equipping the four New York regiments.

All through the summer of 1775, and the winter of 1775-76 the British remained cooped up in Boston, closely watched by Washington, while the world looked on in surprise. New York, soon to be the theatre of events, was neglected. It was a sad, depressing year for her. All business was suspended. The present was unsettled, and the future terrible with forebodings. John Morin Scott, in a letter dated November 15, 1775, thus described the general depression:

" Every office shut up almost but Sam Jones', who will work for 6 /a day and live accordingly. All business stagnated, the city half deserted for fear of a bombardment. A new Congress elected. Those for New York, you will see by the papers, changed for the better. All staunch Whigs now. . . . Nothing from t' other side of the water but a fearful looking for of wrath. Our Continental petition most probably condemned — the bulk of the nation, it is said, against us; and a bloody campaign next summer. But let us be prepared for the worst. Who can prize life without liberty? it is a bauble only fit to be thrown away."

Early in January Washington discovered that Lord Howe had a movement in hand, and, convinced that New York was his objective point, called the attention of Congress to it, and on the 6th sent General Charles Lee thither to take command and fortify the city. Lee was a regularly educated soldier, having been an officer in the British service, and was therefore well adapted for the position. The British movement was, in fact, the expedition of Sir Henry Clinton against the Carolinas, and as it happened, Clinton, his fleet, and General Lee came into New York on the same day. The former, however, remained but a few days, and then departed for the South.

General Lee's first step was to map out a series of fortifications for the defense of the city. His next, to call before him the Tories, who had long been noted for their virulence and bitterness, and administer an iron-clad oath, of which the following, omitting a few forms and repetitions, is a faithful copy:

" I, ——— , here in the presence of Almighty God, as I hope for ease, honor, and comfort in this world, and happiness in the world to come, most earnestly, devoutly, and religiously do swear, that I will neither directly nor indirectly assist the wicked instruments of ministerial tyranny and villainy commonly called the King's troops and navy, by furnishing them with provisions and refreshments of any kind unless authorized by the Continental Congress. I do also swear, by the terrible and Almighty God, that I will neither directly nor indirectly convey any intelligence ... to the enemy, and I also pledge myself if I should by accident get knowledge of such treasons to immediately inform the Committee of Safety, and to take arms and defend my country whenever called upon by the voice of the Continental Congress."

Captain Sears was sent out into Long Island to administer this oath to the Tories there, who had been particularly active. He was pretty successful, for he soon wrote General Lee, that at Newtown he

had administered the oath to four " grate Tories." At Jamaica he sent out scouting parties but had been able "to ketch but five Tories," although, to make amends, they were " of the first rank," all of whom " swallowed the oath." " I can assure your Honor," he concludes, " they are a set of villains in this country, and I believe the better half of them are waiting for support and intend to take up arms against us." On March 12th, Lee began entrenching.

We are now a city of war," wrote one of the letter writers soon after. Lee was soon sent south to take command in that quarter, and Lord Stirling, a brave and efficient officer was appointed in his place.

On March 17, 1776, Howe evacuated Boston. Washington and his generals supposed that he would at once attack New York; but instead he sailed to Halifax to await the coming of a greater armament from England. The patriot army, however, was hastily transferred from Cambridge to New York, as it was evident that that city would be the next point of attack. General Israel Putnam arrived April 4th and made head-quarters in the fine mansion of Captain Kennedy, of the British arms, at No. 1 Broadway. He held command until Washington arrived, which event occurred on the 13th of April, the Commander-in-Chief selecting as head-quarters the Richmond Hill House, later occupied by Vice-President Adams, and still later by Colonel Aaron Burr; and where he was soon joined by Mrs. Washington and his family. "The people here do not seem so apprehensive of the soldiers' landing since the account of the happy fact of our enemies evacuating the city of Boston, on which I congratulate you and every other friend of Liberty," wrote John Varick to his brother, on April 1st.

The summer was devoted mainly to drilling, organizing, and fortifying, for everyone knew that a powerful armament would soon attack the city. Stirring and startling incidents, however, were continually occurring to break the monotony of entrenching. One day, for instance, a party is sent off to break up a camp of Tories who had fortified themselves without the city and were raiding the country. Another day two negroes are arrested for conveying intelligence to Governor Tryon, "that villainous rascal on board the Duchess of Gordon," as one of the letter-writers put it. Another day a letter came from Kinderhook detailing an affair which had recently happened at a quilting frolic there, which convulsed the young officers with mirth, and "heartened" them more than a great victory. At this quilting it seems but one young man was present, the others being in the army. He was a Tory, and very soon began to cast aspersions on Congress, whereupon he was seized by the young women present, stripped to his waist, coated with molasses in lieu of tar, and feathered with the down from the tops of flags or "cat-tails" found in the marshes. The daughter of Parson Buell, a noted patriot and divine of the day, is said to have been a ring-leader in the work.

"Tory rides" were another diversion. "We had some grand Tory rides in this city this week, and in particular yesterday," wrote Peter Elting on June 13th. "Several of them were handled very rough, being carried through the streets on rails, their clothes torn from their backs, and their bodies pretty well mingled with the dust."

Thus the summer flew on, and the momentous Fourth of July, 1776, arrived. The Declaration of Independence was adopted. Washington received an official copy on the 9th of July, with instructions to have it read to the troops. Accordingly, at six o'clock in the evening, the brigades were drawn up on their respective parades, while the instrument was read by the brigade commanders or their aides. One of the brigades was honored by the presence of the Commander-in-Chief. It was drawn up in a hollow square on the historic Common. Within the square Washington sat on horseback, while an aide in a clear voice, read the Declaration. "When it was concluded," says an eye-witness, "three hearty cheers were given." In the city, bells were rung and guns fired in honor of the event, and a multitude of soldiers and citizens gave further expression to their feelings by attacking and demolishing a leaden statue of George III., which had been erected in 1770 on the Bowling Green. With grim irony they mounted the statue on a cart and drew it with oxen into the heart of Connecticut (Litchfield), where the ladies, under the lead of Oliver Wolcott, a famous patriot leader of that State, ran it into bullets for the army. This conversion of King George's statue into bullets wherewith to destroy King George's soldiers formed the butt of joke, lampoon, and pun for many a day.

Next morning, at White Plains, the Provincial Congress listened to the reading of the Declaration, and at its close pledged themselves to sustain it " at the risk of their lives and fortunes." There were men, too, among them, with fortunes and position to lose. To Van Cortlandt, Van Rensselaer, Schuyler, the Morrises, and the Livingstons, that pledge meant the sacrifice of feudal rights and manorial privileges, yet they seem not to have hesitated an instant. They sent a swift messenger to the New York delegates in Congress empowering them to vote for the Declaration. They had it proclaimed by beat of drum in White Plains and ordered that it should be publicly read from the City Hall in Wall Street, within reach of the guns of the British fleet.

The public reading of the Declaration in New York, on July 18th, was one of the great events of the day. Almost the whole city came together and received each noble sentiment with resounding cheers, and on its conclusion a few daring spirits entered the court-room, brought out the royal coat of arms, and burned it in the street. All this was done, it must be remembered, in the face of a powerful enemy, for at that - moment Putnam's videttes might have counted, from their post on Columbia Heights, one hundred and thirty enemy sails whitening the Narrows — the fleet of Sir William Howe from Halifax, with the Boston veterans and reinforcements. Only six days before — on the 12th — two frigates, the Rose and the Phoenix, had dashed past the city, fired upon and returning the fire, and were now anchored above in the Hudson, a watchful enemy in the rear. But in order to know all about this fleet, and what it was doing, or hoped to do here, it will be necessary to cross over to England and take up the threads of events there.

Parliament had met October 26, 1775. The first and most important subject touched on in the king's opening speech was the American rebellion. " The colonists sought to set up an independent empire," he charged. That " they had raised troops, collected a naval force, seized the public revenues, assumed legislative, executive, and judicial powers," were counts in the long indictment, and he asked Parliament for men and means sufficient for a vigorous prosecution of the war. The king conquered, though Burke, Fox, Barre, Conway, Dunning, and others spoke powerfully in favor of America. An army of 25,000 men was voted for the American war, with a fleet and ample supplies. A plan for a campaign was at once adopted. Sir William Howe, with the main body of the army, was to capture and hold New York. Sir Guy Carleton and General Burgoyne were to march from Canada down the Hudson and divide the Eastern colonies from the Middle and Southern, while Lord Cornwallis was to ravage Virginia and the Carolinas. The one hundred and thirty sail now in the Narrows were here in pursuance of that plan. They were joined, about the middle of July, by a large reinforcement from England under Admiral Howe, and then there were three hundred ships of war and transports in the harbor. On August 1st Generals Clinton and Cornwallis came in, having been repulsed at Charleston; and on August 12th the third and last reinforcement arrived in the person of the British Guards and of De Heister's division of Hessians. To explain the presence of these Hessians we will digress briefly. The war was extremely unpopular with the masses in England. Pitt, Burke, and other Whig leaders carried the people with them, and when the king came to ask for volunteers for the American war, he could not find them. Instead, placards were posted in London streets calling for volunteers to join the Americans. Victory to America and the re-establishment of the British constitution was the prevailing toast at Whig banquets. The clever *bon mot* of the American wits, that General Gage, on returning to England, was to be created " Lord Lexington, Baron of Bunker Hill," was nowhere more greatly relished than in London, A bright woman's epigram on Earl Percy, who commanded the British at Concord and Lexington —

" Earl Percy, there as well as here,

The ladies think is very queer;

They give him tea and keep him warm,

For surely he can do no harm "—

was widely quoted in the English newspapers, while the London Morning Chronicle thus wrote of the brave Continentals who stormed Ticonderoga:

" Brave race of men that lately showed

The British fire in you renewed.

May God your land secure, defend,

(Your constant guardian, your best friend,)

Unite your hearts, your councils bless,

And grant your just designs success."

Another straw, indicating the state of popular feeling, is seen in the case of a young fellow who went into a cook-shop in Covent Garden with his companions, and while there proposed to show them how the Americans would serve Boston. " Suppose," said he, that pan over the charcoal fire to be the town, and the sausage in it to be General Gage and the king's troops. In that case they will be served thus ": and he threw a paper of gunpowder under the pan, which blew its contents high into the air.

King George, finding it impossible to recruit his army with English yeomen, turned his attention to foreign mercenaries. At first he tried to buy Russian peasants; but Catherine, Empress of Russia, said she thought it beneath the dignity of her crown to sell her subjects to conquer brave and oppressed people. In the little German principalities along the Rhine, however, the British agent. Colonel Fawcett, was more successful. From the Landgrave of Hesse Cassel he bought 1,200 infantry; from the Duke of Brunswick 3,900, and a few cavalry; and from the Count of Hanau 660, the price paid being $34.50 per man, three wounded men to count as one dead. The arrival of this great armament — much larger than the famous Armada launched by Philip II. of Spain against England in 1588, — while it inspired great terror among non-combatants, does not seem to have discouraged the Continentals.

" I could not get your shoes," wrote Peter Elting to Captain Varick, July 9th, " on account of the alarm on the arrival of the fleet, since which almost all business in town is knocked up. The fleet," he adds, " now lays very quiet at the watering-place waiting a reinforcement from England, when, they say, they shall little regard our batteries. We as little regard them. Our men are in high spirits, and ready to meet them at any hour."

XV. TWO BATTLES.

On the 18th of August it was apparent to all that a battle was at hand. Washington felt it, and issued a stirring address to his army, exhorting them that the time had come when the future of America was to be determined. " The fate of unborn millions will now depend under God on the courage and conduct of this army,", he said. " Our cruel and unrelenting enemy leaves us no choice but a brave resistance or the most abject submission. We have, therefore, to conquer or die! " But though all knew that the blow must soon fall, none could tell with certainty where it would strike. The enemy might sail up the Hudson or the East River, land in Westchester, and attack the city from the rear; he might disembark on Long Island and advance from that quarter; or he might make a direct attack. Howe chose the Long Island approach; but while he is slowly making preparations, let us sketch the position, the numbers, and the personnel of the contending forces. New York at this time contained 25,000 inhabitants and 4,000 houses, the latter built along both rivers, forming an acute angle, thus <. Most of the town was below the present Chambers Street and comprised an area less than one mile square.

But one highway led off the island — the Kingsbridge, or " Post Road," which left Broadway at the present post-office, followed the line of Chatham Street to Chatham Square, thence the Bowery and Fourth Avenue to 14th Street, crossed Union Square diagonally and followed Broadway to Madison Square, then turned northeast and continued on between Fourth and Second avenues to 53rd Street, turned farther east beyond the line of Second Avenue until it reached 92nd Street, where it turned west and entered Central Park, leaving it again at a hollow in the hills called McGowan's Pass from the fact that a man named McGowan had his farmhouse there. This pass was about on the line of 107th Street, and beyond, the road followed Harlem Lane to the end of the island, crossing the Harlem by a long wooden bridge known as the "King's Bridge"; a short distance beyond, it forked, one branch leading to Albany, and the other to Boston. This was the only bridge and road by which an army could leave the island. There was another road called the " Bloomingdale Road," on the west side, which left the Kingsbridge Road at about the present corner of 23rd Street and Fifth Avenue and passed through the district of Bloomingdale to the farm-house of Adrian Hoofland at 108th Street. There was still another road leading up from the city along the present line of Greenwich Street to the village of Greenwich on the Hudson, which stood about on the present line of 14th Street, and which then connected with a lane running northeast with the Bloomingdale Road at 43rd Street.

The reader will please keep these highways in mind, as we shall again recur to them. It was evident that the city and island being surrounded by navigable waters, were entirely at the mercy of a naval armament unless its defenses were sufficiently strong to repulse an attack. Washington had faith in his defenses.

Let us see what they were. On the Hudson River side the principal ones were McDougall's and the Oyster Batteries on a little eminence in the rear of Trinity Church, the first of two, and the last of three guns. Fort George and the Grand Battery came next, on the north line of the present Battery, the first mounting six guns and the last twenty-three. Then on the East River front were the Whitehall Battery on Whitehall Dock, at the foot of the present Whitehall Street; Waterbury's, on the dock at the angle of Catharine and Cherry streets; Badlaw's, between Madison and Monroe; Spencer's, between Clinton and Montgomery; Jones Hill, a little north of the intersection of Broome and Pitt, and connected with Spencer's by a line of redoubts; a circular battery on the corner of Grand and the Bowery, and another corner of Grand and Eldridge. Last, but not least, was the Bayard Hill redoubt, one of the strongest of the city's defenses. It stood on the corner of Grand and Mulberry, and is described as having been " a powerful, irregular heptagonal redoubt mounting eighteen guns, and commanding the city and its approaches." As for barricades, Paris under the Commune presented no more grisly spectacle. Every street leading up from the water was defended by a cordon of boxes and barrels, kegs, mahogany logs, stones, and branches of trees. City Hall Park was quite enclosed by them. There was one across Broadway opposite St. Paul's Church, one at the head of Vesey, of Barclay, Warren, and Murray streets. A cordon of logs closed Beekman Street to travel. There was a right-angled bulwark on the present site of the Tribune building. Another at the point where Centre Street leaves the Common. Frankfort and Chatham were also barred.

But the batteries on Manhattan Island were not the only ones relied on by Washington to protect the city. As can now be seen, Brooklyn and Columbia Heights across the river commanded the city, and there the more powerful works had been constructed. A chain of earthworks, whose sites are now occupied by Brooklyn mansions, was thrown up across the promontory from Gowanus Marsh to Wallabout Bay. First, and nearest Gowanus Creek, was Fort Box, on the line of the present Pacific Street. Fort Greene came next, three hundred yards to the left of Fort Box, between the present State and Schermerhorn streets. It was a star-shaped battery of six guns, the largest in the series. A small circular battery, called " the oblong redoubt," came next; and to the northeast crowning the hill now forming a part of Washington Park, was Fort Putnam. A small redoubt about the middle of the present Cumberland Street completed the series, which were connected throughout by a line of intrenchments, and protected by ditches and abatis. These forts were intended to defend the Heights.

There were also supporting forts — one on Cobble Hill, near the intersection of Court and Atlantic streets; a redoubt at the mill, corner of Degraw and Bond; Fort Defiance, at Red Hook; and Fort Stirling, commanding the East River channel. In reality, the Brooklyn forts were the key to the position.

Swarming like bees upon these fortifications, marching through the streets, drilling on parade, was perhaps the most incongruous and oddly caparisoned army recruited since Falstaff's day. There were the tow frocks and tarnished scarlet regimentals — mementos of the bloody French wars — of the Connecticut troops; the dark-blue coats, with red facings, of the Delaware militia; the green hunting shirts and leggins of the Marylanders. There were the New Jersey riflemen: some in short, red coats and striped trousers; some in blue coats with leather breeches, ending in blue-yarn stockings, and heavy shoes with brass buckles. Now a Pennsylvania regiment marched by in variegated costume: one company clad in brown coats, faced with white, and adorned with huge metal buttons; another, showing blue coats, faced with red; a third, brown coats faced with buff. Many wore buckskin frocks and leggins. Some marched and fought in their shirt-sleeves. The Virginians created some feeling by their superior uniform — white frocks, adorned with ruffles at neck, wrists, and elbows; black, broad-brimmed slouch hats; black stocks, and hair in long queues.

The arms of this impromptu army were quite as diverse and incongruous. The shotgun and old king's arm of the New England farmer, the long " goose gun " of the New York Knickerbocker, the musket of the Jerseyman and Marylander, the deer-slaying rifle of the Pennsylvania and Virginia rangers, were all represented. Very few were furnished with bayonets or proper accoutrements. There were ostensibly 28,000 men in this army, but only 19,000 in reality, the others being on the sick-list. A few had seen service in the French and Indian wars; the regiments of the Continental line had had the benefit of a year's drill; but the others were raw levies hastily summoned from farms and workshops for the defense of the city. The army was divided into five divisions: Putnam's, which comprised the brigades of Clinton, Scott, and Fellows; Heath's division, comprising the brigades of Mifflin, Clinton, Spencer, Parsons, and Wadsworth; Sullivan's division, consisting of Stirling's and McDougall's brigades; Green's division, of Nixon's and Hand's brigades; the Connecticut Militia, under General Wolcott; the Long Island Militia, under General Woodhull; and Knox's division of artillery, in which, as captain of a battery, served Alexander Hamilton. In the same army, serving as aide to General Putnam, was a young man with whom, later, his name was associated — Aaron Burr, a youth of twenty, son of President Burr, of Princeton College, and grandson of the famous divine, Jonathan Edwards. The general officers, with one exception — Spencer, — were young in years, and had had little or no military training. Many of the subordinate officers, though acquitting themselves like men, were but boys in years; Hamilton, for instance, was but nineteen; Burr, as we have seen, twenty; and Nicholas Fish, Scott's brigade-major, but eighteen.

One arm of the patriot power must not go unmentioned — the odd little fleet of schooners, sloops, periaugers, row galleys, and whale boats commanded by Lieutenant-Colonel Benjamin Tupper that patrolled the harbor, and picked up spies, deserters, provision boats, and intelligence, with the greatest impartiality. It was one of the commanders of this fleet who, on reporting the enemy short of provisions, piously added: " May God increase their wants."

Let us now consider briefly the opposing force and express our wonder at the temerity of the patriots in attempting for a moment to resist it. That army was composed mostly of regulars — men trained to arms. There were the Boston garrison, seasoned veterans from the West Indies, picked men from Gibraltar and other strongholds, Scotch who had won fame in a seven years' war, and Hessians whose trade it was to fight. And then the array of officers — Lieutenant-Generals Clinton, Percy, and Cornwallis; Major-Generals Matthews, Robertson, Pigot, Grant, Jones, Vaughn, and Agnew; Brigadier-Generals Leslie, Cleveland, Smith, and Erskine. There were twenty-seven regiments of the line, four battalions of light infantry, four of grenadiers, two of the king's guards, three brigades of artillery, a regiment of light dragoons, 23,000 officers and privates — with the 8,000 Hessians, forming an army of 31,000 men. It was the best-officered, best-equipped army that King George, with the resources of Europe at command, could muster.

Lord Howe, the Commander-in-Chief, was a just and humane man, whose sympathies were with the Americans. He had been given power to offer free pardon to such of the rebels as would submit, and before launching his force against those whom he could but regard as Englishmen, he desired a conference with the leaders. Accordingly, on July 14th he dispatched an officer in a barge with a letter to

Washington. Tupper's alert whale boats, however, met the officer in the harbor, and detained him while they sent a message to head-quarters. In answer to it, Joseph Reed, Washington's adjutant-general, and Colonel Knox came down to treat with the officer. He received them politely, hat in hand. " I have a letter," said he, " from Lord Howe to Mr. Washington." " We have no person in our army with that address," returned Colonel Reed. " Will you not look at the address? " persisted the officer. " No, sir," replied Reed. " I cannot receive that letter." " I am sorry," said the envoy, and returned to the fleet.

In thus declining to receive a letter not bearing his proper title, Washington was not moved by vanity or any question of etiquette: a grave principle was involved. The Americans now considered themselves a free and independent people, entitled to all the rights of belligerents. If so, Washington was as truly a general as Howe. England, however, denied that the Americans were a nation. She contended that they were rebels, traitors, to her authority, liable to trial and summary execution by court-martial whenever caught. For Howe to have addressed Washington as " General " would have been to acknowledge his claims. For Washington to consent to be addressed as plain " Mr." was to relinquish his claims to being considered a belligerent. In this little by-play before the grand drama both actors appear as skilled diplomatists, as well as soldiers. After much talking, it was later arranged that Colonel Patterson, Lord Howe's adjutant-general, should have a personal interview with the American chief. The colonel came in full dress, attended by his aides, to the Kennedy mansion, where Washington and his generals, also in full uniform, received him with stately courtesy. Colonel Patterson, in behalf of Lord Howe, apologized for the address on the former letter, said no disrespect was meant, and produced another with the inscription: " George Washington, Esq., etc., etc., etc.," which, as it implied everything, he hoped would prove satisfactory. " True," replied Washington. " but it also implies anything "; and he added that he could not receive a letter addressed to him as a private person when it related to his public station. Colonel Patterson then tried to communicate orally the contents of the letter. The king desired to conciliate the colonists and had given to Lord Howe and his brother. Admiral Howe, power to pardon past offences. To this Washington replied that " the Americans, having done no wrong, wanted no pardons. They had but maintained their rights as Englishmen." The interview then terminated, nothing having been gained by it.

His offers of pardon being rejected, Lord Howe decided to fight, and to attack by way of Long Island. At dawn on the morning of August 22nd the frigates Rose and Greyhound^ with the bomb ketches Thunder and Carcass, took position within Gravesend Bay to cover the landing. Then 15,000 soldiers, fully equipped, entered the eighty-six flatboats and bateaux that had been provided, and were rowed in ten divisions to the Gravesend wharf, where they were landed without opposition, only a few Dutch farmers and the pickets of Hand's Virginia riflemen witnessing the affair. At this point, Howe was between six and seven miles from the American defenses, although the skirmish line was three miles nearer.

But before describing the army's movements, let us go over the ground it was to contest. Had you crossed Fulton Ferry in August, 1776, Brooklyn Heights would have risen before you in natural outline, uncrowned by buildings. There were a few farm-houses on the slopes and the two noble mansions of Robert and Philip Livingston on Columbia Heights, but neither city nor village. A road, called the

King's Highway, started from the ferry, and following the present line of Fulton Street, passed through Jamaica and continued on to the eastern end of the island. A mile and a half out on this road a little hamlet had clustered round a quaint old Dutch church, standing in the middle of the street. There was another village at Bedford farther on, one at Gowanus, and another at the Wallabout. As you passed the line of the five forts and went on toward New Utrecht Plains, on which the British army now lay, you came, soon after leaving Bedford, to a ridge of hills extending from New York Bay eastward to Montauk Point through the center of the island, and forming its backbone, so to speak. They were from one hundred to one hundred and fifty feet high, often abrupt, and covered with the dense growth of scrub oak, pine, and bushy thickets, which still prevails farther east. Of course, no army could pass these hills. There were, however, four natural depressions or " passes " in the range, through which roads had been constructed — farthest north was the Jamaica Pass, through which the King's Highway ran on its way to Jamaica and the east; then on the south a road from the King's Highway to Flatlands, one from Bedford to Flatbush; and the coast road from Gowanus to the Narrows. These roads led to villages on the plain, — Flatlands, Flatbush, Gravesend, and New Utrecht. On the coast road, at a noted tavern called the Red Lion, Martense Lane, now the south line of Greenwood Cemetery^ diverged to the southeast through a hollow in the hills and connected with the roads on the plain. Jamaica Pass was four miles from the American line, the Flatbush Pass a mile and a half, and the Red Lion tavern nearly three. General Sullivan held the hill passes, which Washington considered the key to the position, with about twenty-five hundred troops, while Putnam, as Commander-in-Chief in the absence of Washington, remained in the fortified camp. Washington was in New York watching the enemy, and on Long Island Putnam was the central figure.

A rugged, striking figure he was, too, — one of the strongest characters of the Revolution. At this time in middle life, a veteran of the French and Indian wars, a good fighter, a stern disciplinarian, rough in manner, like Miles Standish much readier with the sword than the pen, as the letter opposite, probably written while the army was fortifying New York, shows. The apologists of Washington say — without sufficient proof — that it was by his advice that the battle of Long Island was risked and lost.

Howe's first movement was to send Cornwallis with the reserves to seize Flatbush, but not to attempt the pass if held by the enemy. It was held by the Virginia riflemen; so he pushed on and occupied the village of Flatlands. The position of the Americans at this moment was as follows:

Sullivan took post on a wooded hill near the center; Hand's riflemen watched the Hessians at Flatbush; Miles held the Bedford Pass; a detachment under Parsons took post at the Red Lion tavern on the lower road, while videttes were set to patrol the King's Highway, at the Jamaica Pass. The whole patriot force on the skirmish line did not exceed 2,500 men. Putnam, with the main body, lay within the fortified line, where it was thought he could at once push forward a force to any outpost if attacked. His entire army was scarcely a third of that of the enemy's. Howe lay four days before making an advance, studying his ground and awaiting re-enforcements. On the 25th he was joined by De Heister, with two brigades of Hessians, raising his force to 21,000 men, and on the evening of the 26th he began his advance, the

Hessians and reserves under Cornwallis being massed at Flatbush, the main body, commanded by Clinton and Percy, at Flatlands, and Grant's two brigades near the Narrows. The British plan of battle was an admirable one. Grant, on the extreme left, was to engage the Americans at the Red Lion tavern as a feint merely, his orders being not to press the battle until he heard from the other columns on his right. De Heister was to attack at Flatbush Pass, while the main army would steal around to the extreme right, turn the American line by the unguarded Jamaica Pass, gain the hills, and double up the skirmish line on the main body. It was vitally necessary to the success of the plan that the advance of the flanking force should not be discovered. At nine o'clock, of the night of August 26th, it being quite dark, this column began its march " across the country, through the new lots toward Jamaica Pass," as Lord Howe wrote in his report.

At the front were three Flatbush Tories as guides; then came Clinton with the light dragoons and a brigade of light infantry; then Cornwallis and the reserve, with fourteen pieces of field artillery; lastly. Lords Howe and Percy. The force toiled on in the darkness, along the road from Flatlands as far as Shoemaker's Creek, thence through the fields for a mile or two until they reached the Jamaica Road and came to a halt in the open lots in front of Howard's " Half Way " tavern, a little southeast of the pass. Scouts sent forward reported the latter unguarded. Where, then, were the videttes set to guard it? On this particular night they comprised five young American officers of undoubted bravery and patriotism who had volunteered for the dangerous work, — Lieutenants Van Wagener, who had charged with Montgomery at Quebec, Troup, Dunscomb, Gilliland, and Hoogland. Their orders were to patrol the pass. Had they obeyed orders, a patriot defeat might have been averted; but they were young, ardent, burning for distinction, and so must needs go forward on the road in order sooner to discover the enemy's advance, never once considering that a foe might march across the fields and gain the road in their rear. Yet this was what happened; the British came into the road behind and quickly surprised and captured them. It was a greater prize than Lord Howe knew; there were none now to carry the news of his advance to the patriot camp. The young men were at once hurried into the presence of General Clinton, who questioned them minutely as to the troops, the forts, and dispositions of the American commander. But they sturdily refused to answer, claiming the privileges of prisoners of war. " Under other circumstances," said Dunscomb, "you would not dare insult us in this manner." Clinton, angry, called him an " impudent rebel," and threatened to hang him, — a threat which terrified the prisoners but little; " for," as Dunscomb significantly observed, Washington can hang man for man. " The column now marched through the pass and down the King's Road to Bedford, where it arrived at about half-past eight in the morning. It was in the rear of the American left, still undiscovered, and much nearer Putnam's fortified camp than were his outposts on the skirmish lines. A swift push forward and the British might break through the chain of forts and cut off the Americans from their New York supports. In their present position the British could not hope to remain long undiscovered. Miles, who had been marching 'back and forth all the morning in search of them, discovered them at last in full possession of the Jamaica Road, between him and the forts. The British promptly attacked him in the rear, while the Hessians pressed forward in front at Bedford Pass, and drove the troops there back upon Miles; at the same time, cannonading in the direction of the Red

130

Lion inn proved that Grant was on time, and had engaged and overlapped the American right. The patriots were in a trap. Failure to guard the Jamaica Pass had undone them. They did the best thing possible under the circumstances, — broke and fled into the wood, and made their way back to the American lines as best they could. Many were captured, and a few regained the forts.

Meantime the honors of the day had been gained by Stirling, Parsons, and their sturdy troops of the Connecticut, Maryland, and Pennsylvania lines. At two o'clock that morning Grant's advance had driven in the American pickets at the Red Lion tavern. Word was quickly sent to Parsons, who commanded in that quarter, and to Putnam in the camp. Parsons hurried down, and with a squad of twenty men, hastily collected, held the enemy in check for some time. Putnam, who had been ordered to hold the outposts at all hazards, at once sent Lord Stirling with a force of 1,600 men to check the enemy's advance. Stirling found the latter moving down the road nearly half a mile this side the Red Lion on their way to the forts; directly before them was a bridge over a little creek, and on the Brooklyn side rose a small hill known as Blockyesbergh. Stirling seized on the creek and hill as his line of resistance.

The British line of battle was formed on the opposite bank, and as on the right it overlapped the American, Parsons was sent to take possession of a small hill, which would extend the patriot line on the left some three hundred yards. The British first gained this hill, and Parsons made a gallant assault before he could carry it, but at last it was his. The two armies now confronted each other for two hours, it being contrary to orders for Grant to force a battle until he heard the guns of the flanking column. Stirling's men were 1,600 strong, the enemy 7,000, and their bravery in facing in open field an enemy so much superior is worthy of remembrance. Meantime a brisk artillery fire was kept up, and very soon Parsons, on his hill — now the beautiful Battle Hill of Greenwood Cemetery, — was attacked by the enemy, whom, however, he again repulsed.

At ten Grant heard firing at the passes and knew that Howe was in the American rear. He at once began pushing Stirling harder, but the Americans held their ground heroically. Eleven o'clock — half past eleven came, and still no orders to retreat, although Stirling knew from the firing that the enemy were gaining his rear. At last, about noon, he attempted a retreat. It was too late; he was surrounded. Cornwallis, with the 71st Regiment and the Grenadiers, was on the Gowanus Road. Looking about to see how he might save his brave fellows, Stirling saw on his left Gowanus Creek and a marsh that was deemed impassable Across on the opposite shore were the American redoubts and safety. He ordered his men to break ranks and cross the marsh as best they could, while he, with Gist's and half the Maryland battalion, should hold Cornwallis in check, thus giving them time to escape. This plan was carried out. Most of the men escaped across the marsh, whereupon Stirling, seeing they were beyond danger, and finding that his Spartan band was being borne back into a thick wood, gave his men orders to disperse and save themselves. Nine men under Major Gist succeeded in crossing the creek and escaping; but most of them, with the brave Stirling himself, were made prisoners. The greater part of Parsons' brave fellows on Battle Hill were also taken, though the General with quite a number succeeded in hiding himself in a swamp and thence gained the American lines.

Just as Stirling made his bold stand, Washington reached the forts. Smallwood, who had gained the lines with the Marylanders, begged to go to his assistance, but

Washington said the risk was too great. He, however, dispatched Douglas' Connecticut levies and Thomas' Marylanders, with two guns, to a point opposite the mouth of Gowanus Creek, to check the enemy's advance.

Thus ended the battle. The Americans were defeated. The British were close upon their line of forts. Only this thing had been gained. The patriots, as in the case of Stirling's men, had proven that they could meet the British veteran in open line of battle and defeat him in fair fight. Washington ordered over additional troops from New York and Harlem but could not conceal the fact that his army was in bad plight. If the enemy should assault and carry his redoubts, or if the British frigates should sail up and command the ferry in his rear, the capture of his entire force was certain. On the 29th he called a council of his generals to consult on the advisability of retreating to New York. Several reasons were given for the step. The loss in officers and men in the defeat of the 27th had occasioned confusion. The men were tired out with constant watching and alarms; their arms and ammunition had been rendered nearly useless by the rain of the last two days. The enemy was trying to get his ships into the East River. Lastly, Howe was advancing by trenches parallel with the American works, and an assault might soon be expected. It was decided, after long discussion, to retire to New York.

" To conduct a skillful retreat," someone has said, " is equal to winning a great victory." Washington conducted this retreat in the most masterly manner, and in part atoned for his bad generalship in trying to defend the city. As soon as it was resolved to retreat he sent Colonel Trumbull to Assistant Quartermaster Hughes in New York, with orders to at once impress every kind of craft, from Hell Gate to Spuyten Duyvil Creek, that could be kept afloat, and have them all in the " east harbor " by dark. Trumbull was also ordered to send a messenger to General Heath, commanding at Kingsbridge, to impress all the boats in his district, and to man them with the Salem and Marblehead fishermen of his command. The boats were required, it was said, to ferry over some New Jersey troops, who were to take the place of others relieved.

In his general orders to the army, Washington employed the same fiction, — a retreat was not mentioned, — they were to be relieved by fresh New Jersey militia. Every regiment was ordered to be ready to march at dark, knapsack on back, and arms and camp equipage in hand. It was a busy day for General Heath and Colonel Hughes. The entire water-line of Manhattan Island was scoured, and, by sunset, every craft that would float was impressed and moored at the Fulton Ferry dock. It was an odd fleet — sloops, sail-boats, galleys, periaugers, flat-boats, row-boats, whale-boats, — manned by the hardy Salem and Marblehead fishermen. At dark the army was ready, each regiment being drawn up on its parade. First, Hitchcock's Rhode Islanders marched to the ferry, "through mud and mire, and not a ray of light visible," their place being at once supplied by another brigade; and so the retreat went on, the place of each regiment, as it moved, being noiselessly taken by its fellow. Out on the redoubts the camp-fires blazed brightly, and the sentinels called the hours within hearing of the British pickets. Six regiments, under General Mifflin, held these redoubts. At two in the morning, a nearly fatal blunder occurred. An aide, by mistake, brought an order for Mifflin's command to march to the ferry, which was still crowded with the retreating army. On the road, however, the mistake was discovered, and the men gallantly returned to the deserted earthworks. As day broke in the east, the main army and its militia was on the New York side. Mifflin's force still held the forts. How should they be drawn off undetected? The question was answered as if by a special Providence. Ranks of heavy fog-clouds rolled up from the bay and drew around the frowning heights an impervious curtain. Mifflin was safe. As the last outpost retired it heard distinctly the sound of shovel and pickaxe in the British trenches. Before 7 A.M., the entire force was over the river. " Washington," said Colonel Chamberlain, " saw the last man over himself." He had been for nearly forty-eight hours in the saddle. When Howe awoke that morning, he found that an army of nine thousand men, with stores, baggage, and artillery, had been spirited away from under his guns while his army slept.

The 30th and 31st of August, 1776, were gloomy days in New York. Tents, clothes, baggage, all manner of camp equipage, soaked with rain, encumbered the streets and sidewalks. Squads of soldiers moved wearily and dispiritedly about or lingered on the corners. The inhabitants who were unable to flee kept within doors. In a few days, however, the army was reorganized, and order and confidence were restored. The burning question then was, whether to attempt to hold the city against all odds, or to burn it, and retreat to the fastnesses of the Hudson. The matter was debated for several days by Congress (to whom it was referred), and by the generals. At length. Congress gave Washington sole discretion in the matter. On September 12th, he called a council at his head-quarters in the Richmond Hill House, and there it was decided to evacuate the city — without burning it, however, as Congress thought it might be recovered. It was time to retreat; already the British had seized the islands in the Harlem River, with the evident design of capturing Harlem Heights, which commanded the city on the north.

On September 3rd, the frigate Rose of thirty-two guns had sailed by the batteries and up the East River conveying thirty boats which were to be used in the crossing. On the 12th thirty-six more boats passed up, and on the 14th the frigates Roebuck, Phoenix, Orpheus, and Carysfort, with six transports, joined the Rose. On this day all the teams and transports of the Americans had been employed in removing to Kingsbridge the sick, wounded, and stores. Another day and the work would have been done. Unfortunately it had been begun a day too late, for next morning the British moved upon the city, and in the afternoon it fell. The cove that now sets in from the East River at the foot of East Thirty-fourth Street was then known as Kip's Bay. There were several earthworks there, and around arid below it five American brigades were distributed to watch the enemy. Sullivan's division garrisoned the city. Parsons' was at Corlear's Hook below Kip's Bay. Scott's New York brigade was on the Stuyvesant estate near the present Fifteenth Street. Wadsworth, with the Connecticut levies was at Twenty-third Street, Douglas with three Connecticut militia regiments at Kip's Bay. Putnam's division was also in the city guarding the forts and barricades. Washington on the eve of the 14th had left New York and had fixed his head-quarters at the Apthorpe mansion on the Bloomingdale Road, which one may still see, a quaint reminder of old days, at the corner of Ninth Avenue and Ninety-first Street.

Such was the situation on Sunday morning, September 15th. A little after daybreak Douglas, at Kip's Bay, saw the five frigates make sail and slowly move up abreast of his position. " They were so near," said a soldier, " that I could distinctly read the name of the Phoenix which lay a little quartering." But the militia soon had other objects to look at, for presently from the mouth of Newtown Creek, nearly opposite, emerged a flotilla of eighty-four row galleys filled with grenadiers in scarlet uniforms, looking, as the soldier above quoted aptly said, " like a large clover field in full bloom." Slowly the boats came on; as they neared the shore, all at once with a thundering sound the seventy-five guns of the frigates belched a storm of grape-shot on the devoted patriots. " It came like a peal of thunder," says Martin. Sharpshooters stationed in the frigate's tops picked off every man that showed himself. One soldier thought " his head would go with the sound," " but," he added, " we kept the lines until they were almost levelled upon us, when the officers seeing we were exposed to the rake of their guns, gave the order to leave." At the same moment, a little to the left, under cover of the cannon smoke, the flotilla was beached, and the troops threw themselves ashore without opposition. The Americans all along the river front now began a retreat, which soon ended in a panic-stricken flight with the British in hot pursuit. Up the Post Road fled the militia — every man for himself — Parsons, Douglas, Prescott, and Huntington in vain trying to rally and reform them. At the corner of Fourth Avenue and Thirty-sixth Street, with grounds extending through to the Kingsbridge Road (which then ran on the present line of Lexington Avenue), stood the handsome mansion of Robert Murray, a wealthy Quaker merchant of New York. Just above, covering the present line of Forty-second and Forty-third streets, a wide lane crossed the island and connected with the Bloomingdale Road. On the south side of this lane, where it joined the Post Road, was a large cornfield. Washington, at the Apthorpe house, on hearing the firing, leaped to saddle, spurred down the Bloomingdale Road and across by the connecting lane toward the Kingsbridge Road. He had just reached this cornfield as the mob of frightened fugitives came hurrying on, some taking the fields in their haste, some toiling and panting along the road. Parsons' and Fellows' brigades, which had been ordered up to check the rout, also came up at this moment. Washington ordered them to form and make a stand along the line of the Post Road. " Take the walls; take the cornfield," he shouted.

The men ran to the walls, but the vanguard of the enemy just then appearing over the crest of the hill they broke and fled in a panic equal to that of the militia. Washington, Putnam, Parsons, and other officers dashed in among them, endeavoring to rally them, but in vain. The senseless panic that sometimes seizes even brave men in battle was upon them, and as the lines of gleaming bayonets appeared they broke and fled.

Washington at the sight is said to have lost the self-control habitual with him. He dashed in among the confused mass swinging his hat and shouting to them to re-form and make a stand against the enemy; his officers ably seconded him — in vain, however. "The very demons of fear and disorder," said a soldier, " seemed to take full possession of them all and of everything on that day." Seeing that the field was lost, the Commander-in-Chief ordered the retreat continued to Harlem Heights, while he spurred away to make dispositions for defense there.

Meantime what of the soldiers left in the city? At the first note of attack Putnam's division had been put in motion toward Harlem, taking the Bloomingdale Road, which, as has been mentioned, ran along the west side of the island; but the column was forced to move slowly; it was hampered with refugee women and children, by stores, cannon, camp impedimenta; besides, stretching along the country road for two miles, it was very unwieldy, and the sun was intensely hot. To cover its retreat, Silliman with his brigade, and Knox with his artillery took post at Bayard's Hill Fort, which we have described as standing on the bluff north of Canal Street, and as being one of the strongest of the city's defenses. This was perhaps two hours before the rout began at Murray's cornfield. On leaving the retreating force there, Putnam spurred down to look after the fortunes of his column, first detaching his aide, Major Aaron Burr, with a company of dragoons, to bring off Silliman's and Knox's force at Bayard's Hill — a congenial task for Major Burr, who had already distinguished himself by his gallantry. Soon he dashed up to the redoubt and inquired who commanded there. General Knox appeared, and Burr delivered his orders, imploring him to retreat at once, as a column of Hessians was then advancing down the Post Road upon the city, and the fort would inevitably be taken. Knox replied that they would be cut off in any event, and that he preferred to defend the fort. "But," urged the intrepid aide, "it is not bomb proof; you have no water; I would engage to take it with a single howitzer." And turning to the men, he told them that if they remained there, one half of them would surely be shot before night, and the rest hung like dogs; " whereas," said he, " if you will put yourselves under my guidance, I can and will lead you in safety to Harlem." The brigade decided to retreat. Burr led it at once to the main column, then put himself at the head of all, and by lanes and by-ways, through thicket and forest, led it past the British advance to Harlem, while Captain Alexander Hamilton's battery served as rear-guard, and gallantly beat back, on more than one occasion, a squadron of the pursuing enemy.

The credit for this happy escape was accorded Major Burr and gave him great prestige in the army. Had Howe pushed forward his troops, however, he might easily have cut off the column. At the fine old mansion of the Murrays, within half a mile of the road by which the patriots were escaping, his main army was encamped at the time, and he, with Tryon, Clinton, Cornwallis, and others, was sipping Mrs. Murray's rare old Madeira, while his troops prepared and ate the mid-day meal. But perhaps, as was later charged, General Howe had no desire to capture the mass of fugitives.

The army was now out of the city. The battle scene was transferred to Harlem Heights. If one stands upon the high bluff where 119th Street crosses Morningside Park, a few squares north of the Leake and Watts Orphan House, — the site of the proposed grand cathedral, — he can take in the battle-field at a glance. At his feet Harlem Plains, well built over, stretches away to the east. Directly north, across the valley, at about 125th Street, rises a bold promontory, known in 1776 as Point of Rocks, and which sweeps away northwest in a series of rocky points and ledges, three quarters of a mile to the Hudson. On these heights Washington's army was massed on its retreat from the city, the headquarters of the general being fixed at the Morris House, now the Jumel mansion, which one may still see on the rocky height southwest of High Bridge — a fine example in decay of old colonial architecture.

The British were directly opposite on Bloomingdale Heights — where we are supposed to stand, — with their pickets stretched across the upper part of Central Park to Horn Hook on the east, and across Riverside Park to the Hudson on the west. The low land between, showing here and there a farm, but mostly covered with forest, with the crag on which we stand, was the scene of the battle of Harlem Heights. It was the object of the British to capture the heights and thus force the Americans off the island. The latter, however, assumed the aggressive, and brought on the battle. From Point of Rocks Washington with his field-glass could sweep the Harlem Plains, and easily see what the enemy was doing in that quarter. Not so with the forest and broken land along the Hudson. At daylight, therefore, on the morning of the 16th, he dispatched Colonel Thomas Knowlton, one of his bravest officers, with a force of one hundred and twenty picked men, to make a reconnaissance in that direction, and unearth the enemy — if possible capture his advanced guard. This guard comprised two battalions of the light infantry supported by the 42nd Highlanders and was pushed forward nearly to the southern limits of the present Morningside Park. Knowlton led his men down the ravine now marked by Manhattan Street, to the river bank, and then south under cover of the bluffs and forest until he came upon the enemy, when a sharp skirmish occurred; but after firing several rounds Knowlton, finding that the British were pushing north in such a way as to outflank him, began a leisurely retreat. Meantime the enemy had appeared on Harlem Plain, and Washington hurried to the Point of Rocks to direct the movement of troops. Hearing Knowlton's firing to the south he sent Adjutant-General Reed in that direction to see what it meant. Reed soon returned and reported that Knowlton was being pursued by some three hundred of the enemy, whom he was drawing away from their supports and into the patriot lines. Washington then sent forward reinforcements, and the British were driven ingloriously back to their main line. It was a small affair, but it restored to the Americans that esprit du corps which had been banished by the retreat of the preceding day.

The second or main battle began about ten o'clock and lasted till two in the afternoon. Knowlton's men on meeting the enemy had recoiled and made an orderly retreat before a superior force. At ten o clock, as Washington sat on his horse awaiting reports from scouts, Knowlton hurried up and begged for reinforcements to capture his pursuers. At the same moment a body of troopers appeared in the plain below and blew their bugles in the face of the Americans, as if at a fox-hunt. Washington accepted the challenge. He ordered Major Leitch with his Virginia Riflemen to join the Connecticut Rangers under Knowlton and gain the rear of the foe by their right flank, while another detachment engaged them in front. The British, seeing so few enemies before them, pushed down into the valley under the Point of Rocks to engage them. The rattling volleys hurried up the British reserve corps in support; at the same time the riflemen and rangers, by some misunderstanding, struck the right flank of the enemy instead of the rear as had been intended. At this the British leaders became alarmed and ordered up their choicest regiments. Washington responded with detachments of Douglas', Nixon's, Richardson's, and Griffith's regiments, the very troops which had so ingloriously fled the day before, and the battle in the plain became general. Meantime the column under Knowlton and Leitch had attacked with so much spirit that the enemy gave way and was rolled in on Bloomingdale Heights, hotly pursued by the patriots. In the plain, too, the battle had gone against the British, and they also fell back upon the heights, where the combined force made a stubborn stand.

Just here, between Morningside Drive and Ninth Avenue, a little south of the line of 119th Street, Knowlton and Leitch both fell at the head of their troops. An officer stooped over Knowlton as he fell. " Are you badly hurt? " he asked. "Yes," replied the dying patriot; but I value not my life so we win the day." When Morningside Park is laid out, the city would do well to commemorate by a suitable statue the place where these heroes fell. But, though the leaders had fallen, the battle still raged. At last the British were driven from the hill-top as they had been from the valley. About noon, receiving fresh succors, they made a stand in a buckwheat field and held their ground for nearly two hours, but were finally routed and chased for two miles, the Americans mocking their bugles as they pursued.

Thus in victory for the American arms ended the battle of Harlem Heights. It was not a great battle — there were in all barely ten thousand men engaged, — but it was an important one, chiefly because it restored to the patriots that confidence in themselves which had been lost by the inglorious retreat from New York. Washington remained on the heights for three weeks, confronting his foe, and then removed his army to the highlands of the Hudson in the upper part of Westchester County.

XVI. NEW YORK IN CAPTIVITY.

Meantime the city was in the grasp of the invaders. When Howe took possession, September 16th, it bore much the appearance of a dismantled town. Houses and stores were closed, bells removed from churches and public buildings, brass knockers from houses, everything portable and of value the flying people had taken with them. On Saturday, the 21st, at midnight, a fire broke out in a low groggery near Whitehall Street, in the southeastern part of the town, and fanned by a strong south wind, swept like a prairie fire through the city. It ran up Whitehall to Broadway, and up the east side of that thoroughfare to Beaver, where with a change of wind it leaped the street and sped on up the west side, sweeping everything clean to the North River. Trinity Church, with its rectory and charity school, and the Lutheran Church, were soon blackened heaps of ruins. St. Paul's was saved only by the desperate efforts of citizens, who climbed out upon its flat roof and quenched live embers as they fell. The flames were only checked by the open grounds and stone buildings of King's College. *' This fire was so furious and so violently hot that no person could go near it," wrote an eye-witness. " If one was in one street and looked about, the fire broke out already in another street above, and thus it raged all the night, and till about noon," wrote the Rev. Mr. Shewkirk, pastor of the Fulton Street Moravian Church. Four hundred and ninety-three houses, (some accounts say 1,000) and several churches were destroyed. The British jumped to the conclusion that the Americans were burning the town to prevent its serving them as winter quarters, and they bayoneted several worthy citizens who were putting out the fire, and threw others into the flames, under the impression that they were the incendiaries. The patriot leaders indignantly repelled the charge. " By what means it happened, we do not know," wrote Washington to Governor Trumbull the day after the fire, September 23rd, and Colonel Reed wrote to his wife the same day: "There was a resolve in Congress against our injuring it, so that we neither set it on fire, nor made any preparations for the purpose; though I make no doubt it will be charged to us," — as it was by Lord Howe in his official dispatches. This fire incensed the British, and many outrages were committed on the helpless patriots. Among other things, the library and apparatus of King's College, which had been stored in the City Hall, were stolen, and publicly hawked about the streets, or bartered in liquor saloons for a dram.

Following close upon the fire came one of the saddest and most tragical incidents in the city's history — the execution of Captain Nathan Hale as a spy. This young officer, barely twenty-one, a graduate of Yale, and betrothed to a beautiful girl, had volunteered to penetrate the British lines around New York, and gain intelligence of Howe's numbers and position. He went to Fairfield, Connecticut, and, making use of Captain Brewster's whale-boat service, crossed the Sound to Huntington, on the Long Island shore, whence, disguised as a schoolmaster, he easily succeeded in entering the British lines. He succeeded, too, in collecting the information desired, and returned to Huntington Bay, where it had been arranged that a whale-boat should meet him and return with him to the Connecticut shore. A boat was in waiting near the shore, and Captain Hale approached it confidently, only to find that it was a yawl from a British frigate lying near. There was no escape; he submitted to his captors and was sent to New York as a "a prisoner taken within the lines " — that is, as a spy. There was short shrift for a rebel and a spy in the first year of the war.

Howe called a court-martial next day at his headquarters in the fine old Beekman mansion to try him. The prisoner waived a trial, however, and boldly avowed himself a spy in the service of General Washington; and the board at once condemned him to be hung the next day, which was Sunday. Until that time the prisoner was given in charge of the brutal Provost-Marshal Cunningham, and probably confined in the new Gaol, of which we shall say more presently. He asked for pen and paper that he might write a last letter to his mother, but this was denied; for a Bible, but the request was refused. An English officer, however, is said to have interposed, and to have furnished him with the articles desired.

Hale's conduct in the hour of death illustrates in a striking way the spirit of the times. The scene of execution was the Rutgers orchard, a site now covered by the blocks of huge buildings on East Broadway, a little above Franklin Square. As he stood upon a cart under the apple boughs a British officer, one of a group standing near, said, tauntingly: "This is a fine death for a soldier." " Sir," replied Hale, " there is no death which would not be rendered noble in such a glorious cause." His last words form one of the noblest sentiments of humanity, a heritage of the race. Andre, in a similar situation four years later, uttered the sentiments of a soldier, but Hale's last words breathed only the loftiest patriotism. " I only regret," said he, " that I have but one life to lose for my country."

For seven years, or until the return of peace, in 1783, New York remained a captured city; martial law prevailed; the city was made a depot for stores, a rendezvous for troops, the hospital of the British army, and the prison-house of those Americans unfortunate enough to be taken in arms. When the battles attending the capture of the city were over, it is safe to assume that Sir William Howe had, at least, 5,000 prisoners to provide for. To contain so large a number the ordinary prisons were, of course, inadequate, and other places were sought. The Brick Church, the Middle Dutch, the North Dutch, and the French churches, all fine, handsome structures, were despoiled of their fittings, and appropriated to this use. Besides these, King's College, the Sugar House, the new Gaol, the Bridewell, and the old City Hall, were filled with prisoners, and to this array were added, later, the prison ships of the East River.

The sufferings of the poor prisoners through the brutality of Captain Cunningham, Howe's provost marshal, were terrible, and, more than the musket and the sword, depleted the ranks of the patriots.

They who entered the British prisons, like Dante's pilgrims to the Inferno, left hope behind.

In Liberty Street, south of the Middle Dutch Church, stood until forty years back, a dark stone building five stories high, with small, deep windows rising tier above tier like portholes in a hulk. Each floor of this building was divided into two bare, dungeon-like apartments, on the walls of which later visitors were fond of tracing the carved names and dates that had been cut by the knives of the prisoners nearly a century before. This was the old sugar house of the Livingstons. A strong gaol-like door opened on to Liberty Street, and another on the southeast gave entrance to a dismal cellar. While occupied by the prisoners -two English or Hessian sentinels were constantly on guard, lest some desperate captive should attempt to escape. " In the suffocating heat of summer," said William Dunlap, *' I saw every narrow aperture of those stone walls filled with human heads, face above face, seeking a portion of the external air." " Seats, there were none," says another narrator, " and their beds were but straw intermixed with vermin. For many weeks the dead cart visited the prison every morning, into which eight to twelve corpses were flung, and piled up like sticks of wood, and dumped into ditches in the outskirts of the city."

Worse than this were the prison ships, which were at first intended for prisoners taken on the high seas, but later accommodated landsmen as well. The most important were the Jersey, Whitby, Good Hope, Prince of Wales, Falmouth, Scorpion, Strombolo, and Hunter. The Jersey, from the great numbers confined in her, and the fearful mortality among them, had a more ominous fame. It was confidently asserted that no less than 10,644 prisoners perished in her during the war and were buried on the neighboring shore. These fever-infested old hulks were moored in the East River — most of them in the sheltered little bay known as the Wallabout. When a prisoner was brought on board, his name and rank were registered, his weapons and money, if he had any, were taken, and he was ordered below into the hold, where he found a thousand wretched beings racked with disease and emaciated with hunger. He at once joined a " mess " of six persons, and every morning at the ringing of the steward's bell, formed in line, and received his daily ration of biscuit, peas, and beef, or pork. Sometimes oat meal, flour, suet, and butter were added to the bill of fare, but the poor prisoners never saw vegetables. " The peas," we are told, " were damaged, the butter rancid, the biscuit moldy, and often full of worms, the flour sour, the beef and pork unsavory. Not so much the fault of the king, as of his rapacious commissaries, who exchanged good provisions for bad, and by curtailing rations and other expedients, heaped up large fortunes at the expense of the prisoners."

Every morning the poor fellows brought up their beds to be aired, washed down the floors, and spent the day on deck. At sunset the guards cried " Down, rebels, down! " the hatches were fastened over them, and in the stifling fever-infected atmosphere the prisoners lay in rows to sleep. When a man died his fellows sewed his body in his blanket, lowered it into a boat, and accompanied by a guard, rowed ashore, and buried it in a shallow trench in the bank or on the shore. Not unfrequently the prisoners escaped, despite the vigilance of the sentinels. One night, in 1779, ^o" instance, on the Good Hope, nine sea captains and two pirates overpowered the guard, and got away in one of the ship's boats; and in the severe winter of 1780, fifteen prisoners escaped on the ice that bridged the East River.

The officers and more distinguished civilians were confined in the new Gaol in City Hall Park, now the Hall of Records. In this prison were also the headquarters of Captain Cunningham, the provost-marshal of the city, who, by all accounts, was a most cruel and heartless villain. The officers seem to have been treated no better than were the privates. A creditable witness, Mr. John Pintard, clerk of Elias Boudinot, the commissioner appointed by Congress for securing the exchange of prisoners, speaks thus of it:

" An admission into this modern bastile was enough to appal the stoutest heart. On the right hand of the main door was Captain Cunningham's quarters, opposite to which was the guard-room. Within the first barricade was Sergeant O'Keefe's apartment. At the entrance door two sentinels were posted day and night; two more at the first and second barricades, which were grated, barred, and chained; also at the rear door and on the platform of the grated door: and at the foot of the second flight of stairs leading to the rooms and cells in the second and third stories. When a prisoner, escorted by soldiers, was led into the hall the whole guard was paraded, and he was delivered over with all formality to Captain Cunningham or his deputy, and questioned as to his name, rank, size, age, etc., all of which were entered in a record book. What with the bristling of arms, unbolting of bars and locks, clanking of enormous iron chains, and a vestibule as dark as Erebus, the unfortunate captive might well shrink under this infernal sight, and parade of tyrannical power as he crossed the threshold of that door which possibly closed on him for life. The northeast chamber, turning to the left on the second floor, was appropriated to officers and characters of superior rank, and was called Congress Hall. So closely were the prisoners packed that when they laid down at night to rest, when their bones ached on the hard oak planks and they wished to turn, it was altogether by word of command ' right,' "left' being so wedged in as to form almost a solid mass of human bodies."

It is well to recount these sufferings — the price of liberty — to the boys of to-day, that they may value their birthright accordingly.

New York was not a pleasant place of residence during these seven years. Martial law, with its rigors, bore heavily upon the people. They were in constant fear, too, of an attack from the Americans. Then the burned district, added to by another great fire in August, 1778, was covered with a city of tents and cabins that sheltered the vilest banditti of the British enemy, so that no citizen felt himself safe in the streets after dark, while the presence of the hospitals and prison-houses harrowed the souls of the pitiful. Business was suspended; many were in want. No one could leave without a pass from Lord Howe or his subordinates. No one could enter from within the American lines without a permit from General Washington, like that shown in the illustration. Only the wealthier royalists were sad when, on the 25th of November, 1783, the rear-guard of the British army embarked at the Battery, and with crestfallen air rowed away to their ships. At the same hour there marched down from the Bowery the army of occupation. This column was composed of the picked men of the army, heroes of a score of bloody fields; in the van Captain Stokes' troop of dragoons, next an advance guard of light infantry, then, in order, artillery, a battalion of light infantry, the Second Massachusetts Regiment, and a rear-guard, the whole under the command of Major-General Knox. The line of march was down the Bowery to Chatham, through Chatham to Queen (now Pearl), then the principal thoroughfare; through Queen to Wall, and up Wall to Broadway, where, opposite Cape's tavern, at Rector Street, the column halted to receive the civic procession soon to follow. At the same moment, a company of light infantry and one of artillery were detailed to proceed to Fort George, hoist the American colors on its flag-staff, and fire a salute of thirteen guns. The men hurried away, gained the parapet, and, looking on the bay, saw it covered with the boats of the British and Hessians, en route to their ships. But they soon found that the latter had played them a most unmanly trick — the flag-staff had been greased, and the halyards cut, so that it was impossible to hoist their colors. A sailor-boy volunteered to climb the pole, but, after several attempts, was obliged to desist. What was to be done? The flag must be raised before the salute could be fired, and there were the red-coats on the bay laughing at their plight. A happy thought struck the sailor-boy. He called for hammer, nails, a saw, and boards. The latter he cut up into cleats, nailed on the staff above him as he ascended, and so reached the top, where halyards were quickly reeved, and the colors hoisted.

Meantime, in the city, a larger, more imposing procession had been following the route of the military. It started from the Bull's Head tavern, on the present site of the Thalia Theatre, Captain Delavan's Westchester Light Horse in advance; General Washington and George Clinton, Governor of New York, with their suites on horseback; the Lieutenant-Governor and members of the City Council, pro tern four abreast; Knox, Steuben, James Clinton, McDougall, and other general officers, eight abreast; citizens on horseback, eight abreast; and lastly, the Speaker of the Assembly, and citizens on foot. The greatest enthusiasm greeted this body, and, when it halted before Cape's tavern, the military presented arms, the drums beat, and Fort George thundered a salute. Addresses were then made to General and Governor by prominent citizens, and in the evening a grand dinner was given by the Governor at Fraunces' tavern, at which a distinguished company gathered. Governor Clinton chose for his residence the De Peyster mansion, on Queen Street near Cedar, and the government of the new State of New York went into operation without friction. Two months later the Governor's council appointed James Duane the first mayor, and the city government was complete. Thus New York came under the folds of the last flag that was to wave over her.

An army other than that in scarlet uniform followed the retreating British to their ships — the American loyalists, who, having adhered to the crown, had now no part in the new country, and whom the bitter resentment of the Whigs, if not their own pride, would have forced into exile. According to British official reports, dated November 24, 1783, 29,244 men, women, "and children had, up to that date, been furnished transportation to Canada. Not all were loyalists, however; there were soldiers with their families among them, and 3,000 negro slaves which were taken by their masters.

One other scene in the great drama of the Revolution remained to be enacted before the curtain could be rung down for the last time — the leave-taking by the Commander-in-Chief of the officers of his army. This occurred in the " great room " of Fraunces' tavern, the fashionable hostelry of the day, and where Washington had fixed his headquarters. On Thursday, December 4, 1783, the principal officers assembled at the tavern for the final parting. It was a time of farewells. They were never to meet again as soldiers. Washington is said to have been affected to tears. He entered the room where the true and tried comrades were assembled, and, taking a glass of wine in his hand, spoke as follows:

" With a heart full of love and gratitude I now take leave of you. I most devoutly wish that your latter days may be as prosperous and happy as your former ones have been glorious and honorable." Having drank, he continued. " I cannot come to each of you to take my leave but shall be obliged to you if each will come and take me by the hand." Knox, Washington's favorite officer, who stood nearest him, turned and grasped his hand, and while the tears rolled down the cheeks of each, the Commander-in-Chief kissed him. This he did to each one in turn, while tears and sobs stifled utterance. Soon repressing his emotion, however, Washington left the room and walked in silence to Whitehall, followed by a great multitude, and there, at two o'clock, military rank and state laid aside, he entered a barge to proceed to Paulus Hook on his way to Virginia.

142

XVII. CONSTITUTION MAKING.

The colonies were now free, but they were by no means a nation. They were in fact separate, distinct sovereignties, each with prejudices and interests, rights and privileges of its own, which were jealously guarded. The Articles of Confederation, adopted in 1777, were but temporary expedients, and weak at the best. The Continental Congress was little more than an advisory council; it might make laws but it had no power to execute them; it could neither impose duties, nor lay taxes, nor make treaties, nor conduct other necessary diplomatic business. Manifestly some strong central power, general in scope, must be organized to perform these functions. To create that power, to construct a strong, national government and yet preserve unimpaired the rights of the States, was the problem presented to the statesmen of that period; fortunately they were equal to the task. That Washington, Hamilton, Jefferson, Franklin, Madison, Morris, Randolph, Luther Martin, and their confreres were statesmen indeed, the strain of a hundred years has proved.

In February, 1787, in answer to a request from a convention which had been held at Annapolis, Maryland, the preceding September, Congress called a convention of delegates from the several States to meet at Philadelphia in May, 1787, "for the sole and express purpose of revising the Articles of Confederation, and reporting to Congress and the various Legislatures such alterations and new provisions as should be necessary to meet the exigencies of government and preserve the Union." A " revision " was all that the framers of this call contemplated.

The delegates from New York were the eminent lawyers John Lansing, Robert Yates, and Alexander Hamilton. Hamilton favored a strong Federal government, while Lansing and Yates were bitterly opposed to it. The majority in the State Legislature, which elected them, was also opposed to it. New York, as a State, was opposed to any scheme of a national government. Under the Confederacy her great commercial advantages and vast extent of territory gave her a preponderance of power, whereas under a federal form of government she would in some important respects possess no more power than the smallest State. The convention met in May. Fifty-five members were present, representing every State except Rhode Island. A body of men possessing equal genius, learning, and wisdom had probably never before met. Washington was President. Benjamin Franklin, eighty-two years of age, was a delegate from Pennsylvania; Robert Morris, the great financier, and George Read, one of the signers of the Declaration, were his colleagues. South Carolina sent three accomplished lawyers — John Rutledge and the two Pinckneys — Charles C. and Charles — the two first-named educated at Oxford and the Temple. From Virginia came, in addition to Washington, George Wythe, her Chancellor, and his pupil, James Madison, a handsome, graceful man of thirty-seven, who proved himself a leading mind in the convention. Luther Martin, afterward counsel for Aaron Burr in his famous trial for treason, and John Dickinson, who had also been trained in law in the Temple, were the central figures of the Maryland delegation. Governor William Livingston, of New Jersey; Caleb Strong, Elbridge Gerry, and Rufus King, of Massachusetts; William Samuel Johnson, Roger Sherman, and Oliver Ellsworth, of Connecticut, were the greatest minds and purest patriots of their respective States. Hamilton, not yet thirty, with slight, graceful form and boyish face, is generally admitted to have been one of the leading spirits of the body. He had made a study of the science of government; he had a definite plan and matured ideas on the subject to present, while the others, with the possible exception of Madison, had not. The convention sat nearly four months before it could complete its labors. It was soon found to be composed of three parties — ultra Federalists, ultra-Republicans, and a third moderate party occupying middle ground between the two. The Federalists, led by Hamilton, submitted a scheme for a central government, making the States subordinate, and modelled somewhat after the English plan. There was to be a Senate and House of Representatives to make the laws, and a President to execute them. Senators and the President were to be elected for life or during good behavior. Governors of States were to be appointed by the Senate and President and were to have the power of vetoing the acts of the State Legislatures. The Republicans, or Democrats as we should now call them, led by Franklin, opposed this plan. They wished the States to retain all the powers they then possessed, and to have the old Confederation, altered to meet present needs, continue in force. There was much heated discussion between the advocates of the two plans, and for a time it seemed probable that the convention would agree on nothing. At last James Madison, leader of the moderate party, came forward with a plan which combined portions of both systems, and which was the framework of the present Constitution of the United States. This compromise plan was opposed at first by both parties, but, at last, enough of the extremists on both sides to pass it were won over, and on September 17, 1787, it was adopted. It had next to be ratified by nine of the thirteen States, and here came the tug of war. In New York the contest was fierce and bitter. The Republicans, led by Governor George Clinton, opposed even the modified plan. Her delegates, Yates and Lansing, had withdrawn from the convention before it had passed, saying that Hamilton, in advocating it, had exceeded his powers. The objections of the Republicans to the instrument were, that it robbed the States of their sovereignty; that it clothed the President with too much power; and that the people were not sufficiently protected by a Bill of Rights. To these objections Hamilton, Jay, and Madison responded in a series of celebrated papers called The Federalist^ which showed with convincing logic and wonderful force and clearness of statement that the American States could never hope to become anything more than a group of petty, jealous, warring provinces, unless they consented to waive a few of their rights for the public good and unite as one powerful, puissant nation.

A State convention was called for ratifying the Constitution, and met in Poughkeepsie June 17, 1788, with Governor George Clinton as President. From New York City were sent as delegates, Jay, Hamilton, Chancellor Livingston, Richard Morris, the Chief-Justice of New York, and James Duane, the Mayor. The city was in favor of the Constitution. There the influence of Hamilton, Jay, Chancellor Livingston, and other liberal minds was paramount, but in the State at large the prevailing sentiment was against it. Four counties, it was found, had elected Federalists, eight had elected Republicans, and two were divided. There were in all sixty-seven delegates. A long and acrimonious discussion followed. The majority of the delegates were strongly opposed to New York's giving up her advantages as the Empire State. Perhaps they would not have consented at this time had not news come that New Hampshire had adopted the Constitution. New Hampshire made up the requisite majority of nine States; the Constitution had been adopted. New York must therefore accept it or secede from the Confederation. She chose the former alternative, and agreed to ratify the instrument, July 26, 1788. A great popular demonstration in favor of it, held in New York City, July 23rd, is said to have had its influence. This was one of the grandest and most elaborate occasions the city had as yet seen, and was the first instance, it is believed, of trades' guilds appearing as such in public procession in the city. We condense a description of it from the newspapers of the day, which the reader may contrast with those of some modern processions.

At ten in the morning thirteen guns from the federal ship Hamilton gave the signal for the procession to move, the different bodies composing it being already assembled in the City Hall Park. The route was down Broadway to Great Dock Street, thence through Hanover Square, Pearl, Chatham, Division, Arundel, and Bullock streets, to the Bayard House, near Grand Street, where, beneath a rustic temple, a banquet for six thousand guests had been spread. Ten divisions, representing the ten States which had adopted the Constitution, composed the procession. First marched a body of light horse in full regimentals, preceded by a band of trumpeters and a company of artillery with a fieldpiece. Next came Christopher Columbus on horseback, preceded and followed by foresters with axes. The farmers came next, Nicholas Cruger in farmer's dress guiding a plow to which three yoke of oxen were attached, while John Watts, also in farmer's costume, conducted a harrow drawn by both oxen and horses; many farmers followed. Then came a newly invented threshing machine, under the care of Baron Polnitz, threshing and winnowing grain, capable, the old chroniclers say, of threshing and cleaning seventy-two bushels of grain per day. On a splendid gray horse, elegantly caparisoned and led by two colored men in Oriental costume, Anthony White bore the sculptured arms of the United States, and following in full military uniform marched the local Society of the Cincinnati. Then came gardeners in green aprons, tailors attended by a band of music, grain measurers, with banners depicting brimming measures, and underneath the lines:

" Federal measures and measures true

Shall measure out justice to us and you.'

The bakers made a handsome appearance. First came ten apprentices, clad in white aprons with blue sashes, each carrying a large rose decorated with ribbons; then ten journeymen in similar garb preceding a large square platform on wheels drawn by ten bay horses, on which was mounted the federal loaf, which bore the names in full of the ten consenting States, and in the baking of which a whole barrel of flour had been used.

Next marched the brewers and coopers, the latter presenting a striking appearance with their thirteen apprentice boys, each thirteen years of age, dressed in white shirts, trousers, and stockings, and in hats ornamented with thirteen pillars, colored green and white. After the boys came forty-two apprentices, with green oak branches in their hands, and then a stage drawn by four bay horses, with workmen upon it at work on a new cask, which was completed as the procession moved, and long preserved as the " federal cask."

After the stage came one hundred and thirty-eight masters and journeymen coopers, each carrying green oak branches in their right hands, and wearing oaken boughs in their hats. After these came the butchers, the tanners and curriers, the breeches-makers and glovers, the cord-wainers, the carpenters, the furriers, the hatters, the peruke makers and hair-dressers, the florists, whitesmiths, cutlers, confectioners, stone-masons, bricklayers, painters, cabinet-makers, chair-makers,

145

ivory turners, and musical-instrument makers, drum-makers, upholsterers, weavers, paper stainers, civil engineers, shipwrights, blacksmiths, ship-joiners, boat-builders, block and pump-makers, sail-makers and riggers, each with their appropriate emblems.

Heading the seventh division was the " federal ship Hamilton," the great feature of the. procession, " a frigate of thirty-two guns, twenty-seven feet keel, and ten feet beam, with galleries, and everything complete and in proportion, both in hull and rigging, manned with thirty seamen and marines in uniform, commanded by Commodore Nicholson, and drawn by ten horses." This gallant craft played an important part in the procession. Thirteen guns from her deck, as we have seen, gave the signal for the procession to move.

" She then got under way," continues the chronicler, " with her top-sails a-trip and courses in the brails, proceeding in the center of the procession. When abreast of Beaver Street she made the proper signal for a pilot by hoisting a jack at the fore-top mast-head and firing a gun. The pilot-boat appeared upon her weather quarter; the frigate threw her main-top-sail to the mast; the boat hailed and asked the necessary questions; the pilot was received on board, and the boat dismissed. The frigate then filled, and moved abreast of the fort, where the crew discovered the President and Members of Congress. She immediately brought to, and fired a salute of thirteen guns, which was followed by three cheers, and politely answered by the gentlemen of Congress. The procession then moved. When the ship came opposite Mr. Constable's, the crew discovered at the window Mrs. Edgar, who had generously honored the ship with the present of a suit of silk colors. Immediately they manned ship and gave three cheers. When she arrived abreast of Old Slip she was saluted with thirteen guns from his Most Catholic Majesty's packet, then in the harbor, which was politely returned. She then made sail, and proceeded through Queen Street to the fields (City Hall Park), when squalls coming on, and the wind ahead, she beat to windward by short tacks, in which the pilot displayed his skill in navigation, heaving the lead, getting ready for stays, putting the helm a-lee, etc. In the fields she had to descend several hills, in raising which she afforded a delightful prospect to the spectators, her top-sails appearing first, and then her hull, in imitation of a ship at sea, exhibiting an appearance beyond description, splendid and majestic. When she arrived at her station abreast of the dining station, she clewed up her top-sails, and came to, in close order with the rest of the procession, the officers going ashore to dine. At four o'clock she gave the signal for marching by a discharge of thirteen guns, when the procession moved by the lower road. The manner in which the ship made her passage through the narrow part of the road was highly interesting and satisfactory, being obliged to run under her fore-top-sail in a squall and keep in the line of the procession. This was accomplished with great hazard by the good conduct of the commander and the assiduity of the seamen and pilot. She arrived at her moorings abreast of the Bowling Green at half-past five, amidst the acclamations of thousands, and the different orders of procession, as soon as they were dismissed, honored her with three cheers as a mark of approbation for the good conduct of the commodore and crew."

After the frigate, which was near the center of the procession, came a handsome pilot-boat full manned. Then the Marine Society, with its white silk banner, and after it more guilds — the printers, bookbinders, stationers, cartmen, carvers and engravers, coach and harness makers, coppersmiths, tin plate workers, pewterers, goldsmiths and silversmiths, potters, tobacconists, dyers, brushmakers, tallow chandlers, and saddlers, each with banners, devices, and emblazoned symbols of its craft, and with hundreds of its craftsmen clad in gala attire and bearing green oak branches in their hands and boughs in their hats. The ninth division was formed of the gentlemen of the bar in their robes, " two and two," of the Philological Society, faculty and students of the university, and of the merchants of the city. In the tenth and last division marched the physicians, distinguished strangers and gentlemen, and, bringing up the rear, a section of artillery.

The line of procession," to again quote our chronicler, "containing nearly five thousand persons, extended upwards of a mile and a half. The march was slow and majestic, and the appearance of the scene as far surpassed every one's expectation as mere description must fall short of it. While numberless crowds were pressing on every side, the doors and windows of houses were thronged by the fair daughters of Columbia, whose animated smiles and satisfaction contributed not a little to complete the general joy. As this splendid, novel, and interesting exhibition moved along, an unexpected silence reigned throughout the city, which gave a solemnity to the whole transaction. No noise was heard but the deep rumbling of carriage wheels, with the necessary salutes and signals. . . . The whole body having arrived at Bayard's house, were disposed in a line and reviewed; after which, the varied insignia of the procession being left upon the fields, the citizens were conducted to their several dining tables, where they were honored by the company of Congress, of many foreigners of distinction, and the patriotic and respectable clergy of the city."

The building provided for the entertainment consisted of three large pavilions connected by a colonnade of one hundred and fifty feet front, and beautifully decorated with the arms and colors of the nations in alliance with America. Thirteen toasts followed the grand dinner in order as follows: 1st. The United States. 2nd. The States which have ratified the new Constitution. 3rd. The Convention of the State of New York: may it soon add an eleventh pillar to the federal edifice. 4th. General Washington. 5th. His Most Christian Majesty. 6th. His Catholic Majesty. 7th. The States-General of the United Netherlands. 8th. The friendly powers in Europe. 9th. The patriotic framers of the present national Constitution. loth. The memory of those heroes who have fallen in defense of American liberty. nth. Success to agriculture, manufactures, and the sciences. 12th. May trade and navigation flourish. 13th. The day: may the union of the States be perpetual. After each toast ten cannon were fired, and in order " to diffuse the joy to all classes of citizens, an ample proportion of the entertainment was dispatched to the prisoners in gaol. The repast ended, the procession returned in the same manner to its place of setting out; and the citizens were dismissed by half-past five o'clock." A grand display of fireworks in the evening closed the pageant.

On the Saturday following, news reached New York of the adoption of the Constitution by the convention, and again the city was thrown into paroxysms of joy. The bells rang triumphant peals, and the great fort on the Battery, and the federal ship Hamilton fired salutes, while the merchants and citizens went in a body to the homes of Hamilton, Jay, Livingston, and other leading Federalists and testified their approval with cheers. Even the anti-Federalists, it is said, forgot their fears, and cheered as heartily as the rest.

147

Congress formally adopted the Constitution September 13, 1788, and appointed the first Wednesday in January, 1789, as the day when the people should meet to choose electors for their first President; it also provided that the first Congress under the new Constitution should meet in New York on the 4th day of March following. Then there was fresh excitement in the city, for a suitable capitol had to be provided in which Congress might meet. Thirty-two thousand dollars were quickly subscribed, and the old City Hall, which has been described as standing at the corner of Broad and Wall streets, was given into the hands of Major L'Enfant to be remodeled and refurnished. Major L'Enfant was a gallant Frenchman, a skilled engineer and architect, who had offered his services to Congress in the beginning of the Revolution, and who first taught American engineers how to build forts and earthworks. Later he planned our capital city, Washington. When the City Hall came from his hands it was admitted by all critics to be a tasteful and appropriate edifice. The basement story was of the Tuscan order and was pierced with seven openings. Four massive pillars in the center supported four Doric columns and a pediment. The frieze was ingeniously divided to admit thirteen stars in metopes, which, with the American eagle and other insignia in the pediments, the tablets filled with thirteen arrows over the windows, and the olive branches united, marked it as a building designed for national purposes. The two chief apartments were the Senate Chamber and the Hall of Representatives. The former, on the left of the vestibule, was forty feet long, thirty wide, and twenty high, with an arched ceiling. There were three windows in front opening into a gallery (shown in the engraving p. 367) twelve feet deep and guarded by an iron railing. The chamber was decorated with pilasters of an order invented by Major L'Enfant. Tuscan pilasters adorned the lobby, — forty-eight feet long and nineteen wide — by which the chamber was approached. The hall of the House of Representatives, opposite the Senate Chamber, was a spacious apartment sixty-one feet deep, fifty-eight wide, and thirty-six high. In form it was octangular, four of its sides being rounded in the form of niches. Above the lofty windows were placed Ionic columns and pilasters, and in the panels between the windows were carved trophies, and the letters U. S. in a cipher surrounded with laurels. The chair of the Speaker occupied a raised dais, approached by several steps opposite the main entrance, and in front in two semicircular rows were the seats of the members. Two galleries were provided for spectators. We have been thus particular in our description of this building because here the first President of the United States — George Washington — took the oath of office, and because here the first Congress under the Constitution assembled. The first Congress and the first President — truly New York has been honored above her peers.

Congress was to have met on the 4th of March, 1789, but, as the day came, only eight Senators and thirteen Representatives presented themselves — not enough of either branch for a quorum, — the missing members having been delayed by the state of the roads. A great gulf seems to open between us and the year, 1789, when we compare the means of transit then in vogue with those that we enjoy. " Stage-boats " and stage-coaches were the only public conveyances. Six days by sloop and coach were often consumed in the journey from New York to Philadelphia. In March the travelling was especially difficult, and it was not until the 6th of April that the members, toiling slowly forward by stage or on horseback, now mired in the March mud, now water-bound by swollen rivers, reached the capital in sufficient numbers to organize the Congress.

When organized, however, it was not long in learning who had been chosen the first President. Washington had received every vote — the only President unanimously elected. John Adams, of Massachusetts, was elected Vice-President. Washington, apprised by official messenger, left his home in Virginia on the 16th of April for New York. His journey was a triumphal procession; in every city and town crowds gathered spontaneously and hailed him as their deliverer. At Gray's Ferry, near Philadelphia, a civic crown of laurel was dropped upon his head as he passed underneath an arch and through long avenues of laurel transplanted from the neighboring forests. At Trenton, thirteen beautiful maidens strewed flowers in his pathway, and chanted an ode in praise of the hero. At Elizabethtown Point, he was met by a Committee of Congress, with Elias Boudinot at its head, the mayor and recorder of New York, and other officials, and escorted on board an elegant barge, provided for the purpose, and commanded by Commodore Nicholson. As the little vessel moved from the shore, scores of other barges, beautifully decorated with flags and streamers, fell into line, and the procession swept through the narrow strait of the Kill von Kull, and across the beautiful bay to New York, while guns thundered and bands of music played, and the ships in the harbor, literally covered with bunting, dipped their colors in salute to the Chief-Magistrate. At the railing of the ferry stairs on Murray wharf, Governor Clinton stood ready to receive him, and the two, preceded by the military and Committee of Congress, and attended by the mayor and aldermen, the clergy, the foreign ministers, and numbers of distinguished citizens, passed through the crowded streets, amid deafening huzzas, to the Osgood mansion, on the corner of Cherry Street and Franklin Square, which had been prepared for the President's reception. Washington arrived on the 24th of April; John Adams, the Vice-President, on the 22nd. Six days were employed in preparations for the inaugural ceremonies, which, as completing the fabric of a national government, it had been decided should be of the most imposing character. Thunder of guns, therefore, aroused the city on the memorable 30th of April, 1789. At nine o'clock every bell in the city rang merry peals for a few moments and then suddenly ceased. All din of traffic was hushed, and, in its place, vast throngs of eager people in holiday attire filled the streets. New York had never before been so crowded with visitors. They had come from town and country for hundreds of miles around, and every incoming packet on sound and river but added to their numbers. All waited with bated breath the beginning of the ceremonies. After a measured interval the bells began again in slow, solemn tones, summoning the people to the churches to implore the blessing of God on the young nation and its untried President.

After the religious services, the military formed in Cherry Street, opposite the house of the President, and when he came forth, attended by the joint committee of the Senate and House of Representatives, formed in columns and took position at the head of the procession. Following them came the sheriff of the city and county of New York, the committee of the Senate, the President-elect, the committee of the House, Chancellor Robert R. Livingston, Secretary John Jay, Secretary Henry Knox, the Commissioners of the Treasury, and distinguished citizens, in carriages. To the sound of martial music, the procession then swept down Pearl Street to Broad, and up Broad to Wall, where, in front of Federal Hall, the regiments halted and opened ranks on either side, through which Washington and the distinguished company passed into the capitol and up the stairway to the Senate Chamber. Here the Senators and Representatives — dignified, reverend men, everyone chosen for his commanding genius, statesmanship, and public services — awaited the chief. As he entered, John Adams arose, advanced, received him with the stately courtesy of the day, and conducted him to the Vice-President's chair, which he had just vacated; then, after formally introducing him to the august body, he said:

" Sir — The Senate and House of Representatives of the United States are ready to attend you, to take the oath required by the Constitution, which will be administered by the Chancellor of the State of New York."

" I am ready to proceed," was the President's reply. Vice-President Adams then conducted him to the gallery overlooking Wall Street, accompanied by the Senators, the Chancellor in his judicial robes, and other gentlemen. A wonderful sight met the eyes of the distinguished company. Wall and Broad streets were a sea of upturned faces; the windows, balconies, and house-tops were filled with gayly dressed ladies; flags and banners, caressed by the mild spring zephyrs, waved everywhere, all bearing the magic word Washington. From the whole vast throng, it was observed, not a whisper arose. But soon a group of three appeared between the central Doric columns of the gallery— the noble figure of the President on the right, opposite him Chancellor Livingston, in his robes, and between them the Secretary of the Senate, holding upon a crimson cushion an open Bible. Then the Chancellor, in words that reached every ear, repeated the solemn oath: " You do solemnly swear that you will faithfully execute the office of President of the United States, and will, to the best of your ability, preserve, protect, and defend the Constitution of the United States."

I swear," said Washington, as he bent to kiss the Bible, adding with fervor: " So help me God." Chancellor Livingston turned to the multitude and, waving his hand, cried with strong, triumphant voice:

" Long live George Washington, President of the United States! " and from the people arose resounding cheers, while the spires shook with pealing of bells, and over all swelled the thunder of cannon from forts and ships and marshalled ranks. A calm onlooker would have said the city was mad with joy. And truly it had cause.

A great idea was firmly rooted that day — the idea of nationality. No more petty, weak, separated States, but a mighty nation, America, the United States. No doubt to those patriotic men the future opened its ravishing vistas, and they saw beyond our time what this nation hopes to be, — first among peoples, the noblest, strongest, grandest — because the freest — nation of the earth!

PART III. THE FREE CITY
XVIII. THE FIRST TWENTY YEARS.

For a year New York continued to be the capital. — the court town. Washington and his cabinet ministers — Jefferson, Hamilton, and Knox, John Adams, the Vice-President, Chief-Justice Jay, Governor Clinton, and other high officers of government — removed their families to the city and formed the court circle. In the diary left by Washington during this period we gain pleasant glimpses of the inner life of this circle. Official life was then attended with much more of stately ceremonial and court etiquette than is now practiced. The President's intercourse with Congress was modelled after the English form, and his messages to that body were delivered in person, after the fashion of the English kings. In his diary for January 8, 1790, he gives an interesting account of this ceremony. A committee first perfected arrangements. Then, at eleven o'clock, he set out for Federal Hall — where Congress, in joint session, was assembled — " in a coach," he tells us, " drawn by six horses, preceded by Col. Humphreys and Major Johnson, in uniform, on my two white horses, and followed by Messrs. Lear and Nelson in my chariot, and Mr. Lewis, on horse-back, following them. In their rear was the Chief-Justice of the United States and the Secretaries of the Treasury and War Departments (Hamilton and Knox), in their respective carriages and in the order they are named. At the outer door I was met by the door-keepers of the Senate and House, and conducted to the door of the Senate Chamber, and passing from thence to the chair, through the Senate on the right and the House on the left, I took my seat. The gentlemen who attended me followed and took their stand behind the Senators, the whole rising as I entered. After being seated, at which time the members of both Houses also sat, I rose as they also did, and made my speech, delivering one copy to the President of the Senate and another to the Speaker of the House of Representatives; after which, and being a few minutes seated, I retired, bowing on each side to the assembly (who stood) as I passed, and descending to the lower hall, attended as before, I returned with them to my house."

A few days later Congress was ready to return an answer to the President's message, and at his request waited on him at his house in Franklin Square, " the members of both coming in carriages, and the latter, with the Mace, preceding the Speaker." " The address of the Senate was presented by the Vice-President, and that of the House by the Speaker thereof."

In the social amenities of the times, the Chief Magistrate was also a prominent figure. He kept a retinue of servants, horses, and carriages; the silver plate and lighter articles of furniture were transferred from Mount Vernon, first to the Franklin-Square house, and in 1790 to the McComb mansion on Broadway, a little south of Trinity Church, which remained the President's home during his stay in New York. He loved riding, walking, and all forms of manly exercise, and his noble figure — six feet three in height and straight as an arrow — became a familiar object to the citizens. He entertained generously and was entertained with equal hospitality. When Congress called with its answer to the address, twelve favored members, we are told, remained to dine. We read of his going in the post-chaise with Madam Washington to call on the Vice-President and his wife at Richmond Hill. On his return he walked to Rufus King's to make a social call, but neither that statesman nor his wife were at home. Another time he honors Secretary and Mrs. Hamilton, Mr. and Mrs. Rufus King, General and Mrs. Philip Schuyler, Mrs. Greene, and Mrs. Adams with tickets to his private box in the John Street theatre; and when the distinguished party enters, the audience rises, and remains standing until it is seated. In one day we find he made business calls on Chief Justice Jay and Secretary Knox, called informally on Governor Clinton, Mr. Ralph Izard, General Philip Schuyler, and Mrs. Dalton, entertained at dinner Mr. and Mrs. Ralph Izard and son. Dr. Johnson, lady and daughter, and Chief-Justice Jay, and afterward went with Mrs. Washington to the dancing assembly and remained there until ten o'clock. His levees on Tuesday were great social occasions. On the 12th (December, 1789) he " exercised with Mrs. Washington and the children in the coach between breakfast and dinner, — went the fourteen miles' round." This "round" followed the " Old Boston Road " as far as McGowan's Pass, thence westerly to the Bloomingdale Road, lined at that time with villas and country-seats, and back along the banks of the Hudson to the city, — the favorite drive of New Yorkers in those days. On the 14th he "walked round the Battery in the afternoon." On Christmas day, " went to St. Paul's Chapel in the forenoon. The visitors to Mrs. Washington this afternoon were not numerous, but respectable."

New Year's Day introduced a new custom to the courtly Virginian, — the custom of congratulatory calls. Between twelve and three he was visited by the Vice-President, Governor Clinton, the members of the Senate and House of Representatives, the foreign ambassadors, and the principal gentlemen of the city. Later in the day great numbers of ladies and gentlemen gathered to Mrs. Washington's weekly levee, which was held on this day (Friday). In the evening those guests that remained were regaled on plum and plain cake, tea and coffee, and the evening was spent in social intercourse. Washington inquired whether this custom of New Year's calling was a long-established one or otherwise; and on being told that it had been introduced by the Dutch founders of New Amsterdam, remarked that with the influx of emigrants many of the ancient customs and manners of the city would, of necessity, be changed, " but whatever changes take place," said he, " never forget the cordial and cheerful observance of New Year's Day." The houses of Jay, Hamilton, Knox, Vice-President Adams, and Governor Clinton were also centers of social courtesies during this period.

Meantime the question of a site for the permanent capital of the nation was agitating the minds of Congressmen and of the people. New York would undoubtedly have been chosen, but neither State nor city was willing to cede the ten miles square of territory demanded by the general government. Philadelphia was mentioned, but Southern Senators objected because her Quakers " were eternally dogging Southern members with their schemes of emancipation." Maryland, Delaware, and Virginia advocated a site on the Potomac which, as we know, was finally chosen. But while the capital city was being built, Congress decided to hold its sessions in Philadelphia; and when it rose on the 12th of August, 1790, adjourned to meet in Philadelphia the next December, — a decision that caused great dissatisfaction in New York. A print of the day represents Robert Morris marching off to Philadelphia with Federal Hall on his back and the Evil One on the roof of Paulus Hook ferry-house beckoning encouragingly and crying, " This way, Bobby."

Thus New York lost her court circle. President and Senators, legislative processions, weekly levees, court balls, and State pageants faded from her streets, and were seen no more. Not entirely to her disadvantage, however, for her genius was commercial, and along this line her marvelous development was to come. Not then, however; it was not chiefly to commerce, but to politics, that the bold and daring spirits of that day turned. In fact, law and politics were almost the only openings then available to men of genius. Of art, science, literature, there was none; and of commerce, very little. Hence, we find that the great lawyers of that day were statesmen, and the great statesmen were lawyers, Clinton, Hamilton, Burr, Jay, Livingston, Duane — it was so in almost every case.

For a time after the adoption of the Constitution party spirit was stilled, but it very soon revived. There were too many points of differences between the two great parties for them to remain long at peace. These parties were the Federalist and the Republican — the same that had been defined by the contest over the Constitution, but they had now become much stronger, and their creeds were more sharply defined. The Federalist was styled by its opponents " the English party." Its leaders regarded the English constitution as the most perfect ever devised by man. They advocated a national form of government, a powerful standing army, the formality and etiquette of courts, a diplomatic service like that of Europe, the restriction of the suffrage, the encouragement of foreign commerce and of domestic manufactures — the latter by a protective tariff. They disliked France and the French people, and viewed with horror the French Revolution, which was now beginning to attract the attention of the world. The Republicans, on the other hand, advocated simplicity and economy in the government, a doing away with all monarchical forms, the employment of a well-drilled militia instead of a standing army, open sessions of Congress, an extension of the franchise, the encouragement of agriculture and internal trade, rather than of foreign commerce, and they ardently espoused the cause of the French people.

The success of the Constitution, which was largely an embodiment of the federal principle, had placed the Federalists in power, but the Republicans were still numerous and powerful. New York City, under the leadership of Hamilton, Jay, and others, was staunchly Federalist, but the State at large, controlled by Governor George Clinton, was Republican. The differences between the two parties were so great, and the prize in view — the privilege of shaping the destiny of the young nation — so coveted, that their struggle for supremacy became the most bitter and exciting ever known in American politics.

The story has been often told, and we will content ourselves with a brief history of the closing struggle which took place in New York, and in which two famous citizens of the city were the chief actors. These two men were Alexander Hamilton and Aaron Burr; the former a Federalist, the latter a Republican. Both have before appeared in our story, — Hamilton, as one of the chief framers of the Constitution, and as Washington's Secretary of the Treasury, where he had originated the financial policy of the nation. At this time, 1799, he had resigned from the treasury and was practicing law in New York, although his influence with its leaders still gave him almost supreme power in the Federal party. Aaron Burr, whom we last saw leading Silliman's brigade from New York before the British advance, had also studied law, and was now a lawyer in New York, and the only rival of Hamilton at its bar. He had filled several official positions with credit: had been Attorney-General of New York in 1789, Senator from New York, 1791-1797; and, in the presidential contest of 1796, had received thirty electoral votes for President. He had been defeated for reelection to the Senate in 1797 by the Federalists, under Hamilton's leadership, and at once set to work to withdraw New York from their grasp, perceiving clearly that, with the electoral vote of that great State, the Republicans could elect their President in 1800. He laid his plans with matchless tact and carried them out with energy. Presidential electors, at that time, were chosen by the State Legislatures. He therefore caused himself to be elected to the New York Legislature, and, while there, bestowed favors and compliments, and otherwise ingratiated himself with rural members whom he knew to possess great influence with their home constituents; he was also in constant communication with the party leaders in different States and arranged with them for a settled method of procedure in the campaign. Then, as the year 1800 approached, he brought his marvelous powers as an organizer to work, to so discipline and organize the party in New York City as to insure victory. Aaron Burr first taught politicians the resistless power of party organization in winning victories. True, there were other leaders — Edward Livingston, the jurist and statesman, who was given the mayoralty of New York for his services in this campaign; his relative, Judge Brockholst Livingston; ex-Governor George Clinton, the War Governor, and others; but it was generally admitted that Burr's matchless tact and energy won the victory. He began by gathering about him a body-guard of able, ardent, resolute young spirits — men of education and wit, — for the most part without birth or fortune, but ambitious of distinction, and imbued them with his courage and activity. These were the ward-workers, the men who attended to the primaries and caucuses, and saw to getting out a full vote; the "Tenth Legion " — Theodosia. Burr's daughter, called them; " Burr's Myrmidons " they were styled by the Federal leaders. Burr played, too, with rare tact upon the two factions of the party led by the Clintons and the Livingstons.

As the year 1800 drew near, all admitted that the only hope of Republican success lay in carrying New York. That State, at this time, was Federalist. John Jay was Governor. In the election of 1799, the Republican ticket, headed by Aaron Burr, had been beaten by a majority of 900. In April, 1800, the Legislature which was to elect presidential electors was to be chosen. Burr strained every nerve to make this body Republican. The strongest names that could be obtained were nominated — George Clinton, so long Governor of New York, Horatio Gates, the conqueror of Burgoyne, Samuel Osgood, Washington's Postmaster-General, and others whose names were towers of strength. He marshalled his body-guard again and infused into the party in general that discipline and blind fealty which has ever since made New York a Democratic city. He made lists of Republican voters, noting each one's age, habits, residence, health, and temperament; he held ward and general meetings, and addressed them, and watched with a wary eye the movements of his opponent, alert to take advantage of the slightest mistake or accident. Hamilton led the opposition. He, too, put all his heart and soul into the canvas, but although greatly the superior of Burr in depth of intellect and statesmanship, he lacked the latter's tact, executive ability, and mastery over men; he made several grave mistakes which were quickly taken advantage of by his antagonist. As the day approached, the result was felt to be doubtful. The polls opened on the 29th of April, and closed May 2nd. They were days of supreme exertion for the contestants, and of intense excitement. Business was largely suspended. Newspapers and pamphlets were scattered about like autumn leaves. From large platforms the rival chieftains addressed the people; sometimes both occupied the same rostrum, one listening with the deepest interest and courtesy while his opponent spoke, and then replying with all the wit, logic, and eloquence at his command. At sunset, on May 2nd, the polls closed, and before the politicians slept, they knew that the Republicans had carried the city by a majority of 490 votes — which meant that the Republicans would come into power at the next election. Hamilton was vastly chagrined, and the Federal leaders desperate. Thomas Jefferson and Aaron Burr were shortly after nominated for President and Vice-President by the Republicans, Burr receiving the second place for his services in carrying New York. But when the votes were opened, in February, 1801, it was found that there was a tie, the two candidates, Jefferson and Burr, having received exactly the same number of votes. This threw the election into the House, and a fierce contest arose, the Federalists wishing to make Burr President instead of Jefferson, whom they greatly disliked. It is probable that they would have done this, had it not been for Hamilton, who used his powerful influence with the Federal leaders in favor of Jefferson, whose right to the office could not be disputed. The contest ended, at last, in favor of Jefferson. As Vice-President, from 1801 to 1805, Colonel Burr performed his duties to the satisfaction of all and is said to have been the best presiding officer the Senate ever saw. He still maintained his town house and country-seat at Richmond Hill, in New York, and when not in Washington resided there, entertaining generously — two of his guests being the famous French diplomat, Talleyrand, and the author, Volney.

Hamilton, in the meantime, remained in New York, practicing his profession, but none the less watching keenly the course of political events. It was an era of bitter partisan feeling and recrimination. Duels, the result of political quarrels, were frequent. A fierce newspaper war was one of the features. The organ of the Federalists was the Minerva — which later became the Commercial Advertiser of to-day — its editor being Noah Webster, the famous maker of dictionaries. The organ of the Clintonian wing of the Republican party was the American Citizen, edited by James Cheetham, an Englishman, whose fiery philippics were continually involving him in quarrels. Supporting Burr and his wing, and generally regarded as the President's organ, was the Morning Chronicle, edited by Dr. Peter Irving. In that paper, about this time, the delightful author, Washington Irving, first made his bow to the public. His essays, signed " Jonathan Oldstyle," greatly pleased Colonel Burr, who was wont to cut them out and enclose them in letters to his daughter Theodosia. November 16, 1801, appeared the Evening Post, which was generally regarded as the mouthpiece of Hamilton. Its editor, William Coleman, was much the ablest and most reputable journalist of his day. The columns of all these papers bristled with scurrilous attacks on the opposition.

As the days passed, it became evident that Colonel Burr could hope for no further preferment from his party. The tie contest had marked him out to the powerful Virginia faction as a man to be crushed. The Clinton and Livingston interests in New York also combined against him. His name was scarcely mentioned in the presidential contest of 1804. He was then nominated by his friends as an independent candidate for Governor of New York but was signally defeated. If now he could have stifled his political aspirations, and returned to the bar, as Hamilton had done, a brilliant and honorable career might still have been his; but unfortunately he could not endure defeat with patience.

At the close of the campaign of 1804, the manner in which General Hamilton was in the habit of speaking of Colonel Burr had been brought to the latter's attention in a manner that compelled him to take notice of it. During the contest, Cheetham, in his paper, had asked: " Is the Vice-President sunk so low as to submit to be insulted by General Hamilton? A few weeks after, a newspaper containing a letter from a well-known physician — Dr. Charles D. Cooper — was put into Colonel Burr's hands. Two sentences in the letter were marked. One was:

" General Hamilton and Judge Kent have declared in substance that they looked upon Mr. Burr to be a dangerous man, and one who ought not to be trusted with the reins of government." The other was: "I could detail to you a still more despicable opinion which General Hamilton has expressed of Mr. Burr." Colonel Burr at once sent the paper by a friend to General Hamilton, with an indignant letter, in which he demanded "a prompt and unqualified acknowledgment or denial of the use of any expressions which would warrant the assertions of Mr. Cooper."

Several letters passed between the two men. General Hamilton replied that if Colonel Burr would specify any one expression or statement he might have made he would deny or acknowledge it, but he could not undertake to give a general denial or acknowledgment as to what he had or had not said, in the heat of political debate, during a period covering many years. Colonel Burr replied that the expressions attributed to General Hamilton attached dishonor to him and reiterated his demand that General Hamilton should deny ever having said anything that would give color to the assertion of Dr. Cooper. This General Hamilton declined to do, and a challenge was given and accepted. The duel, savage and murderous as we now justly regard it, was then the recognized mode among gentlemen of settling such disputes as this. Both chieftains had recognized it. Hamilton's eldest son had fallen in a duel a few years before. Burr had been a principal in one of the savage affairs. The partisans of both had fought for the honor of their chiefs, with the latter's approval, and there was therefore no other resource but for them to settle their quarrel in the recognized way.

They met on the fatal field of Weehawken, sacred to these encounters, very near where the present tunnel of the West Shore Line debouches upon the water front. At the first fire Hamilton fell mortally wounded; Burr escaped unhurt. The stricken statesman was rowed across the river and carried to the residence of Mr. Bayard at Greenwich; his own beautiful country-seat, "The Grange," which he had built, in 1802, in the upper part of the island, being too far away for one to be conveyed in his dying condition. Servants were hastily sent for surgeons and nurses; Mrs. Hamilton was summoned, and later his children. The fatal meeting occurred at sunrise on July II, 1804. At nine o'clock on that morning a bulletin appeared on the board of the Tontine Coffee-House; "General Hamilton was shot by Colonel Burr this morning in a duel," it said; " the General is thought to be mortally wounded." With every hour came a fresh bulletin, each adding fuel to the flame. In one the General was reported to be slowly sinking; in a second, the arrival of the sorrow-stricken wife and children, the calmness and resignation of the dying man, the over-mastering grief of Mrs. Hamilton were graphically pictured; in a third, the last sad scene, when the seven children were led in to take their last farewell of a dying father.

Next morning a bulletin related the patient's sufferings during the night. At two o'clock another announced his death. The news swept swiftly through the city. Expressions of grief, pity, sympathy, mingled with execrations on the slayer, were heard on every side. At night a meeting of the merchants was held at the Tontine Coffee-House, and it was resolved to close the stores on the day of the funeral, to wear crape for thirty days, and to order the flags on the shipping at half-mast. Next morning the lawyers met and agreed to wear mourning for six weeks. The various military companies, the Tammany Society, the Cincinnati, the students of Columbia College, the St. Andrew's Society, the General Society of Mechanics, and the Corporation of the city all passed resolutions of sympathy and pledged themselves to attend the funeral in a body.

Hamilton died on Thursday afternoon. On Saturday, in Trinity Church, the funeral was held. The city had never seen a more imposing pageant than the funeral cortege, as it moved slow-paced down Broadway amid the booming of minute-guns from the Battery and from British frigates and French men-of-war in the bay. Every organization in the city is said to have participated in the procession. At the church, on a platform, with the four sons of the dead statesman beside him, — the eldest sixteen, the youngest four, — Gouverneur Morris, the life-long friend of Hamilton, stood to deliver the funeral eulogium. Certain of his terse, forcible sentences the men of that generation never forgot.

" You know that he never courted your favor by adulation or the sacrifice of his own judgment. You have seen him contending against you, and saving your dearest interests, as it were, in spite of yourselves. I declare to you before God, in whose presence we are now especially assembled, that in his most private and confidential conversations the single objects of discussion were your freedom and happiness. The care of a rising family and the narrowness of his fortune made it a duty to return to his profession for their support. But, though he was compelled to abandon public life, never, no, never for a moment, did he abandon the public service. He never lost sight of your interests. . . . For himself he feared nothing, but he feared that bad men might, by false profession, acquire your confidence and abuse it to your ruin."

Thus tragically passed from the scene one of the greatest of the great men of the Revolutionary era.

"The Patriot of Incorruptible Integrity,

The Soldier of Approved Valor,

The Statesman of Consummate Wisdom. "

One reads it on his modest tombstone in Trinity Churchyard — a truer panegyric than most. As for his slayer, the popular verdict — whether just or unjust — went against him. He became "a man without a country," socially ostracized, abhorred by Federalist and Republican alike. Good came of the statesman's death, however. It stilled, for a time, the rage of faction, for it was clearly seen that the duel was the outcome of the bitter political strife of the preceding fourteen years, and, as far at least as the States of the North were concerned, it abolished from polite society that savage and barbarous outgrowth of feudalism — the duello.

XIX. A TYPICAL NEW YORK MERCHANT.

Almost immediately on gaining her freedom New York began extending her commerce. Trade with England revived, her ships became familiar objects in French, German, and Russian seas; she tapped the rich commerce of the Mediterranean, and a little later strove with the merchants of Salem and Boston for the rich trade of China and the East. The greatest merchant of this era, and perhaps of any, was John Jacob Astor. His career has so much of inspiration in it for young readers, that we present its leading features in detail. He was born in the German village of Waldorf, near Heidelberg, on the Rhine, in 1763. In the winter of 1784, he arrived in Baltimore, with a small stock of goods which he had brought from London, but with no other " pledges to fortune," except thrift, energy, good habits, and an invincible determination to succeed. A fellow countryman, a furrier by trade, chanced to be on the same ship, and directed the young merchant's attention to the possibilities of the fur trade, the result being that he determined to become a fur merchant. He came on to New York, sold his goods, and invested the proceeds in furs, which were bought of the country traders and merchants as they came in. With these he returned to London, sold them at a profit, and then came back to New York with a view of settling permanently as a fur merchant. He at once set to work to inform himself thoroughly concerning his business. First, he apprenticed himself to a furrier, and learned the mechanical part of the trade. In a few years we find him with a store of his own. But his aspiring mind did not long rest content with the retail tradesman's career. He began to study the extent, capacity, and methods of the fur trade of North America, then nearly as valuable as the gold and silver of the South had been to the Spanish.

Montreal, Canada, he found to be the great fur mart. The rich trade in furs of that vast region later known as the Northwest, stretching from the shores of the Great Lakes to the head-waters of the Mississippi and Missouri, had been first organized by the French traders of Canada; and when the latter country became a British possession, the trade naturally fell into the hands of its conquerors.

At this moment, 1790, there were three rival companies in the field — the Hudson s Bay Company, chartered in 1670, by Charles H., and granted exclusive right to the territory watered by Hudson's Bay and its tributaries; the Northwest Company, founded in 1787, and which garrisoned by its trading-posts the whole region of the upper lakes; and the Mackinaw Company, whose head-quarters were on Mackinac Island, at the mouth of Lake Michigan, and whose posts garrisoned the latter lake, the Fox and Wisconsin rivers, and the great Mississippi and its tributaries.

The animals which produced the furs — chiefly the beaver, fox, mink, otter, and muskrat — were trapped by the Indians. The pelts were then cured and brought in to the " posts " or trading-stations, where they were exchanged for powder, ball, fire-arms, blankets, trinkets, and such other goods as the Indians prized. Then, once a year, in the spring, great fleets of canoes and bateaux, filled with the goods for exchange, would set out from Montreal, ascend the Ottawa River, and thence by other rivers and portages reach Lake Huron, Lake Superior, and the most distant posts, collecting the furs which had been gathered by the post-traders, distributing the goods they had carried out, and at last, when the furs had all been collected, returning with them to Montreal. Our merchant began operations by buying furs from these merchants of the Northwest Company, and shipping them direct to

London — Canada, at that time, not being allowed to trade with any but the mother country.

In 1795, however, a treaty was made with England which allowed American merchants to trade with Canada; and from this time on, Mr. Astor's furs were sent direct from Montreal to New York.

Some he used for the home supply, some were shipped to Europe, but the bulk he began sending to China, where much better prices could be obtained. Thus began Mr. Astor's China trade, which proved immensely profitable. In a few years, having abundant capital, he began asking himself if it were not better to buy his furs of the Indians themselves, and thus save the immense profits made by the Northwest Company. The operations of the Mackinaw Company, he reasoned, were carried on almost entirely within the territory of the United States — a field which he thought belonged of right to citizens of the United States. He determined to occupy this field — a decision which was heartily approved by our government, which had long viewed with alarm the commercial influence possessed by British traders over the tribes within its borders. In 1809, the American Fur Company was chartered by the State of New York, with a capital of one million dollars, and the privilege of increasing it to two. This company was in reality, John Jacob Astor. He owned all of its stock and directed its movements; but in order to cope with the Mackinaw Company, he desired the weight and authority of a government charter. He at once entered the field with energy and began a hearty rivalry with the latter corporation; but the strife and bitterness thus engendered were so great, that in 1811 he was led to purchase the Mackinaw Company and all its posts. Some of the partners of the Northwest Company were engaged with him in the enterprise, and it would no doubt have been very successful had not the war of 1812 broken out and put a stop to his operations. After the war these operations were not resumed, because Congress soon passed a law forbidding British trappers to pursue their vocation within our territory. But before this had happened, Mr. Astor's thoughts were occupied with a grander scheme.

The great navigator, Captain Cook, in his last voyage had discovered that sea otter were numerous on the coast of Oregon. Now sea otter fur was a rarity greatly prized in China, so that, in a few years, there were a score of vessels, chiefly from Boston and Salem, on the northwest coast collecting these furs; and then, when a cargo was gathered, sailing with it to Canton, China. One of these vessels, the Columbia, Captain Gray, of Boston, in 1792, discovered and entered the great river Columbia, which empties into the Pacific in latitude 46° 5' N. and whose head-waters are a thousand miles back in the heart of the continent. No organized company had gained a foothold on this coast except the Russian Fur Company, whose posts were far to the northward of the Columbia. Mr. Astor now conceived the grand plan of establishing a colony of trappers and traders at the mouth of the Columbia, with posts stretching back in the interior along the river and its branches, and also up and down the coast, the whole to be supplied by his vessels, which would receive in return the furs gathered by the trappers. This plan was also confided to government, and President Jefferson, glad to have a chain of American posts established in that untrodden country to form the nuclei of future cities and towns, promised it all the assistance and protection in his power. Mr. Astor at once began preparations. He secured three partners from the Northwest Company, and with Mr. Wilson Hunt, of

New Jersey, formed the Pacific Fur Company. He engaged voyageurs and traders from the western wilderness. He fitted out a fine ship — the Tonquin — and placing her in command of one whom he deemed a competent commander, dispatched her around the Horn to the mouth of the Columbia. She bore three of the partners and everything necessary for the Indian trade and for the infant colony. At the same time a land party was organized under Mr. Hunt, to proceed overland to the head-waters of the Columbia, and thence down that stream to meet the Tonquin at its mouth. The Tonquin sailed September 8, 1810 and reached the Columbia March 22, 1811. Here on Point George, the promontory overlooking the estuary into which the Columbia falls, the partners built the trading post, which in honor of their principal they called Astoria. The Tonquin then made sail and proceeded north on a trading voyage, as ordered by Mr. Astor. Much better would it have been if Captain Thorn, her commander, had obeyed orders in other respects as implicitly. He had been especially cautioned against allowing the coast Indians, who were a fierce and warlike race, to come on board in force. But he disobeyed these orders, and while lying in the harbor of Neweetee, Vancouver's Island, the ship was taken by a large body of the natives, who came on board in friendly guise, but with arms concealed under their mantles. The captain and all of his crew, except Mr. Lewis, the supercargo, and four seamen, were savagely murdered. These five barricaded themselves in the cabin, and with discharge of fire-arms soon cleared the ship. Then, as soon as it became dark, fearing that the savages would return, the four seamen took the ship's boat and set out on their return to Astoria, but Mr. Lewis, who was seriously wounded, refused to go and remained on the ship. He had formed a plan for avenging the butchery of his comrades. Next morning, by friendly signs, he enticed the Indians on board, and when the deck was covered with them, touched a match to the powder magazine and blew ship, Indians, canoes, and himself into fragments. A hundred savages were killed, it is said, in this holocaust. But the four men who had embarked in the ship's boat met a worse fate. They were taken by the Indians, and put to death in revenge, with every refinement of torture that savage ingenuity could suggest. The loss of the Tonquin was the first of a series of mishaps, which, in the end, ruined this well-laid plan.

Mr. Hunt, who left Montreal in August, 1810, with a large party, to come by the overland route, reached his destination, after suffering incredible hardships, ragged, emaciated, with the loss of nearly all of his men and stores. Meantime Mr. Astor, unaware of the loss of the Tonquin, had dispatched, in 1811, a second ship, the Beaver, which found the little colony at Astoria in good health and spirits, and the trading posts, which had been established, well equipped and prosperous. No doubt the enterprise would have proved successful and Oregon have been settled much earlier than she was, had not war (1812-1815) broken out between England and the United States, and put a stop to all industrial enterprises. This war was a commercial war; that is, it was waged to protect American commerce from the exactions and encroachments of England and was fought chiefly on the sea. During the contest New York was blockaded by a British fleet; her commerce was destroyed, and the people lived in constant dread of an attack.

Mr. Astor in those days had little time to think of, and no chance to aid, his struggling colony on the Pacific. But Astoria was soon beyond the reach of assistance, having been surrendered on the 12th of December, 1813, to the British sloop-of-war

Raccoon. It had, however, previously been sold to an agent of the Northwest Company, together with its stock of furs and stores, at about half their value; so that the entire loss did not come upon the partners. Mr. Astor's subsequent enterprises were not of such national importance, although they extended to the remotest seas. Twenty years before his death he retired from commercial ventures and devoted himself to the care of his real-estate interests, which had grown to vast proportions. He developed scholarly tastes during these years, one of his contemporaries tells us, and at his modest mansion, that stood on the block now occupied by the Astor House, delighted to gather the scholars and literary men of the day. Washington Irving always made his home there when in the city; so did Dr. Joseph C. Cogswell, the editor of the New York Review; Fitz-Green Halleck, who was in his employ, often dined with him; and in his will he showed his regard for letters by setting apart the sum of $350,000 as an endowment of the Astor Library. Mr. Astor died in 1848, leaving a fortune valued at forty millions — the fifth largest estate at that time in the world.

CHAPTER XX. COMMERCIAL DEVELOPMENT.

But despite the presence of great merchants, the growth of the city during the first period of freedom (1783-1815) was not so great as might have been expected. In 1674, when she came permanently under the English flag, she had a population of 3,000; in 1783, when she became a free city, she had 23,000 inhabitants, an average yearly increase under English rule of 183. By 1810 this had grown to 95,000, a yearly increase of 2,666. To-day her population, with that of her environs, — Brooklyn and Jersey City, — is estimated at 2,600,000, an average yearly increase since 1810 of 32,532. Her comparatively slow growth during the first period was due to a variety of causes: the disordered condition of Europe, the restrictions of England on her commerce, the war of 1812, and absence of a great producing tributary country. Soon after the war of 1812-15, how-' ever, three beneficent genii came to her aid, roused her to renewed activity, and have since combined to make her one of the queen cities of the world. They were the steamboat, the canal, and the railway. The steamboat came first, — the historic Clermont, — the first ever seen in New York waters, — having paddled her way up the Hudson in August, 1807, frightening half out of their wits the simple countrymen, who thought her some visitant from the infernal regions. Her maker was Robert Fulton, one of the greatest men of his age; of humble parentage, — as most great men are, — born on a farm in Fulton township, Pennsylvania in the year 1763. A painter of ability, but chiefly distinguished for his inventions and discoveries in mechanical science. Steamboats, torpedo boats, canals and canal boats, the ferry-boats that we now use, and the floating docks into which they run without shock were his most useful inventions. It would be more proper to say that he invented a steamboat, for boats propelled by steam had been invented as early as 1543, and John Fitch in 1787 had constructed a steamboat, which made regular trips on the Delaware River between Philadelphia and Burlington. Fulton's design, however, was the first successful steamboat, and in its essential principles is still in use. In making his experiments he was greatly aided in both money and advice by two other eminent Americans, Joel Barlow and Robert R. Livingston, the latter becoming his partner, and advancing money for the building of the Clermont and securing for her the exclusive privilege of navigating the waters of New York when she should be finished. After many trials and discouragements, the Clermont was launched.

The engraving gives a good idea of her general appearance. She was 130 feet long, 16 feet wide, and 4 feet deep. Her steam cylinder was 24 inches in diameter, with a four-foot stroke, and her paddlewheels 15 feet in diameter, with paddles, or floats, 2 feet wide. While the Clermont was being built, many witticisms were indulged in at her builder's expense. Few believed that heavy boats could be propelled against wind and tide by the power of steam; and when it was advertised that the Clermont would sail for Albany on her trial trip, on the morning of August 11, 1807, a great crowd gathered on the dock, eager to witness the inventor's discomfiture. They had nothing but sarcastic remarks for the man with an idea.

" This is the way," wrote Fulton to his friend Mr. Barlow, " that ignorant men compliment what they call philosophers and projectors." But the voyage of the Clermont proved a complete success. She arrived at Clermont, the country-seat of Mr. Livingston, in twenty-four hours, a distance of no miles, and at Albany in eight hours more, making the entire distance of 150 miles against both wind and tide in thirty-two hours, or nearly five miles an hour. The return trip was made in thirty hours. " The power of propelling boats by steam is now fully proved," wrote Fulton in the letter above quoted. And so it was; for, although between the skeleton steamboat of Fulton, and the palatial steamers which now ply on the Hudson and the Sound, a great gap exists, yet their principle was the same; while the splendid ocean steamers, which have utterly changed commercial methods, sprang from the same germ.

The Clermont at once began running regularly as a passenger boat, and, as she made the passage to Albany in thirty-two hours, while the packet sloop required from four to seven days, she had no lack of patronage. Some rival boats were built and put on the river, in defiance of the exclusive right to navigate boats by steam given to Fulton and Livingston. By 1809, there was a regular line of steam packets to Albany. In 1813, there was a triweekly line, leaving New York every Tuesday, Thursday, and Saturday afternoon. Improvements continued to be made, so that, by the year 1817, the time of passage had been reduced to eighteen hours. In 1818, the present steamboat service on the Sound was begun — the Fulton, under Fulton and Livingston's patent, running between New York and New Haven, and the Connecticut, making regular trips to New London. In 1822, the New York and Providence Line was organized. By 1830, there were eighty-six steamboats running on New York waters.

The year before, in 1829, a man came to New York who was destined to give a great impetus to the business of steamboating. His name was Cornelius Vanderbilt, and he had been born at Port Richmond, on Staten Island, thirty-five years before; a poor boy, but strong of body and mind, ambitious, intent on making his fortune. At sixteen, he was master of a sail-boat plying as a ferry between Staten Island and New York. At eighteen, he owned two ferry-boats, and had saved $1,000. The possibilities of the steamboat early attracted his attention, and in 1817, at the age of twenty-three, with $9,000 to his credit, he joined Thomas Gibbons, of New Jersey, in building a small steamer, TJie-Mouse-of-the-Mountain, to run from New Brunswick, New Jersey, to New York; of this boat he was captain, at a salary of $1,000 per year. He was connected with the Gibbons line for twelve years, and when he left it, in 1829, it was paying $40,000 a year. But the monopoly of the Hudson and the Sound, granted Fulton and Livingston, was now broken, and he had a keen ambition to enter that field. He removed to New York in 1829, as has been said, and soon made his presence felt. The steamboat service of the day was wretched. The boats were small and slow, the cabins dirty and ill ventilated. Mr. Vanderbilt built new boats — larger, faster, with many improvements, and lowered the fares; and although he had such competitors as Colonel John Stevens, Dean Richmond, and Daniel Drew, soon distanced them all. In a few years he had boats running to Albany, and to all the important Sound ports. His receipts for the first five years were $30,000 per year, and later double that. Between 1829 and 1848, he owned and operated nearly fifty steamboats, most of which he built himself. The breaking out of the California gold excitement drew him into ocean steamship ventures, and he began a famous contest with the Pacific Mail Steamship Company for the passenger traffic to California, across the Isthmus of Darien, which ended in his being bought off, as there was not trade enough for two. In 1855, he established a line of steamers to Havre, France — larger, swifter, and more elegant than those of the Collins line, then running to

England, and which soon became the favorite of travelers. This line he continued until the breaking out of the war in 1860. While engaged in ocean navigation, he is said to have owned twenty-one steamships, ten of which he built. In his later days, Mr. Vanderbilt withdrew from shipping, and turned his attention entirely to railways. He died in New York, in 1877.

We have wandered somewhat from our subject. Let us return to the second great factor in the city's progress — the Erie Canal. The fact that boats could be towed by steam-power from Albany to New York, no doubt turned men's thoughts to a canal from Albany west to Buffalo, which should connect the Atlantic and the Great Lakes, and give to New York the commerce of half a continent.

Judge Jonas Piatt first brought the project to the attention of the Legislature, in 1810, though it had been before agitated in the public prints. The plan was generally regarded as chimerical, or, if practicable, as being beyond the resources of the State of New York. In the autumn of 1815, however, the war being over, the project was revived, the leading spirit being De Witt Clinton, nephew of the War Governor, Mayor of New York City at the time, and subsequently Governor of the State. A meeting of merchants and others was held at the City Hall, in the autumn of 1815, and a committee, headed by Mayor Clinton, was chosen to prepare a memorial to the Legislature on the subject. This memorial was written by Mayor Clinton and was one of the ablest and most effective of State papers. In glowing terms it depicted the benefits to State and City of the stupendous plan. It would make tributary the Great Lakes and the entire Northwest. Boats laden with the crude products of that vast region would pass through it in endless procession; great manufacturing establishments would spring up; agriculture would establish its granaries, and commerce its warehouses in all directions; villages, towns, and hamlets would line the banks of the canal and the shores of the Hudson. In addition to these prophecies — which soon became facts, — plans and careful estimates of the cost of the proposed work were given, and methods for raising the money were suggested. Monster mass-meetings in its favor were held along the line of the proposed canal. A bill for building it was introduced in the Legislature of 1816, and, after a stormy debate, was passed on April 17th. On July 4th, of the next year, ground was broken for the canal at Rome, midway between the two termini. The work was so magnificent that it awakened intense enthusiasm throughout the State. Subscriptions poured in; most of the right of way was given. The sturdy yeomen along the line worked with willing hands and patriotic hearts, each feeling that every shovelful thrown out brought the bridal of the lakes and ocean nearer and advanced the power and glory of his State. In 1820, the middle section, from Utica to Rome, ninety-six miles, was opened. October 1, 1823, the eastern section to Albany was completed, and two years later the entire canal was declared ready for traffic. The herculean task, that its opponents — and they were many — declared would tax the resources of the nation, had been completed by New York alone in a little more than eight years.

There was more poetry and originality in men's natures then, I think; at least, the celebration of the opening of the canal was one of the most unique and poetic incidents in the history of peoples. There was then no telegraph, so they proceeded to invent one. They stationed cannon — thirty-two pounders, survivors of the Revolution and of the War of 1812 as far as they could be had — at intervals of eight or ten miles along the line of the canal, from Buffalo to Albany, and thence along the banks of the Hudson to New York and Sandy Hook. And they appointed veterans of the wars to man them, too, as far as they could obtain them; the object being to announce to New York and the country between, the precise moment when the waters of Lake Erie were let into the canal, and the little fleet of pioneer boats started on their journey to the Atlantic.

The opening day of the grand celebration was appointed for October 26, 1825, and, the night before, these cannons were loaded with powder and blank cartridges, carefully primed, and put in charge of the veterans, with strict orders to each to fire as soon as he saw the flash or heard the roar of the westward gun. At ten o'clock precisely, on the morning of the 26th, the water was let into the canal, and the boats began their journey. Simultaneously the signal gun was fired. Its report, taken up by the relays of cannon, swept on over the broad reaches of the lake basin to Rochester, across the flats of the Genesee to Syracuse, over the sixty-seven-mile level to Utica, and down the beautiful valley of the Mohawk to Albany. At 11 A.M. precisely, the grim old veteran standing to his piece at Castleton caught the signal gun from Albany, and sent it thundering on to Baltimore. It reached Coxsackie at 11.03; Hudson, one minute later; Catskill, Upper Red Hook, Rhinebeck, and Hyde Park at moment intervals. At 11.09 it was at Poughkeepsie, and the eagles on Storm King flapped their wings joyously, thinking war had come again. Hamburgh, Newburgh, West Point, Fort Montgomery, Stony Point, Sing Sing, Closter's Landing, Fort Washington, Fort Gansevoort, the Battery, Fort Lafayette, took it up in succession, and passed it on, the last station — Sandy Hook — receiving it at 11.21 A.M., twenty-one minutes after it left Albany, and one hour and twenty-one minutes from Buffalo. At twenty-two minutes past eleven, Fort Lafayette began the return fire with a national salute; this the Battery took up at 11.31, and so the line of fire sped back as it had come to the Great Lakes, reaching Buffalo at 12.50 P.M., having passed over 1,100 miles in less than three hours. Much more poetic and impressive seems this roar of cannon than the click of the telegraphic needle.

The Commercial Advertiser, in its issue of that day, thus announced the event:

" The work is done. At twenty minutes past eleven this morning the joyful intelligence was proclaimed to our citizens, by roar of artillery, that the great, the gigantic work of uniting the upper lakes with the ocean was completed, and that exactly an hour and twenty minutes before, the first boat from Erie had entered the canal and commenced its voyage to New York."

Let us return to this boat and to Buffalo. At the moment of the in-rushing of the lake water, a procession of four boats began their journey to New York. First came the Seneca Chief, drawn by four gray horses elegantly caparisoned, and following her the Superior, the Commodore Perry, a freight boat, and the Buffalo of Erie. On board was a distinguished company: De Witt Clinton, now Governor of the State; Lieutenant-Governor Tallmadge, the New York delegation which had come on to extend to the party the hospitalities of the city, and a great company of fair women and brave men, — the invited guests. As they progressed, it seemed as if the entire State of New York had gathered along the line to greet them. At Rochester the canal was carried across the Genesee River by a stone aqueduct of nine arches, each of fifty feet span. Here sentinels, stationed in a small boat to defend the entrance, hailed the flotilla, "Who comes there?" "Your brothers from the West on the waters of the Great Lakes," was the swift reply, and the dialogue continued. " By what means have

165

they been diverted so far from their natural course?" — "Through the channel of the Grand Erie Canal." — "By whose authority and by whom was a work of such magnitude accomplished?" and a chorus of voices from the Seneca Chief answered: " By the authority and by the enterprise of the people of the State of New York." The sentinel boat then gave way, and the fleet proudly entered the spacious basin at the end of the aqueduct amid welcoming salutes of artillery and the acclamations of thousands.

Similar demonstrations awaited the procession all along the line. At Albany there was a congratulatory address, a public dinner, and a grand illumination in the evening. All the steam craft on the Hudson had been gathered there to tow the fleet down the river. It left Albany on November 2nd, the brilliant company increased by the addition of the corporation of Albany as the invited guests of New York. On the morning of the 4th, the flotilla came abreast of the Palisades, with the city in the distance half concealed by the mellow Indian-summer haze. Before sunrise it anchored off the city and was soon approached by the steamer Washington, having the committee of the Common Council and officers of the Governor's Guards on board, and flying the broad pennant of the Corporation. "Where are you from and whither bound? " asked the corporation steamer, as she approached. " From Lake Erie and bound to Sandy Hook," was the reply. The Washington then moved alongside the Seneca Chief, and the committee boarding her. Alderman Coudrey in a graceful speech welcomed the visitors to the city. Some hours later the aquatic procession was formed, and after proceeding to the Navy Yard, and taking on board officers and other guests, moved out to sea. The spectacle, as the vessels were getting into line, is said to have been a brilliant and animated one. Hundreds of ships, frigates, sloops, steamboats, barges, and other craft covered the bay, each bedecked from trucks to keelson with flags and banners, and swarming with humanity, while both shores, the Heights, and the islands in the harbor were lined with applauding spectators.

There were twenty-nine steam vessels of all sorts in the line. Occupying the first place was the Washington, with the mayor, corporation, and distinguished guests on board. The ship Hamlet, chartered by the marine and nautical societies and towed by the Oliver Ellsworth, was noticeable for her display of the flags of all nations. Another feature, described by the old chronicler with fulness of compliment, was the "safety barges" Lady Clinton and Lady Van Rensselaer, towed by the Commerce and filled with the fairest daughters of a city renowned for fair women; the former bore Mrs. Clinton, the governor's lady, and was hung from stem to stern with festoons of evergreen, among which were intertwined roses, china-asters, and other bright-hued flowers. The fleet moved down the bay saluted with guns from the forts on shore, and from the British frigates at anchor, and when nearing the Narrows was met by a pilot-boat, which hailed and announced that it had been sent by Neptune to conduct the fleet to his dominions. The throne of Neptune at this moment was the United States schooner Porpoise, moored just within Sandy Hook, and around which the fleet formed a circle some three miles in circumference. A colloquy ensued between Neptune on his schooner and the visitors, as to the place whence they came and the object of their coming, and when this had been explained to his satisfaction the last act in the pretty drama was performed. Governor Clinton, manly in frame, handsome of face, gallant of spirit, standing on the Seneca Chief, took a keg of lake water, which had been brought from Buffalo, and holding it aloft in full view of all, poured its contents into the briny sea, saying:

" This solemnity, at this place, on the first arrival of vessels from Lake Erie is intended to indicate and commemorate the navigable communication which has been accomplished between our Mediterranean seas and the Atlantic Ocean in about eight years, to the extent of more than four hundred and twenty-five miles, by the wisdom, public spirit, and energy of the people of the State of New York; and may the God of the heavens and the earth smile most propitiously on this work and render it subservient to the best interests of the human race." Dr. Mitchell then poured into the ocean water from the Ganges, Indus, Nile, Thames, and other rivers of the world, and the ceremony was complete. The fleet then returned to the Battery, where the guests disembarked and took part in the land procession, which was a splendid and successful affair, but so much like the great Federal pageant of 1788, that a detailed description is unnecessary. The corporation further commemorated the day by issuing a great number of medals in gold, silver, and white metal. There were fifty-one of the gold medals, which were enclosed in elegant red morocco cases and sent to various monarchs of Europe and to the eminent men of our own country. Among the latter were the three surviving signers of the Declaration, John Adams, Thomas Jefferson, and Charles Carroll of Carrollton.

Thus, the great Erie Canal was opened. Its benefit to New York has been incalculable. In fact, it has been the greatest factor in the city's marvelous commercial growth, pouring into her lap the crude products of a constantly widening area, which form the bulk of her exports, and distributing to this same region the multitudinous articles comprised in her imports. In 1831, however, a competitor appeared, which in a few years completely distanced the canal as a means of locomotion, and, to a great extent, of transportation. In that year the first railroad in New York, and one of the first in the country, was opened between Albany and Schenectady.

A year later, April 24, 1832, the great Erie Railway — the first trunk line, — designed to open communication between New York and the Great Lakes, was chartered. It was completed to Dunkirk, on Lake Erie, in 1851. Meantime, the Mohawk and Hudson (later known as the Albany and Schenectady) had been pushing westward under various names until, by completion of the Buffalo and Lockport Railway in 1854, it formed a continuous line of rail from Albany to Buffalo. These various roads had been merged into one line in 1853, by the name of the New York Central, and that line, by its union, in 1869, with the Hudson River Railroad, formed the second great trunk line between New York and the West. Two years later, in 1871, the Pennsylvania Railroad, which had been opened from Philadelphia to Pittsburg in 1854, leased the United Railways of New Jersey, and formed the third great trunk line. The Baltimore and Ohio, the Delaware and Lackawanna, and the West Shore systems have since been added. These seven great arteries, joined to her position and unexcelled harbor, appear to assure to New York City the commercial supremacy of the world, provided her merchants have the courage and genius to take advantage of them. To a recital of some of their triumphs in the past we can well devote another chapter.

XXI. SHIPS AND SAILORS.

The first shipping enterprise of moment to New York merchants was the founding, in 1816, of the famous packet service between New York and Liverpool, and which contributed not a little to the glory of American shipbuilders and merchants. The merchantmen of that day were also passenger ships. They were clumsy, slow sailors, dingy and shabby in their passenger appointments, and without stated time of sailing, leaving at hap-hazard, whenever their cargoes were complete. By and by, it occurred to certain shrewd merchants of New York — Isaac Wright and Son, Francis Thompson, Benjamin Marshall, and Jeremiah Thompson — that a line of ships unrivalled for strength, speed, and beauty, and with a regular schedule of sailings, would soon drive the old merchantmen from the trade. They therefore founded the famous " Black Ball Line," still a fountain of happy memories to the old merchants and sea-captains, who haunt the shipping-offices about Burling Slip and South Street and talk of past glories. There were four packets of this line at first, subsequently increased to twelve, each a thing of beauty, and a joy to the American heart; one of them sailed regularly on the 1st of every month. They were so successful that, in 1821, a rival Liverpool line — the Red Star — was established by Byrnes, Grimble, & Co., with four ships — Manhattan, Hercules, Panther and Meteor, and sailing on the 24th of every month. Stimulated by this competition, the proprietors of the Black Ball Line added four new vessels and advertised a sailing on the 1st and 16th of every month. Then began an era of shipbuilding: Fish, Grinnell, & Co., and Thaddeus Phelps, & Co., founded the Swallow-Tail Line — so called from its forked pennant, — with departures on the 8th of every month, and the city papers proudly announced that New York had the exclusive and distinguished privilege of a fast weekly service to Liverpool. These packets were noble ships, of from 600 to 1,500 tons each, and made the run from New York to Liverpool in twenty-three days, and the return trip in forty. Once the Canada, of the Black Ball Line, beat the record by making the outward voyage in fifteen days and eighteen hours.

In 1823 a London Line was established by Grinnell, Minturn, & Co., with sailings every month. A line of packets to Havre, France, was also established, about 1822, by Francis Depau, with four ships. These various lines of packets aided greatly in building up the city. They shortened and cheapened communication between her and Europe, and they drove the clumsy French and English traders from the seas, thus throwing the carrying trade into American bottoms. They also proved mines of wealth to their captains, agents, and builders, — for each owned a share; the captain usually an eighth, the builder another eighth, the agent an eighth, the rigger another fraction — that all might have an interest in the success of the voyage. Gradually larger and finer vessels were built, the Palestine and Amazon of 1,800 tons each being the largest as well as the last of their race. It is a tradition of South Street that the latter had once made the voyage to Portsmouth, England, in fourteen days — a great feat for a sailing vessel, although the Independence, the Montezuma, the Patrick Henry, and the Southampton had performed the voyage to Liverpool in the same period. The packets remained in commission until the war of 1860 drove American ships from the ocean. Some were utilized as transports, some were sunk in Southern harbors to blockade them, a few may still be seen at our wharves.

As fine specimens of naval architecture, however, the packet ships were quite thrown in the shade by the Canton and California clippers of 1840-55. The clipper ships originated in Baltimore about 1840, in answer to the demands of the China tea trade. Merchants found that tea deteriorated in quality with every day spent on the ocean — besides a cargo was of such great value that every day saved represented quite an item in interest and insurance — hence the demand for swift ships. The first clippers built in New York were for those famous China merchants, William H. Aspinwall, N. L. & G. Griswold, and A. A. Low & Brother, and were small, swift vessels of from 600 to 900 tons burthen. In 1849, however, came the California gold excitement and brought at once the golden age of the clipper service. For one half the distance to China — San Francisco — a return cargo could be secured. This comprised bulky articles, passengers' baggage, provisions, machinery of the mines, etc., and created a demand for larger ships. This brought into existence those triumphs of the shipbuilder's art — the Challenge, of 2,000 tons, built by William Webb in 1851 for N. L. & G. Griswold; the Invincible, of 2,150 tons; the Comet, of 1,209 tons; and the Sword Fish, of 1,150 tons. Other famous sea rovers followed: the Tornado, the Flying Cloud, the Black Squall, the Sovereign of the Seas, and others, so that of the 157 vessels of all grades that entered San Francisco in 1852, 70 were clippers. Mr. Sheldon, in his article before referred to, has given so spirited an account of the exploits of the clippers that we copy it as the best that can be said on the subject:

" That clipper epoch was an epoch to be proud of. And we were proud of it. The New York newspapers abounded in such head-lines in large type as these: ' Quickest Trip on Record,' ' Shortest Passage to San Francisco,' ' Unparalleled Speed,' ' Quickest Voyage Yet,' 'A Clipper as Is a Clipper,' 'Extraordinary Dispatch,' 'The Quickest Voyage to China,' 'The Contest of the Clippers,' 'Great Passage from San Francisco,' 'Race Round the World.' The clipper ship Surprise, built in East Boston by Mr. Hall, and owned by A. A. Low & Bro., having sailed to San Francisco in ninety-six days — then the shortest time on record (Mr. W. H, Aspinwall's Sea Witch had run the course in ninety-seven days) — a San Francisco journal said: ' One of our most distinguished merchants made a bet with a friend some weeks since that the Surprise would make the passage in ninety-six days — ^just the time she has consumed to a day. Yesterday morning, full of confidence, he mounted his old nag, and rode over to the north beach to get the first glimpse of the looked-for clipper. The fog, however, was rather thick outside, and after looking awhile he turned back to town, but had not arrived at his counting-room before he heard that the Surprise had passed the Golden Gate, and by eleven o'clock Captain Dumaresq was in his old friend's counting-room on Sansome Street. She has brought 1,800 tons of cargo, which may be estimated at a value of $200,000. Her manifest is twenty-five feet long.' Her greatest run was 284 miles in twenty-four hours, and she reefed her topsails but twice during the voyage of 16,308 miles She soon left San Francisco for London, by way of Canton, and on reaching the English capital her receipts for freights had entirely paid her cost and running expenses, besides netting her owners a clear profit of $50,000. At Canton her freight for London was engaged at £6 sterling a ton, while the English ships were taking their freight at £3 and £4 a ton; and this was the second season that the preference had been given to American ships at advanced rates, their shorter passages enabling shippers to receive prompt returns from their investments, to save interest, and to secure an early market. ' If ships,' said a California newspaper, ' can be built to make such trips as this, steamers for long passages will be at a discount. California has done much toward the commencement of a new era in shipbuilding when the heavy, clumsy models of past days have given way to the new and beautiful one of the Surprise and others of the same build.' ' The Californians,' said a New York newspaper, 'are in ecstasies over our clipper ships, which come and depart like so many winged Pegasuses. There are now on the way to the Pacific, and ready to start for that portion of the world, as splendid vessels as the eye ever rested upon, and commanded by men whose knowledge of their profession cannot be excelled, and each determined to do his utmost to be first in this clipper contest.'

" The whole country, indeed, was stirred by the beauty, the speed, and the triumphs of these American clippers. The Houqua, Captain Daniel McKenzie, built by Brown, & Bell for A. A. Low & Bro., made the trip from Shanghai to New York, in 1850, in eighty-eight days, then the shortest ever made between these ports. The Samuel Russell, Captain N, B. Palmer, owned by the same firm, sailed in one day in 1851, on her voyage home from Whampoa, China, 318 miles, or thirteen and a quarter miles an hour, — a speed greater than had been obtained by any ocean steamer. For thirty days in succession, from the 8th of November to the 7th of December, she averaged 226 miles a day, covering in that period 6,722 miles, or one half the entire distance between China and New York. On another occasion, while going to Canton, she sailed 328 miles in one day. ' Now, sir,' wrote one of her skippers, ' I humbly submit if that is not a feat to boast of — if that is not an achievement to entitle a ship to be classed among clippers 1 ' On her return voyage she had the honor of reporting in New York the news of her own arrival at Canton. The Flying Cloud, 1,782 tons, built by Donald McKay, of East Boston, commanded by Captain Josiah P. Creesy, of Marblehead, went, in 1851, to San Francisco from New York in eighty-four days — the fastest trip ever made by a sailing vessel, and twelve days shorter than that of the Surprise. Lieutenant Maury, of the United States Naval Observatory at Washington, reported that the greatest distance ever performed from noon to noon on the ocean was 433 ¼ statute miles, by the clipper ship Flying Cloud, in her celebrated passage ' of eighty-four days from New York to San Francisco, 'which yet stands unequalled.' The Northern Light, of Boston, left San Francisco on the 13th of March, 1853, and reached Boston on the 29th of May following, thus sailing more than 16,000 miles in seventy-seven days, an average of over 200 miles a day. Splendid is the record of the Sovereign of the Seas, commanded by Captain L. McKay, and built by his brother Donald McKay. This noble vessel left New York for San Francisco in August, 1851, with freight, for carrying which she would receive $84,000 — a marvelous sum to-day — a barrel of flour on her arrival selling for $44, and when off Valparaiso in a storm was dismasted, everything above the mast-heads of her fore and main-masts being carried away. In fourteen days she was rigged at sea, and proceeding on her way to California, reached her destination in 102 days from New York, in spite of the accident and detention — the best passage ever made at that season of the year. Seventy feet of her fore-mast and main-mast were gone, and also four sails on each mast. Having discharged her cargo, the clipper sailed for Honolulu, and loaded with oil for New York, which she reached in eighty-two days — a passage never equaled. For 10,000 miles she sailed without tacking or wearing, and in ten consecutive days she made 3,300 miles. Loading again immediately for Liverpool, she left on a Saturday, the 18th of June, 1852. On Sunday, the 26th, she was becalmed on the Banks of Newfoundland; but at midnight a breeze sprung up, and on the following Saturday, at 5 o'clock P.M., she dropped anchor in the Mersey — another passage never equaled. She had sailed from the Banks to Liverpool in about five days and a half, and from New York to Liverpool in the unprecedented time of thirteen days and nineteen hours. One day she sailed 340 miles; on the same day the Cunard steamer Canada, which had left Boston almost simultaneously with the Sovereign of the Seas, made only 306 miles. To-day, thirty years afterward, it is enlivening to read in the newspapers of that time the editorial articles on the splendid performances of that splendid ship. But her story is not told yet. On the 10th of May, 1853, Lieutenant M. F. Maury reported to the Hon. James C. Dobbin, Secretary of the Navy, that the clipper-ship Sovereign of the Seas, 2,421 tons, on a voyage from San Francisco, had made 'the enormous run of 6,245 miles in twenty-two days, a daily average of 238.9 miles, and that the greatest distance traversed from noon of one day to the noon of the next day was 419 miles. After his illustrious performances on the ocean. Captain McKay is now a shipping merchant in South Street, New York City. His brother, Donald McKay, the builder, died some time since in Boston. For the meritorious work of rigging his vessel at sea when dismasted off Valparaiso, Captain McKay was presented by Walter R. Jones, president of the Atlantic Mutual Insurance Company, on behalf of the underwriters, with a massive and costly silver dinner service.

" Captain Samuel Samuels became famous in the clipper Dreadnought, and it used to be said that with a strong wind nothing ever passed her, — not even a steamer. Built in Newburyport for Governor E. D. Morgan, Captain Samuels, and others, she was named after the famous vessel in Admiral Nelson's fleet, her owners sending to England to get the right spelling of the name, which they found to be Dreadnought, and not Dreadnaught. Her keel was laid in June, 1853, and her first return trip from Liverpool made in February, 1854. On that voyage she scudded into celebrity by reaching Sandy Hook as soon as the Cunard steamer Canada, which had left Liverpool one day earlier, reached Boston. In 1859 she made the 3,000 miles from Sandy Hook to Rock Light, Liverpool, in thirteen days and eight hours; and in 1860 went from Sandy Hook to Queenstown, 2,760 miles, in the unequalled sailing time of nine days and seventeen hours. How often a first-class steamship has been longer in going the same distance! "

Such were some of the triumphs of our early marine; and how galling to national pride the contrast between that day and this! In 1853, American ships securing cargoes in English home ports amid the fiercest competition. In 1888, almost every pound of America's exports afloat in British bottoms, and scarcely an American vessel in commission in the foreign trade.

XXII. MINOR EVENTS — 1784-1860.

Some minor events of interest in the period passed over remain to be noticed.

Soon after the close of the war, in May, 1784, King's College was re-chartered by the State of New York, under the title Columbia. It cannot be said to have been fairly reorganized, however, until 1787, when the first president under the new regime, William Samuel Johnson, was elected. He was a son of Dr. Johnson, the first president of King's, an able and scholarly man. De Witt Clinton, later famous in the annals of the State, was the first student. The college buildings continued on the original site until 1857, when they were found to be too far down town, and the present site, between Madison and Fourth Avenues and Forty-Ninth and Fiftieth streets, was chosen.

In 1790, the new Trinity Church, built on the site of the one burned in 1776, was dedicated with appropriate ceremonies. Washington and his family were present in the pew set apart for the President's use; many other high officers of government were also present.

The city treasurer at this time was Daniel Phoenix, an eminent merchant and shrewd financier. During his term of office, the city issued the paper money shown below — the first instance, we believe, of the issue of such currency by the corporation, although as early as 1771 the colony had issued ten-, five-, and two-pound notes, which became a circulating medium. The decade between 1800 and 1810 was marked by a growing interest in letters and in art. In 1804, the New York Historical Society was founded by Mayor De Witt Clinton, Judge Egbert Benson, and others. Four years later, in 1808, the American Academy of Fine Arts was incorporated, with Chancellor Livingston as president, and the famous painter, John Trumbull, as vice-president. In 1809, "The History of New York," by Diedrich Knickerbocker, appeared, and was received with the greatest favor and enthusiasm. Busy merchants and lawyers read it by chapters in the pauses of business. Grave magistrates are even said to have taken it upon the bench with them. Sir Walter Scott, after reading it, wrote to a friend in New York that he had never seen anything so closely resembling the style of Dean Swift as the annals of Diedrich Knickerbocker. Some pains were taken to preserve the secret of its authorship, but it soon leaked out that the author was a briefless barrister of the city — one Washington Irving — but twenty-six years of age, and who had never written anything of note before, save some bright pieces in the Morning Chronicle, and in a weekly journal called Salmagundi, which made its appearance in 1807, and was edited and written chiefly by our author and his friend, James Kirke Paulding.

In 1812, the present City Hall, having been nine years in building, was completed. The same year war against Great Britain was declared, and the resources of the city were taxed to their utmost in raising troops and fortifying her harbor against an expected attack by the British fleet. Within four months after the declaration of war, she also equipped and sent to sea twenty-six privateers, carrying 212 guns, and 2,239 men. In 1813, her harbor was blockaded by British war-vessels, and continued to be with more or less thoroughness until the treaty of peace at Ghent, December 24, 1814, put an end to the war.

Nearly all the victories of that war were gained on the ocean. On August 19, 1812, Commodore Isaac Hull, in the frigate Constitution^ encountered the British frigate Guerriere, off the mouth of the St. Lawrence River, and in a gallant action of fifteen

172

minutes, captured his enemy. Six days before. Commodore David Porter, in the Essex, had captured the British sloop-of-war Alert, in an action lasting eight minutes. October 18th, of the same year, John Paul Jones, in the little Wasp, captured the British sloop-of-war Frolic, and this was followed on the 25th by the capture of the British war frigate Macedonian by the frigate United States, under command of Commodore Decatur. New York honored the heroes of these victories. Her citizens presented swords to Commodore Hull and his officers. The corporation ordered for the Commodore a richly embossed gold box, on which was engraved a picture of the action between the Constitution and Guerriere, and also asked him to sit for the portrait which now graces the Governor's Room in the City Hall. And on the 26th of December, at the moment that Commodore William Bainbridge was adding another leaf to American naval laurels by his capture of the Java, off the Brazil coast, the citizens of New York gave a grand banquet in honor of the heroes, Hull, Jones, and Decatur. Five hundred guests sat down at the tables, which were spread in the City Hotel, on Broadway near Trinity Church, a famous hostelry of that day.

Mayor De Witt Clinton presided, with Decatur on his right hand and Hull on his left. The room was " colonnaded round with the masts of ships entwined with laurel and bearing the flags of all the world." A miniature ship, flying the American flag at masthead, was placed upon each table, and, covering one side of the room, was the main-sail of a ship, 33 x 16 feet, which was drawn back as the third toast, " Our Navy," was drunk, and revealed an immense transparency on which the three battles of Hull, Jones, and Decatur were depicted. Many patriotic toasts were drunken after this, and many patriotic speeches made in reply to them. Banquet songs, praising the achievements of American sailors, were also sung. A few weeks later—January 7, 1813, — at the same place, Decatur's gallant crew were honored with a banquet. Another red-letter day of this period was that on which Decatur, in the victorious United States, with the conquered Macedonian in his train, came sweeping through the Sound and East River into port. Thousands covered the river banks, the docks, the buildings, and shipping, and cheer after cheer mingled with the thunder of cannon in greeting the victors.

At the close of the War of 1812, New York contained about one hundred thousand people. Her rapid progress northward toward Kingsbridge, levelling the crags and filling the vales as she advanced, dates from this period. Then it was that old citizens, returning after a few years' residence abroad, found her transformed. Marble palaces and temples stood on the site of former goat pastures. Crags and hills were levelled, ponds and marshes filled up. In the map of 1804, it will be seen that, at that time, Grand Street, west of Broadway, was far out of town, and that, on the east, the city was solidly built up but one block above it.

The Collect (marked 35 on the map) still lay in placid beauty, scene of boating parties in summer and of skating frolics in winter. As the city crept toward it (and, indeed, sometime after it had leaped the low, flat marshes along the line of what is now Canal Street) many plans for removing the pond were broached and discussed. Some proposed draining it by a canal along the present Canal Street from the East to the North River; others advocated filling its bed with rocks and clean earth excavated in the process of removing the crags above. The former expedient was at length adopted, commencing in 1809 a drainage canal was dug through the marshes, and a street laid out on either side, street and canal forming a spacious thoroughfare one hundred feet broad, and which naturally took the name of Canal Street. A double row of shade trees were set out along the canal, and the street was for years one of the finest in the city. But before this was accomplished, the city line had advanced far up the island, and by 1825 had reached Astor Place. I cannot better indicate the transformation since that day than by repeating the reminiscences of a gentleman born nearly eighty years ago in this city, indulged in one mellow autumn day, as we rode slowly down Broadway from Astor Place:

"In 1825," he began, "all north of Astor Place was open country, a region of farms and farm-houses, gardens, and apple orchards. An old high-peaked barn stood on the present site of Grace Church, and above, quite up to the powder-house (now Union Square), there were but two dwellings, as I remember, old stone farmhouses with attics. Lafayette Place was not, and near where the Astor Library now stands, extending through from the Bowery to Broadway, and south nearly to Bond Street, was the Vauxhall Garden, a delightful spot, with flowers, and lawns, and shade trees, where the New Yorkers of 1825 resorted to see the fireworks, partake of cakes and ale, and hear the band play on summer evenings. Nearly opposite, in the triangular-shaped park formed by the intersection of Third and Fourth Avenues, stood Peter Cooper's grocery store, and more than one quart of blackberries have I exchanged there for the seductive taffy or bunch of raisins.

" Bleecker Street was my great blackberry preserve when a boy," he said, as we came opposite that thoroughfare. " What luscious berries grew beside the walls on either side, and roses — no such roses bloom nowadays! Upper Broadway was then a country road: by 1830, however, lower Broadway had become almost as crowded and noisy as now. I remember that when the Broadway stages were first put on — about 1830 I think — they were very popular and multiplied beyond calculation. Rival stage companies were quickly organized, and the street was filled with their vehicles. Jams at the corner of Fulton and Broadway were frequent, and what with the shouting of the drivers and hoarse commands of the policemen were very amusing. The street venders then were quite as numerous as now, and, I think, more picturesque and interesting. Some bore trays containing baked pears swimming in molasses, which they offered for sale; others sold hot corn. The sandman was a verity in those days. The bar-rooms, restaurants, and many of the kitchens had sanded floors, and men in long white frocks with two-wheeled carts, peddling Rockaway sand, were familiar objects on the streets. Then there were the darkeys who sold bundles of straw for filling the beds, and an old blind man who sold door-mats made of picked tar rope. I knew a man in those days who acquired quite a fortune by peddling pure spring water about the city at two cents a pail. Sometimes we crossed the ferry to visit friends in Brooklyn. You would laugh at the ferry-boats of my earlier years. They had open decks with an awning stretched over them, and benches around the sides, and were propelled by horse power. From four to sixteen horses were required, and they walked around a shaft in the center of the boat, turning it as sailors turn a capstan, and this shaft by gearing turned the paddle-wheels."

As we came to City Hall Park my friend's animation and interest increased.

"The City Hall," he said, "then only a few years built, stood between two prisons, the Bridewell and the Gaol. On the Chambers Street side of the park were three buildings, all under one roof. Nearest Broadway was the American Museum, a great favorite with the little people of that day; then the Academy of Fine Arts, and last the Almshouse, the artist and showman of that day being not far from the almshouse in more senses than one. Next, still going east, you came to the Rotunda of John Vanderlyn. Vanderlyn, you remember, had been discovered by Colonel Burr in an interior town, covering his master's blacksmith shop with charcoal sketches, and had been sent by Burr to Paris and Rome for instruction in art. His ' Marius amid the Ruins of Carthage ' had taken the prize at Paris under Napoleon, and he returned to New York comparatively famous. The city, thinking to do something for American art, built the Rotunda, and gave Vanderlyn the lease of it for a studio, and for the exhibition of his pictures. He showed there his ' Marius,' 'Ariadne,' and the 'Garden of Versailles,' the latter a panorama taking up two sides of the room.

" I could give you a volume of reminiscences about the old American Museum. It had been removed to the site of the present Herald building, and had ruined several owners, when P. T. Barnum got hold of it, and made a success of it. The fashionable place of amusement in my day was the Old Park Theatre, which stood on the south side of the park, near the site of the present World building. I have seen there Edmund Kean and Charles Matthews, the great actors of that day. The Old Park Theatre was burned on the morning of the 25th of May, 1820, but John Jacob Astor and John K. Beekman rebuilt, on the old site, in 1820-1, a much handsomer building. The park was a beautiful place in those days, with its flowers, and trees, and well-kept lawns. Tammany Hall, the cradle of the present powerful organization, was on the east, on the corner of Frankfort Street. Aaron Burr had an office in the Hall. The south side of the square, where now are the great newspaper offices, was then covered with low, one-story buildings — cigar stores, beer saloons, and the like. The modern giants of the press had not been thought of. I have seen them grow from infancy. The Sun was founded first, in 1833; next, the Herald, in 1835; the Tribune, in 1841; the Times, in 1851; and the World, in 1860."

My friend was loth to leave the spot, so many associations were connected with it. We passed Wall Street and Trinity Church, with their stirring and patriotic memories, and came out upon the Battery.

" This," said he, "is another historic place, and ought to be reclaimed. How absurd to give the fairest, breeziest spot in the city to emigrants, who could much better be accommodated at Communipaw. When I was young," he continued, " the Battery was the fashionable promenade. Castle Garden then was a frowning fort, with black muzzles of guns looking seaward through embrasures eight feet thick. The fort is there still, though few people know it. In those days we called it Fort Clinton. It was built about 1807, when the attacks of England on our commerce made it evident that we should have to whip her again to secure decent treatment. Later it was turned into a summer garden, and entertainments were held there. Here Jenny Lind, under the auspices of the great Barnum, made her debut in this country. I remember it perfectly. She arrived on September 1, 1850, by the Collins Line steamer Atlantic, and gave her first concert on Wednesday, September nth, and a second on the 13th. Four thousand people crowded into the garden to hear her sing."

We walked eastward towards the Staten Island Ferry-house.

" It was from the Battery," he continued, "that Washington took boat for Paulus Hook on his way to Virginia, and here we received Lafayette on his second visit to this country in 1824. He came on the French packet Cadmus and was met off Staten Island by a delegation of the City Fathers, headed by our handsome, courtly Mayor

175

William Paulding. Next day was made a fete day in his honor. From twelve to one the bells rang merry peals. No travel or traffic was allowed on Broadway below Chambers Street. At nine o'clock, the Corporation of the city, the Chamber of Commerce, the officers of the army and navy, and the Society of the Cincinnati proceeded to Staten Island and escorted to the city the man whom the American people delighted to honor. The cortege landed at Castle Garden upon a carpeted stairway, above which sprang an arch richly decorated with laurel and the flags of all nations. I remember Lafayette — a small, delicate man, — and the shouts of thousands and the salutes of artillery that greeted him. In a few moments he entered a carriage, to which four horses were attached, and proceeded up Broadway to the City Hall, where he was formally welcomed by Mayor Paulding. A public illumination in the evening completed the ceremonies."

XXIII. NEW YORK IN THE CIVIL WAR.

When war threatened, in the exciting days of 1860-61, the voice of New York was for peace. As a commercial community, she was, from the nature of things, conservative — averse to change. Debts to the amount of millions of dollars were due her at the South. War would confiscate every dollar. So as the irrepressible conflict drew near, her merchants made serious efforts to ward it off, — to effect a compromise, patch up a peace. On January 12, 1861, a memorial, signed by hundreds of her business men, was sent to Congress, praying that the pending difficulties might be settled on the basis of the Crittenden compromise. On the 18th, another memorial, with 40,000 names attached, praying for a peaceable solution of the difficulties, was endorsed by a meeting held in the Chamber of Commerce, and forwarded to Washington. A mass-meeting was held at Cooper Institute, at which three delegates were appointed to confer with the delegates of the six States that had seceded, with a view to healing the breach, and a Peace Society, with the venerable Prof. S. F. B. Morse, the inventor of the telegraph, at its head, was formed, with the same object in view. Meantime, Fernando Wood, the Mayor of the city, had broached his plan for erecting New York into a free and independent State. His words seem to us ironical, but they were uttered soberly — so infectious was the heresy of secession. In a message to the Common Council, dated January 7, 1861, he wrote:

" Why should not New York City, instead of supporting by her contributions in revenues, two thirds of the expenses of the United States, become also equally independent? As a free city, with but a nominal duty on imports, her local government could be supported without taxes upon her people. Thus we could live free from taxes, and have cheap goods nearly duty free. . . . When disunion has become a fixed and certain fact, why may not New York disrupt the bonds which bind her to a corrupt and venal master? " and so on.

But the brilliant reasoner failed to carry his argument to its logical conclusion: for if the state had a right to secede from the nation, and the city from the state, then the ward could secede from the city, the district from the ward, and each family could set up a government of its own; and so there would be an end, not only of the nation, the state, and the city, but of all law, order, and government. Yet the Common Council thought so well of this very illogical message, that they ordered three thousand copies printed for general circulation. At length, on April 12th, Fort Sumter was fired on. The stars and stripes bowed to the palmetto. In a moment the current of popular feeling in New York was turned. The feeling of citizenship, of nationality, revived. The old flag had been fired on, and Democrats vied with Republicans in sentiments of patriotism and loyalty. At a great mass-meeting held in Union Square, on April 20th, Mayor Fernando Wood, in an eloquent speech, declared with Jackson, that " the Union must and should be preserved." The air was surcharged with patriotism and military ardor. Fife, drum, and bugle, troops mustering in the armories, parading on the squares, tenting in the parks, marching rank on rank through the streets to embark for the front, were the daily sights and sounds all through the bright spring days of 1861. Bryant, the honored poet of New York, voiced the general sentiment, when he wrote:

" Lay down the axe, fling by the spade,
Leave in its track the toiling plough.
The rifle and the bayonet blade

For arms like yours are fitter now.
And let the hands that ply the pen
Quit the light task, and learn to wield
The horseman's crooked brand, and rein
The charger on the battle-field."

The Seventh Regiment, Colonel Lefferts, the pride of the city, was the first to leave, embarking on April 19th. Next day three more gallant regiments — the Sixth, Colonel Pinckney; the Twelfth, Colonel Butterworth; and the Seventy-first, Colonel Vosburg, marched away. In ten days New York City alone had sent 8,000 men to the front. To care for these troops and their families, and aid the government in its work, it was quickly seen that organized effort would be necessary, and on April 20th — the day after the Seventh left for the front — at a grand mass meeting held in Union Square a Committee of Safety was appointed to organize a Union Defense Committee. Of the latter committee Hon. John A. Dix, recently a member of President Buchanan's cabinet, was made chairman; William M. Evarts, subsequently Secretary of State, secretary; and Theodore Dehon, treasurer, while the most prominent citizens were enrolled as members. This committee performed excellent service. During the war it aided in organizing and equipping forty-nine regiments comprising about 40,000 men and disbursed a million of dollars in caring for the troops and their families.

While the patriotic sons of New York were marching to battle, the loyal women of the city were asking what they could do for their comfort and relief in sickness, or when suffering from wounds. Some of them applied to the Rev. Henry W. Bellows, a leading Unitarian clergyman of the city, for advice, and, at his suggestion, a meeting was called late in April, 1861, at which a Central Relief Association was organized. To give the movement wider scope a public meeting was held at Cooper Institute on the 29th, which was addressed by Vice-President Hamlin and others. At this meeting an organization called The Women's Central Relief Association was formed, which soon had branch societies in every one of the Northern States. But the ladies soon found that they needed government sanction and authority in their work, and so, on the 6th of June following, the Secretary of War appointed a commission of six competent gentlemen, with Dr. Bellows at its head, " for inquiry and advice in respect to the sanitary needs of the United States forces." This commission was called the United States Sanitary Commission. The ladies worked under its authority. They held " sanitary fairs" in all the great cities, which yielded immense sums, and they collected private contributions of money, clothing, delicacies, lint, bandages, and other supplies for the hospitals. The New York branch alone is said to have sent to the army $15,000,000 in supplies and $5,000,000 in money. The same year, at the suggestion of Mr. Vincent Colyer, a well-known artist, the Christian Commission was organized in New York, and soon spread throughout the country, its object being to attend to the moral and spiritual welfare of the soldiers. Meantime Miss Dorothea L. Dix had offered herself to government for gratuitous service in the hospitals and became the leader of a noble band of devoted and patriotic women, who in this way served their country quite as effectively as their brothers who bore the musket and girded on the sword. It was a great honor to New York to have originated the Sanitary Commission, the Christian Commission, and the American Order of Florence Nightingales.

The war went on with varying fortunes. The city filled her quota under the various calls of the President for troops. At last a draft became necessary, and in May, 1863, one of 300,000 men was ordered. There were many in the city, who had vowed to resist such an order, if made, and their resolution was strengthened by the seditious utterances of certain politicians of the Peace Party, and also by the fact that at this time Governor Seymour had ordered the city militia away to help beat back Lee, who was invading Pennsylvania. The draft began July nth at the Provost-Marshal's office and proceeded quietly the first day; but on the second an organized mob attacked the office and wrecked it, and then began a three days' reign of terror. New York then discovered that she sheltered a band of savages, capable of atrocities that might make the fiercest warrior of the dark continent blush. The mob attacked the police, insulted women, chased colored people — men, women, and children — through the streets, and when they caught them hanged them to the nearest lamp-post; they sacked houses, burned the colored orphan asylum; trampled underfoot the national flag; and burned, murdered, and robbed with impunity. Secretary of War Stanton at once ordered back the New York troops, but ere they arrived the rioters had been quelled by the combined force of the police, the citizens, and the small military force which had been left in the city. Two millions of dollars' worth of property had been destroyed in the three days, and one thousand of the rioters are said to have been killed.

The great event of 1864 was the Sanitary Fair of the 5th of April, which netted nearly one million dollars for the relief of the soldiers in the field.

In 1865 one event stands out conspicuously, — the death of President Lincoln, who was shot by John Wilkes Booth on the evening of April 14th. The news reached New York at 7:30 on the morning of the 15th, and elicited sentiments of deepest grief and horror. Stores were closed, business was suspended, and buildings were draped in emblems of mourning. A few days later the city received, with every mark of reverence and respect, the remains of the slain patriot. Funeral honors such as had never before been paid to a citizen by a free city were tendered. The body lay in state on a splendid catafalque in the City Hall, guarded by veterans of the army. On the afternoon of the 26th the funeral party was escorted to the railway station, on its way to Illinois, by soldiers and civic societies that filled the streets for five miles; later an immense concourse of citizens gathered in Union Square and listened to funeral orations by William Cullen Bryant and George Bancroft. In this spring of 1865 the return of the veterans, with tattered banners and honorable scars, closed the record of the civil war.

XXIV. THE MOUSE IN THE CHEESE.

I HAVE read somewhere a description of a great state dinner in an old Dutch city. A famous cheese had been made for this dinner, but as the attendants cut into it they found that a sagacious mouse had tunneled her way inside, and with her family had begun housekeeping there; so that when the good people looked for toothsomeness and regalement they found only vermin and foulness. One morning in July, 1871, the people of New York awoke to the fact that there were mice in their municipal cheese; in other words, that a large per cent, of the money which they — honest, hard-working taxpayers — had raised to support the city government and pay for such public improvements as were necessary, was being stolen by the very men who had sworn to expend it economically and for the city's best interest. This was one of the gravest crimes that could be committed in a free state; it added treachery and perjury to the crime of theft, it tarnished the fair fame of the city, and it tended to bring government by the people into disrepute. The master-spirit of the conspirators was William M. Tweed, a coarse, pushing, aggressive person, who several years before had left the ranks of honest labor to become a politician. He cultivated that corrupt, degraded class, which under the leadership of the saloon-keeper has so debauched our city politics, and soon acquired such influence over it that he became its master. By the aid of this clientage he was elected to various offices, each a little higher than the last, until finally he became Chairman of the Board of Supervisors and Deputy Street Commissioner, which virtually placed him at the head of the public works of the city and gave him unlimited control of the public expenditures. He now formed a scheme of plundering, which for boldness and gigantic proportions has never been equaled in the history of peculation. Taking the officers of the city into his confidence, he formed that band of conspirators against the public till which the newspapers, with their happy facility for coining apt terms, named "The Ring," His method of procedure was simple yet shrewd. For everything done for, or furnished to the city — opening, paving, or cleaning of streets, park improvements, public buildings, supplies furnished the city — a sum ranging from sixty to eighty-five per cent, in excess of the real cost was charged in the bills, the excess being divided among the conspirators; if now and then an honest contractor ventured to remonstrate against presenting bills so much above the cost, he was threatened with loss of his contract, but generally the contractors were slaves of the ring. Tweed now projected public improvements on a grand scale. He lived in an ostentatious way. He gave munificently to public charities; for a time he was quite the lion of the city.

The new County Court-house formed the most striking example of the stealings of the ring. The Legislature had authorized the city to build it at a cost of $250,000; by 1871, though unfinished, it had cost $8,000,000, nearly $7,000,000 of which had gone into the pockets of the conspirators. In the few months of the ring's existence, it was estimated that it stole $20,000,000, — enough to have built the Brooklyn Bridge, or given twenty free libraries ample endowments, or provided beds in twenty well-appointed hospitals.

But detection and punishment visited the conspirators at last, singularly enough by means which they themselves provided, with a fatuity for which we cannot account. The fraudulent bills were entered in a book entitled " County Liabilities," which was kept among the records of the auditor's office. One day, an honest clerk in this office, who owed his position to John J. O'Brien, High Sheriff of New York, came upon this book, copied the bills, and gave the copy to his patron, O'Brien. The latter called the attention of Tweed to them and threatened to give the copy to the newspapers unless the ring paid a bill long due him by the city; and, as they failed to pay, he, some months after, gave the copy to the New York Times. Now the newspapers of the city had long been calling public attention to the fact that the warrants drawn upon the treasury were far in excess of the expenditure, and we can imagine with what avidity the Times seized upon this morsel. Next morning it startled the city with the announcement in large display type " Secret Accounts. Proofs of Undoubted Frauds Brought to Light," and followed it with double-leaded columns of figures, giving item by item the amounts stolen by the ring. For several days it continued to publish double-leaded columns of extracts from " County Liabilities," and, on Saturday, July 29th, finished with a supplement printed in English and German, in which the several series of figures were brought together and tabulated. The Tribune, Herald, and other great dailies ably seconded the Times. Thomas Nast, by his cartoons in Harper s Weekly, dealt telling blows at the ring. The conspirators were dumbfounded but thought to brazen it out. " What are you going to do about it? asked Tweed, defiantly; words that have since become a proverb for brazen insolence. The indignant people thought they would do something and appointed seventy of their wisest and best citizens as a committee to bring the thieves to justice. Most of the latter became frightened and fled to Europe. Tweed remained, was arrested, indicted for perjury and grand larceny, found guilty, and sentenced to a long term of imprisonment in the penitentiary on Blackwell's Island. In 1875, his friends secured his release on bail, but he was at once re-arrested on a civil suit to recover six millions of dollars stolen from the city treasury. Not being able to find the bail required — three million dollars — he was placed in Ludlow Street Jail, from which he shortly after escaped and fled to Europe. He was traced to Spain, however, and arrested there; the Spanish authorities thinking that so great a rogue ought not to be at large, surrendered him. He was brought back, tried on the civil suit, and a verdict of $6,537,000 returned against him by the jury. He was unable or unwilling to pay this, and remained in prison until his death, in January, 1878, — a miserable end, and one that carries a moral with it.

The Tweed incident was a dark blot on the city's escutcheon; others quite as foul have since been added, and the end is not yet. They have furnished the English Saturday Review and other Tory journals texts for many discourses on the evil effects of free institutions. The Tory friends one meets in London are fond of instancing it as an example of the failure of democracy.

It is useless to shut our eyes to the fact that New York is badly governed; but equally true is it that this government was not put in power by American votes; nor is it the outcome of American institutions. European laws and European social conditions are responsible for it. Ghetto and Judenstrasse had first to exist before the slums of New York were possible. New York has, in fact, become a sieve that catches the riff-raff of all nations. Between three and four hundred thousand emigrants, of various nationalities, arrive at New York every year. Of these, the strong, thrifty, ambitious push forward to the West, while the vicious, ignorant, lazy, ne'er-do-wells, the mentally, morally, and physically diseased remain in New York. There were, in 1880, 478,670 foreign-born persons in New York. Many of them cannot read nor write. Many cannot even speak our language. They never heard of our Constitution, nor of any one of the traditions of our government; yet, on election day, under the lead of the local boss, the voters among them flock to the polls, and their vote counts for as much as that of the native-born American. These European outcasts make Tweed rings possible, and elect boodle aldermen. The honest student of political science will find in them, and not in our free institutions, the genesis of the city's disgraceful government.

Again, the topography of New York is an important factor in producing this result. On a long, narrow island, swept by navigable waters, bearing the commerce of the world, land acquires an enormous value. Only the very rich and the very poor can live on Manhattan Island — the poor, because they are content with little space; the rich, because they can buy all they need. As a result, the great middle class — the true conservator of society — is driven to seek homes outside the city; and as the poor outnumber the rich, the city government is entrusted, practically, to the inmates of the great tenement hives. How these alarming conditions may best be removed, is a question for the coming generation to solve. Undoubtedly when we have statesmen for our rulers, several things will be done. Unrestricted immigration will be stopped. The crowded tenement hives will be torn down, and their inmates removed to model houses, where more than his natural right to six feet of space will be allowed each tenant; and lastly, the city's bounds will be enlarged to include Brooklyn and her suburban villages, the towns of Westchester County along the Hudson and the Sound, and if the consent of New Jersey can be obtained, Jersey City and the entire peninsula between New York and Newark Bay, With so wide a territory, the formation of " rings " would be much more difficult, and the votes of the middle class would be enlisted in the cause of good government.

XXV. THE TRIUMPHS OF ART.

The latter days of the city have been marked by two great triumphs of art — the Brooklyn Bridge and the Bartholdi Statue. As an engineering feat, the former stands unrivalled; and its office of connecting the two great cities of New York and Brooklyn, making them practically one, adds to its distinction. It is a monument to the genius of the great engineer, John A. Roebling, who conceived it, and to his son, Washington A. Roebling, who, on his father's death, before his plans could be carried out, took charge of the work, and carried it to successful completion. A charter for a Bridge Company to build this great work was granted by the New York Legislature, in 1867. The company was organized in May, of that year, and in January, 1870, began the construction of the bridge. The towers, each 272 feet above tide water, were first built. Then, May 29, 1877, the first little wire, to serve as a nucleus for the pioneer cable, was run out from the towers. When 5,269 of these galvanized steel, oil-coated wires had been laid side by side — not twisted — and bound, the first of the four great cables— 3,455 feet long, and capable of sustaining a weight of 12,200 tons — was complete.

All were at last completed, and then came the suspending from them of the roadway and the building of the massive approaches of masonry on either side.

On May 24, 1883, after thirteen years of labor, the structure was opened to the public. Impressive ceremonies attended the event. The President and his cabinet, Governors of States, and distinguished guests attended. The harbor was filled with merchant vessels gay with bunting, and seven frigates of the North Atlantic squadron participated. The Seventh Regiment, Colonel Emmons Clark, escorted the distinguished visitors to the New York end of the bridge. As this was reached the flagship Tennessee began a general salute, which was completed by the other frigates, the Navy Yard, and Castle William on Governor's Island. Meantime the party proceeded to the center of the bridge, where it was met by the municipal authorities of Brooklyn, and escorted to the Brooklyn station, in which a great company had gathered. Here the ceremonies opened with prayer by Bishop Littlejohn, of Brooklyn. An oration by Hon. Abram S. Hewitt; of New York, and an address by Rev. Dr. Storrs, of Brooklyn, followed. A reception at the house of Chief Engineer Roebling, in Brooklyn, and a general display of fireworks in the evening, completed the ceremonies.

The noble statue of Liberty Enlightening the World is intended to typify at once the genius of America and the benefits of liberty to mankind. It is the creation of M. Frederic Auguste Bartholdi, an eminent French sculptor, who was born some fifty-three years ago at Colmar, in Alsace, France. What adds to its interest is the fact that it is a tribute of respect and esteem from the French people to the people of the United States. The conception is said to have first taken form in the sculptor's mind as he sailed up the noble harbor in the ship that bore him from France. He said:

" We will rear here, before the eves of the millions of strangers seeking a home in the New World, a colossal statue of Liberty; in her upstretched hand the torch enlightening the world; in her other hand the Book of Laws, to remind them that true liberty is only found in obedience to law; and the people of France shall present the statue in memory of the ancient friendship subsisting between the two countries."

This was in 1870. After travelling throughout our country for several months and finding hearty encouragement for his project, Bartholdi returned to France, where his proposed work excited the warmest enthusiasm of the people. They willingly contributed the material, and the statue was begun at once and made rapid progress. The head was completed and exhibited at the Paris Exposition of 1878. On October 24, 1881 — the anniversary of the battle of Yorktown, — the pieces of the framework and base were put in place, and on July 4, 1884, M. De Lesseps, the president of the French committee for procuring funds, officially presented the statue to the Hon. Levi P. Morton, our Minister to France. In his speech at the time, M. De Lesseps said that the statue was " the gift of France, the contributions of one hundred and eighty cities, forty general councils, a large number of societies, and of over one hundred thousand subscribers." At the same time the French government provided a national vessel, the here, for transporting the statue to our shores. Meantime a pedestal for the statue had to be erected, and it was proposed that the American people should provide this by popular subscription, as the French had done with the statue, and an American committee was formed. Congress had authorized President Hayes to set apart a site for the statue, and he designated Bedloe's Island in New York harbor, about a mile southwest of the Battery. Ground was first broken for the pedestal in April, 1883, and the latter was completed in April, 1886, a solid mass of masonry, 154 feet 10 inches high — about three and a half feet higher than the goddess which was to crown it. This statue was not cast of bronze, but was built up of repousse', or sheets of hammered copper. The sheets were packed in cases, and put on board the French vessel here, which arrived off Sandy Hook in the latter part of June, 1886. There she was met by the North Atlantic squadron and escorted up the bay, while the forts fired salutes, and the city bells rang joyous peals in her honor.

The work of putting the statue together was completed in October, 1886, under the direction of General Charles P. Stone, of the United States army. The ceremonies attending the dedication on October 28, 1886, are familiar to the youngest reader, and need not be detailed here.

APPENDICES.

APPENDIX A. MAYORS OF NEW YORK SINCE THE REVOLUTION.

David Matthews, 1776-1784. James Duane, 1784-1789. Richard Varick, 1789-1801. Edward Livingston, 1801-1803. De Witt Clinton, 1803-1807. Marinus Willett, 1807-1808. De Witt Clinton, 1808-1810. Jacob Radcliff, 1810-1811. De Witt Clinton, 1811-1815. John Ferguson, 1815. Jacob Radcliff, 1815-1818. Cadwallader D. Colden, 1818-1821. Stephen Allen, 1821-1824. William Paulding, 1824-1826. Phillip Hone, 1826-1827. William Paulding, 1827-1829. Walter Bowne, 1829-1833. Gideon Lee, 1833-1834. Cornelius W. Lawrence, 1834-1837. Aaron Clark, 1837-1839. Isaac L. Varian, 1839-1841. Robert H. Morris, 1841-1844. James Harper, 1844-1847. William V. Brady, 1847-1848. William F. Havemeyer, 1848-1849. Caleb S. Woodhull, 1849-1851. Ambrose C. Kingsland, 1851-1853. Jacob A. Westervelt, 1853-1855. Fernando Wood, 1855-1858. Daniel N. Tieman, 1858-1860. Fernando Wood, 1860-1862. George Opydyke, 1862-1864. C. Godfrey Gunther, 1864-1866. John T. Hoffman, 1866-1868. Thomas Coman (Acting Mayor), 1868. A. Oakey Hall, 1869-1871. William F. Havemeyer, 1873-1874. William H. Wickham, 1875-1877. Smith Ely, 1877-1879. Edward Cooper, 1879-1880. William R. Grace, 1881-1883. Franklin Edson, 1883-1885. William R. Grace, 1885-1887. Abram S. Hewitt, 1887

APPENDIX B. NOTABLE AND CURIOUS EVENTS IN THE HISTORY OF NEW YORK, ARRANGED CHRONOLOGICALLY.

1609. (Sept. 6th.) Hudson discovers Manhattan Island.

1613. Trading-port of four houses established on the island by Amsterdam merchants.

1614. Fort Amsterdam erected.

1621. Dutch West India Company chartered, and territory of New Netherland committed to its care.

1624. Peter Minuit, first Director, arrives.

1626. Buys Manhattan Island (22,000 acres in area) of the Indians for $24 in merchandise.

1632. Minuit succeeded by Wouter Van Twiller.

1633. First schoolmaster (Adam Roelantsen) arrived, and the first church built. 1635. Fort Amsterdam finished at cost of $1,688.

1638. William Kieft succeeds Van Twiller as Director.

1642. Stone tavern (later Stadt Huys) built at head of Coenties Slip.

1647. Petrus Stuyvesant succeeds Kieft as Director.

1650. First lawyer (Dirck Van Schellyen) began practice.

1652. First city charter granted.

1653. Palisades along line of Wall Street erected as defense against the English. The first magistrates appointed.

1656. City first surveyed, and the streets — 17 — mapped; 120 houses and 1,000 inhabitants then in the city.

1657. Average price of city lots, $50.

1658. Streets paved with stone. Rattle watch of eight men appointed. Rent of an average house $14 per year. Fire buckets, hooks, and ladders furnished.

1664. City taken by the English. Population, 1,500.

1665. Jury trials first established.

1668. Francis Lovelace succeeds Colonel Nicolls as Governor.

1673. City retaken by the Dutch.

1674. Re-ceded to the English.

1678. An Admiralty Court established, and citizens given the exclusive right to export bread and flour. Three ships and fifteen sloops and barques owned in the city.

1683. Dougan's charter granted. City divided into six wards.

1685. Assessed value of property, £75,694.

1686. City seal presented.

1688. Wall Street laid out, 36 feet wide.

1691. Leisler hanged.

1692. Pine, Cedar, and adjoining streets laid out through the old Damen farm.

1693. First printing-press established by William Brad ford. Bell-man or town-crier appointed and furnished with livery dress. The city builds a bridge over Spuyten Duyvil creek.

1696. First Trinity Church erected.

1697. First regular night-watch established. Streets lighted by extending a lantern on a pole from every seventh house.

1699. City Hall in Wall Street erected.

1702. Free Grammar School established.

1703. Trinity Churchyard granted to the church by the city. A cage, pillory, and stocks for the punishment of criminals erected before the City Hall.

1707. Broadway paved from Trinity Church to Bowling Green.

1710. Lutheran Church erected corner Broadway and Rector Street.

1716. A public clock of four dials first put up in the city on the City Hall, presented by Stephen De Lancey.

1719. Presbyterian Church in Wall Street erected.

1725. The first newspaper — The New York Gazette — published by William Bradford.

1728. Jews' burial ground opened near Chatham Square.

1729. Dutch Church in Nassau Street (old Post-Office)

1730. Stages to Philadelphia once a fortnight in winter.

1731. A library of 1,622 volumes bequeathed by Rev. Dr. Wellington, of England, opened in the city, nucleus of the present Society Library. Two fire engines brought from London, and a fire department of twenty-four men organized. City divided into seven wards.

1734. A work-house erected in the present Park. Zenger's Weekly Journal established.

1740-1. Hard winter. Snow six feet on a level. Hudson frozen over at New York.

1743. The Postboy, newspaper established by James Parker.

1750. Beekman Street laid out and paved. Thames and John streets paved.

1751. Moravian Chapel built in Fulton Street.

1752. First Merchants' Exchange built at foot of Broad Street.

1754. The Walton House, on Pearl Street, erected by William Walton, a merchant. Present Society Library established.

1755. Staten Island Ferry established.

1757. (May.) Troops embark against Canada.

1760. A public clock presented by John Watts to the Exchange.

1761. Fulton Street (then Partition) regulated and paved.

1762. Public lamps and lamp-posts erected.

1763. Powle's Hook (Jersey City) Ferry established.

1764. The first Methodist Church (in John Street) erected. Coal thought of as fuel. Sandy Hook Light-house first lighted.

1768. Brick Church (Beekman Street) opened.

1769. Robert Murray, of New York, reputed the largest shipowner in America.

1770. Chamber of Commerce incorporated by Royal Charter.

1773. Lots on corner of Nassau and Pine valued at £150 each.

1773(Sept.) Corner-stone of New York Hospital laid by Governor Tryon.

1774. Hoboken Ferry established. Chatham Street so named.

1784. (May.) King's College re-chartered by State of New York and named Columbia College. William Samuel Johnson, first president, elected 1787.

1785. (May.) Ship Empress returned, — the first vessel ever sent from the United States to China. Sir John Temple, first Consul-General from George III., arrived.

1795. Yellow-fever introduced by a British frigate; 732 deaths occurred from the disease. Society Library opened its first building, corner of Nassau and Cedar.

1804. New York Historical Society organized (November 20th) by Mayor De Witt Clinton, Judge Egbert Benson, Rev. Drs. Samuel Miller, John N. Mason, John N. Abeel, William Linn, Dr. David Hosack, Anthony Bleecker, Samuel Bayard, Peter G. Stuyvesant, and John Pintard.

1806. First Free School opened. Washington Irving admitted to the bar.

1807. College of Physicians and Surgeons chartered.

1808. American Academy of Fine Arts incorporated. Chancellor Livingston, president; John Trumbull, vice-president.

1809. Knickerbocker's "History of New York" appeared,

1812. Present City Hall completed. War with England declared. New York within four months sent 26 privateers to sea, carrying 212 guns, 2,239 men.

1813. New York blockaded by British fleet.

1815. (Feb. 11th.) News of the treaty of peace at Ghent received.

1816. American Bible Society formed.

1820. Apprentices' Library founded.

1821. Mercantile Library founded.

1824. Lafayette, revisiting America, arrived in New York.

1831. University of the City of New York founded. Leake and Watts' Orphan Asylum founded by Hon. John Watts. Opened for the admission of orphans in 1843.

1833. New York Sun founded by Benjamin H. Day.

1835. New York Herald founded by James Gordon Bennett.

1836. Union Theological Seminary founded.

1841. New York Tribune founded by Horace Greeley.

1842. Croton Aqueduct opened. Celebration of the event July 4th.

1845. Magnetic telegraph opened between New York and Philadelphia.

1848. Astor Library founded by bequest of John Jacob Astor.

1851. New York Times founded by Henry J. Raymond. Kossuth, the Hungarian patriot, visited New York.

1853. World Fair in Crystal Palace on Murray Hill.

1856. Site of Central Park (862 acres) purchased for nearly five and one half million dollars

1858. Corner-stone of St. Patrick's Cathedral laid. Atlantic cable laid.

1860. New York World founded by Manton Marble.

1862. Corner-stone of New York Academy of Design laid.

1870. East River Bridge begun.

1883. Bridge opened to the Public.

1886. Bartholdi statue dedicated.

www.ingramcontent.com/pod-product-compliance
Lightning Source LLC
LaVergne TN
LVHW052024080426
835513LV00018B/2153